ADVENTURES BEYOND THE BODY

Adventures

HOW TO   Beyond

EXPERIENCE   the

OUT-OF-BODY TRAVEL   Body

William Buhlman

HarperOne
A Division of HarperCollinsPublishers

HarperOne

ADVENTURES BEYOND THE BODY: *How to Experience Out-of-Body Travel.* Copyright © 1996 by William L. Buhlman. All rights reserved. Printed in the United States of America. No part of this book may be used or reproduced in any manner whatsoever without written permission except in the case of brief quotations embodied in critical articles and reviews. For information, address HarperCollins Publishers, 195 Broadway, New York, NY 10007.

HarperCollins Web site: http://www.harpercollins.com

HarperCollins®, ☎®, and HarperOne™ are trademarks of HarperCollins Publishers.

FIRST EDITION

Library of Congress Cataloging-in-Publication Data

Buhlman, William L.
Adventures beyond the body : how to experience out-of-body travel / William L. Buhlman. — 1st ed.
Includes index.
ISBN: 978-0-06-251371-7
1. Astral projections. 2. Physics—Philosophy. 3. Quantum theory—Miscellanea. I. Title.
BF1389.A7B84   1996
133.9—dc20   95-25921

22 23 24 25 26 LBC 51 50 49 48 47

To my wife, Susan, and our children, Alex and Eric, with all my love.

CONTENTS

Preface   ix

Acknowledgments   xi

PART 1

EXPLORING THE   1 First Journeys   3

MYSTERIOUS   2 Meetings Out-of-Body   37

PART 2

SOLVING OUR   3 The New Frontier   75

GREATEST   4 Transformative Qualities   129

MYSTERIES   5 Developing Your Natural Ability   143

                     6 Exploration Techniques   171

                     7 Mastering the Experience   211

                     8 Advanced Explorations   233

                     Conclusion   269

                     Glossary   271

                     Out-of-Body Survey   277

                     Index   281

                     Permissions   292

Five hundred years ago, a few courageous explorers crossed an ocean in search of a new land—a mysterious land hidden by an unexplored and uncharted ocean. Many people considered this journey a waste of time and resources. After all, modern civilization had flourished for centuries without this kind of exploration.

Against all odds this handful of explorers ventured forward, their burning desire for discovery propelling them into the unknown. They abandoned the comforts of home to embark on a journey beyond the known horizons. Facing both their own and society's fears and doubts, they continued their course, finally achieving their goal of discovery.

Today we face the same kind of exploration—an unexplored ocean of energy waiting to be conquered by individuals who possess the foresight and courage to go beyond the limits of their physical horizons. As in the past, the explorer's vision must extend past the physical shoreline. As in the past, the explorer must possess the internal drive and determination to travel beyond the known limits of society and science. He or she must travel alone, far from the masses who cling to the firm security of land.

As in the past, explorers are driven by one thing—the need to discover for themselves, because accepting anything less than firsthand knowledge is settling for the beliefs and assumptions of the landlocked.

Today each of us has an opportunity to go beyond the physical shoreline and become an explorer. This great adventure is available for all of us to share.

My heartfelt thanks go out to the people who have helped to make this book a reality. To Kate Tacie, thank you for your excellent word processing and computer skills. You always responded quickly and flawlessly. Loretta and John Drury, your creativity in computer graphics brought my concepts to life. Thanks to William Birchfield, whose patience in translating computer programs was tried, but true. To my agent, Nat Sobel, for having faith in the potential of this project, thank you. Sol Lewis, I thank you for inviting me to participate in the Michigan Metaphysical Society with you. Thanks to Jerry Castle for his hypnotherapy insights and expertise. Debbie Aronson, your comments about the original manuscript were valued.

I would especially like to thank the many participants of my workshops and lectures. The sharing of your personal out-of-body experiences has proved invaluable. In addition, I would like to thank Kevin Bentley for his valued comments and assistance.

And a special thanks goes to Michelle Griffith. Your friendship and enthusiasm helped to bring this book from someday to today.

Part 1

EXPLORING

THE

MYSTERIOUS

First Journeys

The most beautiful experience we can have is the mysterious. It is the fundamental emotion which stands at the cradle of true art and true science. Whoever does not know it and can no longer wonder, no longer marvel, is as good as dead, and his eyes are dimmed.

Albert Einstein wrote these words many years ago, and they are forever etched in my mind. Twenty years ago I firmly believed that the physical world we see and experience was the only reality. I believed what my eyes told me—life possessed no hidden mysteries, only countless forms of matter living and dying. The facts were clear; there was no evidence or proof of nonphysical worlds or our continued existence after death. I questioned the intelligence of anyone softheaded enough to accept the illogical concepts of heaven, God, and immortality. In my mind these were fairy tales created to comfort the weak and manipulate the masses. For me, life was simple to understand: the world consisted of solid matter and form, and the concepts of life after death and heaven were feeble human attempts to create hope where none existed.

I possessed the arrogant knowledge of a man who judges the world with his physical senses alone. I supported my conclusions with the overwhelming observations provided by science and technology. After all, if something mysterious was there, science would certainly be aware of it.

My firm convictions of reality and life continued until June of 1972. During a conversation with a neighbor, our discussion turned to the possibilities of life after death and the existence of heaven. I proceeded to present my agnostic viewpoints with vigor. To my surprise my neighbor didn't contest my conclusions; instead, he related an experience that he had had several weeks before. One evening just after drifting to sleep, he was shocked to discover himself floating above his body. Completely awake and aware, he became frightened and instantly fell back into his physical body. Excited, he told me it wasn't a dream or his imagination, but a fully conscious experience.

Intrigued by his experience, I decided to investigate this strange phenomenon for myself. After several days of research I discovered numerous references to out-of-body experiences throughout history. With some searching I found a book on the topic that actually described how out-of-body experiences are induced. The entire subject seemed extremely weird, and I considered the book the result of an overly active imagination.

Out of curiosity, I decided to try one of the out-of-body techniques before sleep. After repeated daily attempts, I began to feel a little ridiculous. In three weeks the only thing I experienced out of the norm was an increase in my dream recall. I became more and more convinced that this entire subject was nothing more than an intense or vivid dream stimulated by the so-called out-of-body techniques.

Then, one night about eleven o'clock I drifted to sleep during my out-of-body technique and began dreaming that I was sitting at a round table with several people. They all seemed to be asking me questions related to my self-development and state of consciousness. At that moment in the dream I began to feel extremely dizzy, and a strange numbness, like from Novocain, began to spread throughout my body. Unable to keep my head up, I passed out, hitting my head on the table. Instantly I was awake, fully conscious, lying in bed facing the wall. I could hear an unusual buzzing sound and felt somehow different. Extending my arm, I reached for the wall in front of me. I stared in amazement as my hand actually entered the wall; I could feel the vibrational energy of it as if I was touching its very molecular structure. Only then did the overwhelming reality hit me, *My God, I'm not in my body.*

Excited, my only thought was, *It's real. My God, it's real!* Lying in bed, I stared at my hand in disbelief. When I tried clenching my fist, I could feel the pressure of my grip; my hand felt completely solid, but the physical wall in front of me looked and felt like a dense, vaporous material with form.

Determined to stand, I began to move effortlessly to the foot of my bed, my mind racing with the reality of it all. Standing, I quickly touched my arms and legs, checking to see if I was solid, and to my surprise I was completely solid, completely real. But around me, the familiar physical objects in my room no longer appeared completely real or solid; instead, they now looked like three-dimensional mirages. Glancing down, I noticed a large lump in my bed. Amazed, I could see that it was the sleeping form of my physical body silently facing the wall.

As I focused my vision on the opposite side of the room, the wall seemed to fade slowly from view. In front of me I could see a wide, green field extending far beyond my room. Looking around, I noticed a figure silently watching me from about ten yards away. It was a tall man with dark hair, a beard, and a purple robe. Startled by his presence, I became frightened and instantly "snapped back" into my physical body. With a jolt I was in my body, and a strange feeling of numbness and tingling faded as I opened my eyes. Excited, I sat up, my mind exploding with the realization of what had just occurred. I knew it was absolutely real, not a dream or my imagination. My entire ego awareness had been present.

Suddenly, everything I had ever learned about my existence and the world around me had to be reappraised. I had always seriously doubted that anything beyond the physical world existed. Now my entire viewpoint changed. Now I absolutely knew that other worlds do exist and that people like myself must live there. Most important, I now knew that my physical body was just a temporary vehicle for the real me inside, and that with practice I could separate from it at will.

Excited about my discovery, I grabbed a pen and paper and wrote down exactly what had occurred. A flood of questions filled my mind. Why is the vast majority of the human race unaware of this phenomenon? Why aren't the various sciences and religions investigating it? Is it possible that this unseen world is the "heaven" referred to in religious texts? Why isn't our government exploring this apparent parallel energy world? Is it possible that our overwhelming dependence on physical perceptions has led us to overlook an incredible avenue of exploration and discovery?

As the initial shock of my first experience sank in, I realized that my life could never be the same again. The more I pondered the significance of my experience, the more profound I realized it to be. All my agnostic beliefs had been swept away in a single night. I knew that I had to reappraise everything that I had learned since childhood, everything that I had assumed to be true. My comfortable conclusions about science, psychology, religion, and my existence had obviously been based on incomplete information. I felt excited, but also uneasy—my familiar concepts of reality no longer seemed relevant. Increasingly, I felt in a void. On several occasions when I talked to friends about my experience, they found it too bizarre to take seriously. In 1972 the term *out-of-body experience* had not even been coined; back then, the most common description was astral projection. No one that I knew at the time had even heard of astral projection, and if you told people you had left your body, they immediately thought that you were on drugs or losing your mind. I quickly discovered that I had to keep my experiences to myself or face some degree of disbelief and even ridicule.

After my first out-of-body experience, my mind was overflowing with endless possibilities and questions. Desperate for information and guidance, I spent several weeks in libraries and bookstores searching for whatever knowledge was available on the topic. I quickly found that little was available; only a handful of books had been written on the subject, and some of these were decades old and out of print. By the end of July 1972, I realized that I was on my own.

I decided to focus on the one technique that had worked for me before. This technique involved visualizing a physical location that I knew well as I drifted off to sleep. As before, I pictured my mother's living room with as much detail as possible. At first it seemed difficult, but after a few weeks I could picture the room's details with increasing clarity; the furniture, patterns in fabrics, textures, even small imperfections in wood and paint began to be clear in my mind. I realized that the more I pictured myself within the room interacting with the physical objects, the more detailed my visualizations would become. With practice I learned to physically walk around the room and memorize specific items that it contained. I also learned the importance of "feeling" the environment with my mind: the feel of carpet on my feet; the sensation of sitting in a chair, walking, turning on a lamp, or even opening the door. The more detailed and involved I was within my visualization, the more effective were my results. Although it was challenging at first, after a while it became fun to make my visualizations come alive in my mind. At this point I decided to keep a journal to record my out-of-body experiences.

Journal Entry, August 6, 1972

I awakened at 4:00 A.M. after three and a half hours of sleep and started to read a book about out-of-body experiences. After reading for about fifteen minutes, I became sleepy and decided to visualize my mother's living room. I selected this because I knew it extremely well. Within the living room are several items I had made in grade school: a metal ashtray, a wooden doorstop, and a watercolor of the ocean. As I pictured the room in my mind, I slowly moved my attention to the items I had made. As vividly as I could, I imagined myself walking around the living room looking at the furniture and the various things I had made. As I focused on the items, I began to see the room surprisingly well. I moved my focus from item to item and visualized myself touching each object. As I became mentally immersed in the sensations and sights of the living room, I drifted off to sleep.

In seconds I'm shaken awake by intense vibrations and a roaring sound throughout my body. It feels like I'm in the middle of a jet engine and my body and mind are about to vibrate apart. I'm shocked and scared by the intensity of the vibrations and sounds and snap back to my body. As I open my eyes, I realize that I'm completely numb and that a strange tingling sensation is spreading throughout my body. Over the next few minutes, my normal physical sensations slowly return. I can't believe the intensity of the vibrations.

I lay in bed and wonder what these vibrations and sounds are and what causes them. I know they're not physical sensations. I can only guess that they're somehow connected to my nonphysical form, possibly my conscious recognition of the transfer of my awareness from my physical to my nonphysical body. Maybe I'm simply conscious of a vibrational shift or transition that's necessary to have out-of-body experiences. Whatever it is, it can definitely scare the hell out of you. Even so, I'm determined to find out what's behind these strange vibrations. There must be a logical explanation.

For the next week nothing happened. I started to doubt myself and my ability to have the experience. Then one evening about eleven o'clock I dozed off while visualizing my mother's living room. Within minutes I was startled awake by a piercing buzzing sound and vibrations throughout my body. Opening my eyes, I realized that I was half in and half out of my body. My first reaction was fear. An overwhelming panic flooded my mind and I instantly snapped back into my body. Upon opening my physical eyes, I discovered that my physical body was numb and tingling; as before, this sensation slowly dissipated and my normal physical feelings returned. I sat up in bed shocked by the intensity of the vibrations and sounds. I clearly remember saying aloud, "What the hell was that?"

As I reviewed the experience I realized that I was completely unprepared. An instinctual fear seemed to flow through me at the first hints of separation.

For two nights nothing unusual occurred. Then on the third night I awakened to a weird numbness and vibration spreading from the back of my neck to the rest of my body. I tried my best to stay calm and reduce my fear, but I couldn't. I felt as though I was completely out of control and vulnerable. Startled, I spontaneously thought about my physical body and the vibrations slowly subsided. As my physical sensations returned, I felt disappointed that I'd missed a great opportunity to explore. In an effort to save the moment, I calmed down, focused my thoughts away from my physical body, and began to encourage the vibrations to return. (I did this by concentrating on the vibrational sensations I had just experienced at the back of my neck.)

After about fifteen minutes, as I gradually relaxed and again drifted between sleep and wakefulness, the vibrations began to return. They started at the back of my neck, then slowly spread to my whole body until I was vibrating at what felt like a higher frequency or energy level. This time I remained calm, my anxiety level decreasing as I recognized that the vibrational sensations were somewhat enjoyable when I was prepared. A high-pitched buzzing seemed to resonate in my body, and I felt energized and light as a feather. With a thought of floating I could feel myself moving upward. I was completely weightless, and for the first time the sensations were absolutely wonderful. I floated up to the ceiling and touched it with my hand. Amazed, I realized that I was touching the energy substance of the ceiling. Pressing my hand into the hazy molecular structure, I felt the tingling vibrational energy of the ceiling. As I withdrew my hand from the ceiling, I noticed that my arm sparkled like a thousand points of brilliant blue and white lights. Out of curiosity, I reached out my other hand and grasped my outstretched arm, and to my surprise it was solid to the touch. Focusing on my arm, I became mesmerized by the depth and beauty of the lights. I realized that my arm appeared to be a universe of stars. It's strange to describe, but I felt drawn into a universe that was me. At that instant I snapped back into my body, and the numbness and tingling sensations quickly subsided as I opened my eyes in awe.

Journal Entry, October 4, 1972

I silently repeat an affirmation, "Now I'm out-of-body," for ten to fifteen minutes as I grow increasingly sleepy. As much as possible, I intensify my affirmations as I drift off to sleep.

Almost instantly I'm awakened by intense vibrations and an electrical-like buzzing throughout my body. I'm startled, and an intense wave of fear surges through me. I calm myself down by repeating, "I'm protected by the light." My initial fear slowly dissipates as I visualize myself surrounded by a globe of protective light. I think of floating and feel myself lift up and out of my physical body. I feel light as a feather and float slowly upward. As I float away from my body I realize that the vibrations and buzzing have diminished to a slight humming sensation. Feeling more secure, I open my eyes and find myself staring at the ceiling two feet in front of me. I'm surprised that I've floated that high and instinctively think about looking at my body on the bed. Instantly, I snap back to my physical body and feel a strange vibration as my physical sensations quickly return.

As I lie in bed reviewing the experience, I realize that my thoughts directed toward my physical body must have snapped me back. I know it's possible to view my physical body, because during my first out-of-body experience I distinctly saw it. I suspect the key to observing our physical bodies is to remain as mentally and emotionally detached as possible, but more important, we must keep our thoughts directed away from our physical bodies; the slightest thought focused on the body will immediately snap us back to it. In retrospect, I should have thought about turning over as I floated; then I could have observed my physical body without any thoughts being focused on it.

Journal Entry, October 12, 1972

I wake up at 3:15 after three and a half hours of sleep (two REM periods) and move to the sofa in the living room. After about forty minutes of reading, I become sleepy and begin to do a different visualization. I picture myself as a bright orange balloon filling with helium. I can feel myself becoming lighter and lighter as the balloon expands. I intensify and hold my visualization as long as possible. Drifting off to sleep I awaken to the sensation of intense vibrations and buzzing throughout my body. I recognize that I'm ready to separate and immediately think about floating. The vibrations and sounds rapidly diminish as I separate and float up to the ceiling. Out of instinct I reach out my arms to touch the ceiling, but instead of touching, my hands slowly enter the tingling vibrational substance of the ceiling. I can feel a slight resistance as my hands and arms move through the ceiling. Moving slowly upward, my body enters and passes through the insulation, rafters, and attic. An intense excitement flows through me as I pass through the roof and float at the top of the house.

I think of standing and I'm instantly upright, standing at the highest peak of the house. As I look around, I can clearly see the TV antenna and chimney. Even though it's the middle of the night, the sky and everything around me are partially lighted by a luminescent silvery glow.

Standing at the top of the house, I have a sudden urge to fly. I spread my arms, glide down from the roof, and fly over my backyard. I slowly descend until I'm flying about four feet above the ground. For some reason I feel as if I'm getting heavier and continue descending until I'm just inches above the grass. I think "control" but it's too late. With a thud I crash face first onto the lawn. At that instant I'm back in my physical body. My physical sensations return and I wonder why I lost control. Why did I become so heavy?

Journal Entry, November 2, 1972

I awaken to the sound and sensations of intense buzzing. It feels as if my body and mind are vibrating apart. At first I'm startled by the intensity of the vibrations, but slowly I calm myself and focus my full attention on the idea of floating away from my physical body. In seconds I float up and out of my body and hover several feet above it. I notice that the buzzing noise and vibrations immediately subside after complete separation. The sound and vibrations are replaced by a serene feeling of calm. It feels as if I'm weightless and floating like a cloud. I think of moving to the door and I seem to automatically float to that destination. I feel an overwhelming sense of freedom I've never known before. Spontaneously I decide to fly and think about flying through the roof. Instantly I fly straight up through the ceiling and pass through the roof like a rocket. I'm thrilled by the response and begin to understand that my thoughts are the energy of my personal propulsion. I spread my arms and level off several hundred feet in the air. Below me I can clearly see the buildings and roads of my neighborhood. I feel a slight tugging sensation as I fly higher and higher over the city of Baltimore. The tugging sensation increases and I think of my body. Instantly, I snap back to my body. My physical body is numb and tingling as I open my eyes.

As my out-of-body experiences continued, I became fascinated with the nonphysical energy structures I observed. With each experience my questions seemed to grow until I became obsessed with trying to understand the nature of the nonphysical forms that I had encountered. In an attempt to comprehend the relationship between the physical and nonphysical environments, I developed a series of crude experiments. For example, every day I would balance a pencil or pen at the very edge of my nightstand. My purpose was to see if I could somehow move the physical object with my nonphysical body. I quickly discovered that this simple experiment was more difficult than it appeared. My biggest obstacle was attempting to focus on my experiment. At the moment of separation my mind would race with unlimited possibilities, and my experiment seemed insignificant compared with the many wonders that were available.

Each experience increased my realization that my nonphysical state of consciousness was extremely sensitive and responsive to the slightest thought. My prevailing conscious and subconscious thoughts would instantly propel me in a specific direction. I quickly learned that my subconscious mind exerts much more influence and control over my actions than I ever imagined. Often, a completely spontaneous thought would create an immediate reaction. For example, if I thought about flying, which I often did, I would immediately fly through the ceiling or wall and glide over my neighborhood.

Gradually, I realized that gaining full conscious control during the first seconds after separation was absolutely essential. To accomplish this I experimented with different ways to gain control. At first I tried focusing my full attention on my hand or arm just after separation. I hoped that this would concentrate my thoughts on a single idea and give me the immediate control that I was seeking. This created a strange sensation of being immersed within myself. Though exhilarating, the end result was not control but a feeling of being mesmerized and then drawn into a sparkling universe of brilliant blue stars.

Unhappy with the results, I decided to try grabbing my non-physical arm and focusing on the sensations of my grip. I was somewhat surprised to discover that the feel of my nonphysical arm was amazingly solid. My nonphysical body possessed an inherent vibrational quality; it felt completely solid, but I could feel the mild vibrational energy of my arm's substance. I quickly discovered that my energy-body was indeed "real" in every respect, appearing to be an exact duplicate of my physical body. I also found that when my thoughts were focused on my nonphysical body I began to feel myself drawn inward, as if I were being pulled into a vacuum deep inside myself.

Over a period of several months I repeated this procedure of self-examination, and through trial and error I learned about my nonphysical body. With repeated observations I began to realize that my nonphysical form was like an energy mold—in effect, conscious energy that had assumed a temporary form. The body I experienced when out-of-body appeared to be the result of my mind's expectations and self-concept. In addition, I recognized that focusing on my nonphysical body created a strong tendency for me to be drawn inward to areas I could not begin to comprehend. I knew that I needed another method for gaining conscious control.

After almost a year I was becoming frustrated by numerous failed attempts to gain full control when I finally discovered that I was making this entire process more involved than it needed to be. During an afternoon out-of-body experience, I spontaneously shouted, "Control now!" Immediately I felt an enhancement of my analytical mind. As I stood by the foot of my bed, my vision improved but remained slightly out-of-focus, so I shouted, "Clarity now!" My vision instantly snapped into focus. I felt a rush of energy and awareness flow through my body and mind. I was thrilled. For the first time I felt in complete control: my entire

16   self-awareness was present, and I actually felt more aware than in my normal physical state of consciousness. My thoughts were crystal clear and vibrantly alive.

I suddenly realized that the key to control was simply to demand full conscious control immediately after separation. I also began to understand the importance of focusing my thoughts and the need to be extremely specific when making requests. On one occasion, just after separation, I said aloud, "I request full waking consciousness," and instantly snapped back into my physical body. I found that the controlling portion of my mind takes my thoughts literally. My poor choice of the word *waking* was immediately interpreted to mean physical waking. After several months of experimenting with different phrases, I began to recognize that I had unintentionally programmed myself to think "control" during each out-of-body experience. I soon discovered myself doing it automatically as I floated up and away from my body. After a year of trial and error, I knew I was finally on the right track.

Throughout this period I continued my pencil experiments. During several out-of-body experiences, I tried to move the pencil balanced on the nightstand and was surprised to find that the vibrational frequency (density) of my nonphysical body seemed to determine whether the pencil or even the entire room was visible to me. Slowly I came to understand that the environment I was observing was not the physical world, as I had assumed. I realized that the structures I normally observed when out-of-body were nonphysical structures. Gradually, it all started to fit together. Now I finally understood why there were slight variations between the nonphysical and physical furniture and other objects. For example, the nonphysical walls were often a different color, and the shapes and styles of some of the furniture and rugs were different. Much of this was minor but nevertheless noticeable.

For me to be able to see my normal physical surroundings, my internal vibrational rate had to be relatively dense, or slow. I also noticed that the very act of requesting consciousness and clarity seemed to automatically increase the internal frequency of my nonphysical body.

In an effort to make my experiments more realistic, I balanced pencils at three different areas that I normally passed upon leaving my body. My hope was that I would notice the pencils, at the side of bed or at the foot of the bed, as I moved past them. Looking back, I realize that it probably looked a little strange. On one occasion I remember my mother asking me, "What's with the pencils?" Just imagine trying to explain this to your mother without sounding like a nut.

After several weeks, I finally focused on one of the pencils after separation. As I moved to the side of bed, I concentrated on the pencil at the edge of my dresser. At first my vision seemed foggy, somehow out of sync, so I said aloud, "Clarity now!" Instantly my vision snapped in focus. I could clearly see the pencil in front of me; however, it appeared like a three-dimensional hazy form with substance. I moved closer, touched it with my hand, and felt a slight vibrational sensation as my fingers passed through the substance of the pencil. Somewhat frustrated, I tried again but experienced the same results. Focusing my attention, I realized that my nonphysical body was obviously less dense than the pencil, and spontaneously said aloud, "I need to be denser." With a jolt I shot back into my physical body. As my physical sensations returned, I couldn't help but laugh: I had received my request. I had to remember that requests made when out-of-body are taken literally. There seems to be little room for interpretation or shades of gray. I would have to remember to be extremely specific with each request. Maybe something like "I wish to move this pencil" would have been more effective.

In a related experience some years later, I was practicing self-hypnosis with a single lighted candle. After separation I stood by the candle and decided to blow it out. To my surprise it went out immediately. Upon returning to my physical body, I opened my eyes to find that the physical candle was still burning. After some thought I realized that I must have blown out a candle in what I now know is the parallel dimension closest to the physical. This dimension is a relatively dense energy duplicate of the physical world.

This simple experiment is important because it provides evidence that the environments and objects encountered during out-of-body experiences exist independently of the physical universe. It appears that we are not observing the physical world from a different perspective, as many believe, but are interacting in a separate but parallel dimension of energy.

Journal Entry, June 21, 1973

I wake up at 5:00 A.M. and move to the sofa. After reading for about fifteen minutes I become sleepy and decide to try something new. I grab a sheet of paper and begin to write out-of-body affirmations. "Now I'm out-of-body." As I write, I verbally repeat them to myself. After writing fifty or so I can barely keep my eyes open. As I drift to sleep, I continue the affirmations in my mind.

I'm startled awake by a strange numbness and vibrations throughout my body. I stay as calm as possible and focus on the sensations of floating upward. After several seconds, I feel myself lift up and out of my body. I stand beside my body and walk to the window. I feel somehow out of focus and request clarity. There's only a small improvement so I repeat my request, and this time I'm more demanding: "I need clarity now!" Instantly, my awareness becomes crystal clear. My body feels lighter and more energized. I feel vibrantly awake and aware and decide to try to fly. Stretching out my arms, I take a small leap and fly through the ceiling and roof, until I'm several hundred feet above my neighborhood. I rotate my arms slightly and level off. It's absolutely exhilarating. I feel completely free as I glide over the town of Catonsville. Even though it's night, the landscape is illuminated by a silvery glow. Below me the houses and streets appear like a Christmas garden. Suddenly, I feel a tugging sensation at my back and spontaneously think of my body. The thought of my body snaps me back to it with a jolt. I awaken with a slight numbness and tingling throughout my body.

Journal Entry, July 3, 1973

I awaken to the sound and sensation of intense buzzing. It feels as if my body and mind are inside an engine. At first I'm startled by the intensity of the vibrations, but slowly I calm myself and direct my full attention to the idea of floating from my body. Immediately I separate and float upward to the ceiling. After separation I notice that the loud, roaring noise has faded. As I float about four feet above my body, the vibrations are replaced by a feeling of calm. It feels as if I'm weightless and floating like a cloud. With a single thought of moving to the door. I seem to be automatically propelled to that destination.

Focusing my thought, I think of the living room and float directly there. I can't believe how easy and natural it is. I think of standing and I'm standing in the living room examining my surroundings. Everything around me looks familiar, except that the walls are now light yellow instead of white and some of the furniture is slightly different from its physical counterpart. For example, an antique lion-head rocking chair looks the same but the coffee table looks different. The physical table is a modern style, while its nonphysical counterpart looks like an eighteenth-century antique.

As I stare at my surroundings I realize that I can see through the hazy outline of the physical walls. When I focus on the living room wall, it appears to become increasingly vaporous in its form and substance and slowly disappears. In front of me is an entirely new environment, a sprawling meadow extending as far as I can see. I step forward several steps and enter the new terrain. As I look out into the meadow I notice the figure of a man standing about twenty yards away. He's watching me intently but does not approach. For several moments I stare in his direction. He has dark hair and a close-cropped beard and wears a purple robe that extends to his knees. He acknowledges my stare by nodding his head and flashing a small smile. The entire situation is overwhelming. I feel uneasy and unsure of what to do next. Should I walk over and communicate with this stranger or avoid him? My dilemma is quickly resolved when I snap back into my physical body.

As I lie in bed it hits me that this man might be the same person I saw during my first out-of-body experience. The more I review his appearance, the more convinced I am that this man is not just a nonphysical resident "passing by"; he seems to be watching my every move. It is also apparent that he had no intention of approaching or communicating with me. I suspect that he knew that any movement on his part toward me would probably have scared me; just the sight of someone standing there was unsettling enough.

For several days, curiosity concerning this man fills my mind. What are his intentions and purpose? I wonder if he is some sort of guide observing my progress. In addition, I wonder if everyone having out-of-body experiences has someone observing their progress. He obviously did not wish to interfere; in fact, he seemed almost surprised when I finally did see him. I can only speculate that he probably was observing my out-of-body experiences from a slightly different vibrational level in order to remain unobserved. When I focused my attention I must have raised my vibrational rate and was then able to see beyond my normal physical-like surroundings.

Comparing this to my first experience, I realize that they were similar in many respects. The main difference was that my control and vision were better this time.

The more I thought about my experiences, the more I realized that everything I believed to be fact or truth had to be reappraised. For example, the long-standing "fact" that our consciousness is the result of electrochemical activity within the brain was now a laughable conclusion resulting from obviously incomplete information. Now I knew that the brain had to serve some other function, possibly as a biological transfer device between the nonphysical mind and the physical body. It became clear that the physical brain is similar to a computer's hard drive, storing information and memories needed to support and operate our temporary biological vehicle.

As my out-of-body experiences continued, this observation was confirmed time and again. One thing was certain, I could think without my physical brain; I could create, analyze, and recall thoughts. I also recognized that there were definite differences. For example, when out-of-body I was more spontaneous and single-minded than in my physical body. I felt somehow motivated to do things I wouldn't ever consider while in my body. For example, I would often think about flying and then instantly fly out of the room and glide around my neighborhood, or find myself flying over strange landscapes I couldn't begin to identify. I sometimes suspected that I was being directed by a more expansive, unknown part of myself. Often my spontaneous thoughts would lead me to situations and experiences that provided insight

22 into areas or events that were related to my past or present. On numerous occasions I didn't understand the reason for these experiences until weeks or even years later.

The next experience had a profound effect on me. For the first time I truly realized the unlimited potential of nonphysical explorations.

Journal Entry, July 9, 1973

Around noon I decide to take a nap. I visualize my mother's living room as I drift off to sleep. A sensation of numbness and tingling energy spreads throughout my body. I enjoy the sensation and easily lift out of my body. A feeling of excitement flows through me as I move to the foot of the bed.

As I look around, I have a sudden urge to see the young woman in the apartment above mine. Instantly I float upward and feel my head and shoulders enter the ceiling. For some unknown reason I encounter an intense resistance and can't pass through the ceiling. For a moment I'm stuck in the ceiling and I begin to panic. I say aloud, "Down," and instantly move down to the floor.

With a feeling of relief I calm down and center myself. I walk to my bedroom door and step into it. As I move through the door I feel a slight tingling sensation but encounter no problems; up close the door has a misty, hazy appearance. Walking normally, I enter the living room and am heading toward the front door when suddenly, to my right, I clearly hear a man's voice calling my name.

"Willie."

Startled, I look around and stare at a man sitting on the sofa. He appears to be in his late twenties and somehow seems familiar.

"Willie, it's good to see you."

I recognize his voice and immediately know that it's my uncle Hilton in front of me. Shocked by his presence, I just stare at him as he speaks.

"I bet you're surprised to see me."

He chuckles as he continues. "Had a little trouble with the ceiling."

I step closer and ask, "Uncle Hilton, is that you?"

He smiles again. "Yes, it's me."

I look at him closely. He appears twenty years younger and much thinner than when he died.

He seems amused by my stare and says, "Hey, I'm just as surprised to see you as you are to see me."

His tone becomes more serious. "Willie, how did you learn to do this?"

I'm surprised by his question and respond, "I just tried it and it worked."

"There aren't many who can do what you do. All of us are quite surprised." He gazes at me, waiting for my reply.

As I look at him, the reality of the situation is overwhelming. For some reason I feel a sudden inner need to fly.

"Uncle Hilton, I have to go."

He smiles and nods as I move to the door.

I easily step through the front door and see a broad green field before me. (My physical surroundings are an apartment complex.) I step outside and extend my arms above me. My impulse to fly seems to propel me into the air like a rocket. I spread my arms, level off, and experiment with controlling my flight. As I look around, I can clearly see Route 40 below me. I decide to follow the road and fly west several hundred feet above the ground. Intense exhilaration and freedom radiate from every part of my being. Looking down, I can clearly see the road, homes, and even entire subdivisions. As I pass over

Ellicott City, I feel a tugging sensation at the center of my back and think of my body. In a flash I snap back in my physical body and can feel a slight tingling and numbness that quickly dissipate.

As soon as my physical senses return, I find my mother's old photo albums and search for a picture of my dead uncle. Turning the pages wildly, I finally locate a photograph of him as a young man in his twenties. Without a doubt the thirty-year-old photograph before me is the exact image of the man I just met.

As I review this experience, a couple of things become clear. First, we obviously continue after death. Even though I have known this since my first out-of-body experience, it becomes even more apparent when you actually see and speak with a deceased person you have known. There is simply no way I could be mistaken; the man with whom I just had a conversation was definitely my uncle.

Second, it strikes me that my uncle appeared to be in the prime of life—I would guess late twenties. In fact, he was so young I couldn't immediately (at least visually) recognize him. It was his distinctive voice and his calling me "Willie" that really made it clear who he was. My deceased uncle is the only person who ever called me Willie; everyone else called me William or Bill.

When my uncle died, he was fifty-four years old and considerably overweight; yet when I saw him, he appeared young, thin, and vibrantly healthy. It seems likely that after we shed our physical body at death, we assume the energy form molded or influenced by our concept of ourselves. Since I've learned that nonphysical energies are naturally thought-responsive, it seems reasonable that our thoughts and self-image would influence our personal energy. It appears likely that we may assume the nonphysical form that most fits our self-conception.

If this is the case, I can't help but wonder what I look like when I leave my body. Do I look the same as my physical body? I also wonder if my form would change if I intentionally altered my self-image. It sounds kind of bizarre, but it seems possible that our nonphysical shape and form may also be a temporary vehicle, just like the physical body. I seriously wonder what would happen if (when out-of-body) I concentrated on changing the shape and form of my nonphysical body.

For several weeks, the meeting with my deceased uncle filled my mind. I was sure that he had seemed surprised and curious about my ability to leave my body, yet I also knew that he had appeared to be waiting for me—he seemed to know that I would walk into the living room. Maybe that was the reason I couldn't go through the ceiling when I tried. It's possible that I was being somehow directed to the living room. In addition, I had a strange sense that someone had been sitting next to him. It's hard to explain, but I had felt someone else there, and I was sure that for a brief moment I had seen the subtle outline of a woman.

I continued to follow the pattern that had worked for me in the past. I would wake up at seven o'clock and get ready for a college class at nine o'clock. After my class I would come back to my mother's apartment and read until I became sleepy. Generally about noon I would begin to do my out-of-body technique. I continued to experiment with different methods but found that the simplest one worked best. I would go to my room, lie in bed, and visualize myself walking around the living room examining all the small details associated with the room. Often I would pick out three or four objects in the room and do my best to picture them clearly in my mind. I didn't understand or even think about the mechanics of what I was doing; I only knew that it worked.

An estimated 30 percent of the time, after dozing off I would find myself sitting up, floating, or rolling sideways out of my body. The sensations during separation were normally similar: a buzzing sound accompanied by an internal high-energy or vibrational feeling spreading through my body. At the peak of the vibrations I would mentally direct myself away from my body by sitting up or rolling out of my body. I preferred sitting up because rolling out would often cause a disjointed or disoriented feeling. I discovered that the easiest way was simply to sit up and step away from my body. I seemed to maintain more conscious control over my nonphysical energy-body this way. It's possible that the physical-like movements associated with walking had a grounding effect.

Journal Entry, September 14, 1973

As I become sleepy, I mentally repeat my regular affirmation, "Now I'm out of body." At the same time I visualize objects in my mother's living room. After about fifteen minutes, I drift off.

Suddenly, I'm startled awake by the sound of a gunshot near my head. My body is completely numb and an overwhelming flood of energy is flowing through me. I'm scared and instinctively think of my physical body. With a jolt I'm back in my body, looking around the room for the source of the sound. After my physical sensations return, I realize that I've handled this experience poorly. I suspect that the gunshot was an internal sound, probably caused by the act of separating from my physical body, and that I may have separated from a connecting point located somewhere in my head.

There is a theory that all of us are connected to our physical bodies at seven energy locations and that a loud popping sound may indicate a separation occurring at or near the pineal gland. Currently I have no evidence to support this theory, but I must admit that my experience is remarkably similar to sounds reported by Sylvan Muldoon and Paul Twitchell.

Little research exists on the sensations and sounds associated with out-of-body experiences. I hope that in the near future this will change. When we consider the vast potential for knowledge available, it's only reasonable that more research should be conducted. I firmly believe that additional research would uncover new insights into the unseen nature and source of consciousness.

Journal Entry, October 25, 1973

I become increasingly relaxed and drowsy as I repeat an out-of-body affirmation, "Now I'm out-of-body." The next thing I know, I'm sitting up in bed completely aware and looking around my room. Vibrations flow through me as I lift and separate from my body, walk through my bedroom wall, and enter a new environment. I am walking on a sidewalk or path of some kind, and all around me is a wide, flat expanse. In the distance a radio tower extends as far as I can see. I have a strong urge to go to it and say to myself, "I must make it to the tower." Instantly I am closer to it. Directly in front of me are dozens of old metal trash cans blocking my way. I begin to push them aside and ask aloud, "What do these things represent?" At that instant, a series of vivid pictures appears in my mind; I can't tell if it's originating from within me or somehow outside of me. "Very good, you're starting to understand. You are in a higher vibratory region, a thought-responsive environment. Your perceptions of your surroundings are created by your mind. Your mind is interpreting the environment according to the reference points and forms it can relate to."

My mind overflows with excitement. For the first time, I understand the obvious. The sidewalk is my path, the direction of my life. The trash cans are all the garbage that slows my progress: my fears, limits, and attachments. All these things must be removed from my path for me to move forward and achieve my spiritual goals.

I stare at the trash cans for a moment; they appear old and battered. With a feeling of intense joy and satisfaction I toss the trash cans out of my way. A surge of energy flows through me as I clear my path of the obstacles. I feel empowered and filled with energy as I step toward the radio tower and discover that I'm directly beside it. I look for the entrance but can't find one anywhere. As I walk around the perimeter, I suddenly feel an intense tugging sensation. I know I have to return to my body.

With a single thought of my physical body I'm instantly within it. I open my eyes and realize that my bladder is full. I'm a little upset with myself for not planning better. Now I'm really curious about the radio tower and exactly what it represented. Why couldn't I find the door? I have an idea but I need confirmation. More important, I wonder about the communication I received. It's difficult to explain, but it was very clear in my mind; it seemed more like pictures than words. Even more important, I realize that this experience is different from all previous ones. I entered a completely different environment, a nonphysical world that appeared separate from the physical-like surroundings that I normally experience. In addition, the surroundings seemed to respond easily to my thoughts. I felt somehow different, lighter, more energized. I don't really understand, but I suspect that this is important.

Journal Entry, November 12, 1973

I feel a slight vibration and a sense of rapid motion. I'm suddenly in an ornate cathedral, standing in front of a tall pulpit. I feel completely comfortable and quickly climb the steps to the pulpit. I'm prepared to address the crowd, but as I look down I realize that no one is present. Confused and unsure of what to do next, I snap back into my body and find myself sitting up in bed fully awake and aware. Surprised, I think to myself, *That's strange; I've never had an out-of-body experience while sitting up.* Then it hits me—I'm not in my physical body at all. I look around and see that my physical body is lying in the bed, sound asleep. A wave of excitement surges through me as I realize that the cathedral experience occurred in a completely different energy-body. For the first time it becomes clear: the "feel" of the two nonphysical bodies are dramatically different. The energy-body I'm in now is much denser, almost physical when compared with the lightness of the second energy-body.

With that experience, I realized that the first (dense) nonphysical body is actually an energy duplicate of the physical, while the second possesses a finer vibratory rate, like pure energy, ready to respond to the slightest thought. The more I thought about my realization, the more excited I became. I knew I had made a major breakthrough because now I understood how limited the first energy-body really is. This also explained why my abilities and perceptions varied so much when out-of-body. In theory, I should be able to consciously move from one energy form to the next. In a sense, I should be able to jettison the first body and move to the second at will. I couldn't wait to have my next experience and test out my theory.

For a week I tried without success; then finally it happened. After sleeping for five hours, I awoke at 6:00 A.M. and moved to the sofa. After about fifteen minutes of reading, I became drowsy and repeated my favorite affirmation, "Now I'm out-of-body," forty to fifty times as I drifted off to sleep.

I immediately recognized the vibrational state, lifted out of my physical body, and took several steps to the door. Instead of walking through the door as I normally would, I requested clarity and firmly asked to experience my second energy form: "I move to my higher body." I felt a surge of energy and was instantly in a completely new environment. I was absolutely thrilled; it had worked.

I felt energized and light as a feather; my mind came alive with possibilities. Out of habit I asked for clarity and my mind became crystal clear. For the first time I truly understood what being conscious meant. My thoughts became faster, more vibrant and alive than ever before. It's difficult to describe, but I felt incredibly expansive, without fears or limits. I realized that the physical state of consciousness is a dull perception, like a hazy dream. In addition, I recognized that the first nonphysical body is very similar to the physical.

Looking back at this experience, I remembered a gradual change of my nonphysical body as I moved inward. It became clear that as I increased my personal energy frequency, I automatically moved inward within the interior, nonphysical regions of the universe. This discovery has significance for all of us. Not only our frequency and density but also our nonphysical shape and form change as we explore inward. After experiencing this change on a number of occasions, I could no longer ignore the importance of the discovery. Our bodies' personal energy frequency is directly related to the frequency of our immediate surroundings. As a result, when we alter our personal energy frequency we automatically move to the nonphysical energy level of the universe that corresponds to our own internal frequency. Once I gained some degree of self-control over my nonphysical explorations, I began to experiment with consciously altering my personal frequency rate. I discovered that this can be achieved by simply requesting an energy change when out-of-body.

For two years I had believed that I was moving laterally from one area to another within the same dimension, but now the startling truth was apparent. I was not moving laterally but inwardly within the universe from one energy environment to another. Lateral motion felt different; it was generally more physical-like in its sensations. After repeated trial and error, I arrived at a series of observations. First, when we request a change in our non-physical energy-body, it will immediately respond to our focused request or demand. Second, when we make a request to raise our vibratory rate or move inward, our consciousness automatically propels us into a higher-frequency area of the universe. And third, our internal frequency always corresponds to the frequency rate of the new dimension or environment that we are experiencing.

With practice it's possible to consciously alter and control the personal vibrational frequency of our nonphysical body. This process is the key to true control and unlimited freedom when out-of-body. With this knowledge it's possible to move from one energy dimension to another with full conscious control, but more important, it gives us the ability to explore the entire multi-dimensional universe. This inner motion, when controlled, provides us with the capability to become fully conscious inter-dimensional beings. The following is an example.

Journal Entry, March 12, 1974

I repeat my regular affirmations at noon, "Now I'm out-of-body," and slowly drift off. Within seconds I feel the vibrational state, will myself away from my sleeping physical body, and move to the foot of the bed. I immediately demand "Clarity now!" and my vision improves. Feeling centered, I stand at the foot of my bed and say aloud, "I move inward." I feel an immediate sensation of rapid inner motion—I'm being drawn into a vacuum deep within myself. The sensation of motion is so intense that I shout "Stop!" Instantly I stop moving and realize that I'm in a new environment. I am outdoors in a beautiful parklike setting. My vision is hazy so I repeat my clarity demand, "Clarity now!" My vision and thoughts seem to snap into place. My body feels lighter and vibrantly energetic. I attempt to stay calm as my thoughts race. I look down and feel my body. I have a distinctive shape and form much like my normal nonphysical body; however, this form somehow feels lighter and more energized than my first energy-body.

Excited with my success, I say aloud, "I move to the next level." Instantly I'm drawn inward at incredible speed. I can barely hold on and my fear begins to build. Within seconds the inner motion abruptly stops and I'm floating in another strange environment. This time few objects are visible, but I feel intense energy radiating around me. As I look around, I realize that I don't need to turn my head; I seem to see wherever I direct my thoughts, and I can see in every direction simultaneously. I look down at my body but see nothing that I can describe; I'm a 360-degree viewpoint without form or substance. I feel an overpowering sense of energy and knowledge flowing through me. My entire being is immersed in a sea of pure energy and unconditional love.

For what feels like hours I enjoy the soothing sensations of floating in this ocean of pure living light. Not wishing to return to my physical body, I hold my focus as long as possible. Finally I return to my body and look at the clock. I'm surprised—I was gone for less than forty minutes.

As I reviewed my experiences I tried to arrive at a clearer understanding of my nonphysical existence. Certain similarities and differences between my physical and nonphysical body were now apparent.

For example, I realized that my sight when out-of-body was very similar to the physical. The only noticeable difference was in its clarity. My vision just after separation was often blurry and out of sync. I could quickly improve it, however, by demanding "Clarity now." I found it essential to do this during each out-of-body experience and often repeated my request several times during a single out-of-body experience.

I noticed that I relied heavily on my sense of sight. The other senses seemed almost unimportant in comparison. In retrospect, I believe this may owe to my current physical dependence on vision. Each of us is different; some of us may focus more on hearing or touch than on vision. I suspect that each of us would probably lean upon one sense more heavily than the others. For example, a professional musician might focus on hearing and a dancer might tend to focus on touch.

I also recognized that breathing was no longer necessary and that the sensations of temperature appeared nonexistent. Even though I experienced no sensation of temperature, I did have a sense of touch and could feel objects and even feel my grip. In addition, while my sense of hearing remained much the same, my sense of taste appeared to be absent. Later I was to discover that all five senses are available if we focus upon them.

With experience I came to understand that all of our nonphysical senses are created and controlled by our minds. I seriously question whether our nonphysical bodies contain any natural or inherent ability to perceive at all. Our thoughts mold the nonphysical body in accordance to our current self-image. I grew to understand that my physical body was only a temporary vehicle for expression. In time I came to realize that this also applies to our nonphysical bodies.

I recognized that my nonphysical form was in many ways an energy duplicate of my physical body. My overall size and shape remained the same; however, the energy substances I was made of were quite different. Instead of molecules, my nonphysical body appeared to be made of countless tiny points of interconnected light. On two occasions I tried to look into a mirror (a physical mirror) when out-of-body but could see nothing.

My curiosity about the appearance, construction, and substance of my nonphysical body increased with each out-of-body adventure. Even though I could easily observe my hand and arm when out-of-body, seeing my entire form proved to be a challenge. Finally, after ten years of out-of-body experiences, the following occurred.

Journal Entry, October 2, 1982

I hear the buzzing, enginelike sounds and will myself out-of-body. I step to the bedroom door and automatically request "Clarity now!" My vision improves and I step through the door, into the living room. Still feeling a little out of sync, I verbally repeat my request with more emphasis, "Clarity now!" I feel my awareness and vision snap into place. My thoughts are clear and I make a verbal demand, "I need to see the form I'm in now!" Instantly I feel an intense sensation of being drawn within myself. I'm suddenly different, weightless as though I'm floating in space. As I look forward I see a sparkling, bluish white form. For some reason, I seem to know that I'm looking at my nonphysical body from a different perspective. I stare in amazement at this form before me that shines and flows with energy and light. It looks like an energy mold created from a million tiny points of light; it radiates a bluish glow but appears to have a defined outer structure. The body of light before me is naked and is identical to my physical form. Even though my body looks firm, there is a noticeable energy motion and radiation present. I can see what appears to be an ocean of blue stars throughout my body. It's difficult to describe because the stars are stable, yet moving at the same time; the light and energy of my body appear to change and flow almost like the waves of an ocean.

As I stare at the body of light, it hits me that I must be in another body. Yet I can't perceive any form or substance; I'm like a viewpoint in space without shape or form of any kind. As I reflect upon my new state of being, I feel a sensation of rapid motion and I'm instantly back within my physical body.

Lying still and reviewing my experience, I'm struck by an inescapable conclusion: I must possess multiple energy-bodies. The form I just experienced was noticeably lighter (less dense) than even my second nonphysical body. I realize that the traditional view of our possessing two bodies—a physical body and a spiritual body—is far too simplistic; we are much more complex than this. Just as there are multiple nonphysical energy dimensions within the universe, each of us must consist of multiple energy-bodies or vehicles of expression.

Now I seriously wonder just how many nonphysical bodies or forms this involves. I suspect that there must be one within each dimension of the universe and that all of these are interrelated and connected, just as the physical body is connected to its first nonphysical (spiritual) body.

Journal Entry, October 17, 1983

I feel a strange vibration and tingling throughout my body. Recognizing that I must be in the vibrational state, I focus all my attention on the sensation of floating out of my physical body. Within seconds I float up and away from my body and slowly glide feet first toward the bedroom door. With a sense of absolute amazement I enter the structure of the door and feel its vibrational energy as I float effortlessly through it, keeping my eyes open. The door looks like an energy fog shaped and formed into an ethereal mold.

After floating through the door, I think of standing and I'm instantly in the living room, standing next to the sofa and looking around the room. As I look around I notice that a strange small form appears to be following me. Staring, I recognize our beagle puppy, McGregor. I'm amazed because I've never seen an animal when out-of-body. He appears surprisingly natural and solid as he wags his tail and looks up at me. I notice that his eyes are shining and then I see something else:

there's a thin filament like a spider's web stretching from his body and extending back toward the bedroom. Out of curiosity I bend down and touch the thin silvery strand. Instantly, the puppy disappears. I'm startled by the rapid change and snap back to my physical body.

As my numbness quickly fades, I can feel the dog physically jump up on the bed. I lie still and review the experience, attempting to put it into perspective. Now more than ever, I realize how little we know about ourselves and our world. I feel like a naive schoolboy who has just seen the real world for the first time. It strikes me how arrogant we are to assume we know anything. We, who don't know what we are, why we're here, or even where we go, consider ourselves the dominant, intelligent rulers of the world. It's truly ironic just how deceived we are.

It's even more laughable that we hold so many firm convictions and conclusions concerning things we don't see or understand. Now more than ever, I'm convinced that out-of-body exploration can provide the answers to the many mysteries of our existence.

CHAPTER 2

Meetings Out-of-Body

Any sufficiently advanced technology is indistinguishable from magic.

—Arthur C. Clarke

Journal Entry, February 21, 1985

I enter the vibrational state and feel waves of energy flowing through my body. It's a soothing sensation of energy radiating from deep within me. As I focus on the vibrational changes, I feel pulses of energy flowing through me and a distinct sensation of hands gently touching my body. At first I'm startled, but I quickly realize that the sensation is comforting and even enjoyable once I get accustomed to it. The waves of energy seem to increase and decrease in a rhythmical sequence, and I can feel myself becoming lighter and lighter until I'm completely detached from my body. I recognize that I'm floating just out of phase with my physical body and could easily separate at any moment; however, I also sense that I should remain still and allow the vibrational process to continue. I can feel the subtle touch of hands as they move from the bottoms of my feet upward along my entire body. Each touch creates waves of energy resonating through me. It feels as though my internal vibrational rate is being adjusted to a new energy level or frequency, and I sense that the person or persons next to me are doing a form of "energy work" on me. For over twenty minutes the energy currents systematically move and flow through my nonphysical body. My body and mind seem to resonate with the energy waves, and I feel an overwhelming sense of peace and unity throughout my being. Slowly the waves of energy dissipate and my physical sensations return.

My mind is racing with questions: What is this? What is the purpose? What entity or entities are touching me? One thing is certain, I felt noticeably light and airy for several hours afterward. My entire body felt as though it was vibrating at a higher or finer rate. I strongly suspect that I've just experienced a vibrational or frequency adjustment of my nonphysical being. I can only imagine that I may have needed this energy adjustment in order to expand or enhance my nonphysical explorations.

Even though no one communicated with me, I know that this process was an important energy adjustment required for my personal development. I also realize that these energy sensations were completely different from the vibrations I normally experience during the vibrational phase before separation. I received a strong sense of direction and purpose as the hands of energy touched me. I believe that it was one or possibly two entities working on me. Like unseen chiropractors, they seemed to know precisely what they were doing; each touch altered my internal vibrational rate at a specific point within my nonphysical body and created energy waves resonating deep within me. Though startling at first, this was a thoroughly enjoyable experience that I know will occur again.

Journal Entry, December 5, 1986

I lie in bed visualizing my living room and repeating to myself, "Now I'm out-of-body," for approximately fifteen minutes. After drifting off to sleep, I feel the vibrations and spontaneously do a sideways roll out of my body. I fall to the floor and open my eyes. Everything is blurry and I feel extremely heavy and out of sync. I crawl a few feet and say aloud, "I'm light as a feather." I feel a surge of inner energy and I'm instantly lighter and able to stand. As I move away from my bed my vision remains poor, so I make another request, "Clarity now." My vision seems to snap into focus and I immediately stride forward through the wall of my room and into a bright green environment. Looking around, I realize that I'm in an open meadow. I feel somewhat confused by the rapid change of surroundings and spontaneously call aloud, "Where am I?" I suddenly feel the presence of someone close by, and a series of vivid pictures enters my mind. "You have raised your vibrational rate when you asked for lightness and again when you asked for clarity. You have entered a higher-frequency environment that is very close to the physical."

I'm amazed at the clarity of the images entering my mind. It's difficult to describe, but they're visual representations of ideas—not words. The communication is far more direct and precise than words.

I understand the meaning and look for the source. I can feel the energy radiation of someone directly in front of me but can see nothing. Out of curiosity I call out, "Who are you?"

Again the images stream in my mind. "I'm an old friend who is observing your progress."

The feelings instilled in the images are warm and friendly. I'm completely at ease and firmly make a request, "I want to see you."

I watch in amazement as the hazy outline of an image appears. A transparent hologram of a man becomes increasingly dense before me. He has dark hair and a short beard and wears a long purple robe. He's about five-feet-ten-inches tall, and a broad smile radiates from his face. At first I'm startled by the reality of his rapid materialization, but he seems to sense my discomfort and a series of comforting images appears in my mind: "No need for fear. You and I are old friends." I somehow sense his friendship and calm down.

As I stare at this man, he seems pleased to see me. He seems to know my thoughts and responds to the questions that fill my mind. "I'm just as you; the only difference is I don't possess a physical vehicle.

"We are friends from long ago and have worked together on numerous projects within the interior. . . . You and I have explored far beyond the second membrane. Now you are exploring the dense region again. . . . You have a strange fascination with the physical, one that I don't share." There is a brief pause as my questions form.

"I'm acting as one of your guides. You have several different individuals assisting you in different aspects of your life. In a way, each person assisting you is a specialist in a given area of existence. You and I love to explore inward, so I am here to assist in that part of your life. . . . You were correct in your conclusion: a guide would never interfere in the natural evolution of an individual's personal development. We realize that we must remain unobserved unless assistance is requested. Even then, we must appraise the situation and its consequences before we act."

My mind is overflowing with endless questions. The being before me seems to understand and anticipate my thoughts.

His calming thought-images pinpoint specific questions as he continues.

"Each person who has an out-of-body or near-death experience has a guide present during the experience. Assistance is always available but it must be requested. . . . There is nothing to fear, but many are still unaware that their thoughts manifest their reality. As you now know, this can happen instantly. The end result can be startling to the novice explorer. Most physical inhabitants possess little control over their thoughts."

After a brief pause, he continues. "As you are learning, thought control and focus are absolutely essential. This is especially true as you explore deeper within the interior of the universe. Your control is getting better, but you still have fears to overcome. . . . You felt your fears when I became visible to you; I could tell that you were wobbling in your energy field and close to reentering your body. . . . Always remember, when we conquer our fears we gain our liberation. . . . Very shortly, you will experience some new ways to confront your fears, both in the dense body and in your higher-frequency bodies. Each experience will serve a purpose; each obstacle is a blessing in disguise."

At that instant I snap back into my physical body and open my eyes. I feel like I'm being prepared for something to come, but I don't have a clue what it could be. I feel a strange sense of friendship with this man. I sense his positive intentions and feel somehow more prepared to face the unknown. His last images echo in my mind: "Each obstacle is a blessing in disguise." I can't help but wonder if he's explaining my past or preparing me for my future.

As I review this experience, I can't help but notice some similarities between my nonphysical friend and the guide described in Paul Twitchell's books. Even though the two resemble each other, it seems unlikely that they are the same person. Over the years, I have met several out-of-body explorers who have described a similar-appearing nonphysical guide. The reason for this is unknown, but I wonder whether our existing concept of a nonphysical guide or event may influence what we experience when out-of-body.

Journal Entry, January 3, 1987

I feel the vibrations and lift out. I'm standing in my bedroom and, looking around, I see that the surroundings are similar but not exact. The woodwork and walls are different from those of my physical home. I move to the door and step through it. Instantly, I'm in a new environment. A woman that I somehow seem to know approaches me. She's tall, with long brown hair and sparkling eyes.

She steps close to me and smiles, "I've missed you."

Spontaneously I respond, "Me too."

She kisses me and warmly takes my hands. Suddenly, we're in another environment. A magnificent parklike setting comes into focus. We stand together at the edge of a crystal blue-green pond. Everything around me—the trees, the grass, the pond—are vibrantly alive. As I look at the woman, an intense feeling of love swells inside me.

She stares at me and holds both my hands. "You travel so much. I need you here."

I hold her close. "I'm here now."

Her face and body seem to shine like ten thousand points of light. We kiss and a surge of energy floods into my mind. Our bodies and minds come together in an intense explosion of pure energy and joy. Our thoughts merge and touch one another in a thousand subtle ways. I feel immersed in her mind as she and I become as one. The ecstasy is beyond words. For the first time, I feel complete and whole.

I think to myself, *My God, I don't want it to end.*

With a jolt, I'm snapped back into my body. My entire being seems to vibrate at a lighter, finer level than I've ever known before. Even my physical body feels different—somehow brighter, lighter, and energized beyond my conception. I lie in bed and enjoy the waves of energy that flow throughout my body and mind. The sensations last for several minutes. I remain still and enjoy every moment.

For many weeks after this experience, I pondered its meaning. Was this sex in the inner worlds or was it a unification of my conscious mind with a higher aspect of myself? I feel that I should know the answer, but I don't.

Journal Entry, October 15, 1988

I repeat my regular affirmation as I drift to sleep, "Now I'm out-of-body." Within seconds I'm floating above my body and direct myself to the foot of the bed. Out of habit I say aloud, "Clarity now." Instantly my awareness becomes clear and I spontaneously think about exploring. There's a sense of rapid motion and I'm standing in a magnificent parklike courtyard. As I focus, I see around me a dozen people riding bikes and roller-skating. The courtyard is the size of a football field, with several large trees and a stone-wall border about eight feet high. I notice that one woman is pushing a baby stroller and two boys are throwing a ball back and forth. The entire environment feels happy and relaxed. I'm especially interested in the baby stroller—I've never seen an infant when out-of-body. To my surprise a smiling, red-haired girl about twelve years old skates over to me and asks, "You're new here, aren't you?"

I respond, "I guess I am."

Out of nowhere it starts to rain and everyone in the courtyard scrambles for cover. I'm amazed. In fifteen years, I've never seen weather changes when out-of-body.

The girl stares at me and points to shelter under a tree. "Come on. Let's go over there."

I can't believe how real the softly falling rain seems. As I enjoy feeling it flow down my face, I wonder if this is a consensus environment. Out of curiosity I focus all my attention on stopping the rain. The girl stares at me as if I'm crazy.

"What are you doing?"

"I'm stopping the rain."

Instantly the rain stops. The girl continues to stare and asks, "Are you a traveler?"

I feel a slight tugging sensation at the center of my back and know I have to leave.

"I've got to go."

She looks deeply disappointed and says, "Will you come back?"

As I look at her face I snap back into my physical body. A tingling sensation quickly fades as my physical senses return.

Opening my eyes, I can vividly see the girl's face in my mind. For some unknown reason I miss her. I feel I know her but I can't remember how or where. It's kind of frustrating because I know there's a connection. I've realized for some time that coincidence is nonexistent. I also wonder about her question, "Are you a traveler?"

Journal Entry, September 16, 1989

As I drift off to sleep, I repeat my normal affirmation, "Now I'm out of body," thirty to forty times. As much as possible, I intensify and hold my affirmation as my last conscious thought before going to sleep. I awaken to a slight vibration and sense of rapid motion. After several seconds I find myself standing in a multileveled parking structure. In the distance I can see ramps heading up and down. As I look around, an unusual sight attracts my attention. A shiny new car is half-buried in a pile of dirt. It looks so strange that I'm drawn to it. I think to myself, *Who would do this to a beautiful new car?* For some reason, I have an overpowering need to look inside and begin to brush the dirt away from the windows and doors. As I work, I realize that this is a huge job before me. Even so, I continue to dig handfuls of dirt away from the windows. Finally, a window is clear and I peer inside. Instead of a normal interior, I see a radiant white light permeating the inside of the car. The light seems vibrantly alive with energy and life. I feel an intense inner connection to the light and an overwhelming need to open the car door. With increased intensity, my hands tear at the dirt and slowly clear another window.

Out of nowhere a car pulls up beside me with a young man inside. I immediately sense that we know each other quite well, but I can't remember how or when. He smiles as he speaks.

"You've got a lot of work ahead of you."

Surprised by his presence, I nod in agreement and walk over to his car.

"Would you like to help?"

He seems amused by my request and replies, "Each of us must free ourselves."

His words seem to ring in my mind as I instantly snap back to my physical body. My physical senses quickly return as I ponder the experience.

More than ever, I realize that my mind is interpreting my out-of-body experiences based upon my current physical concepts, symbols, and images. It's apparent that a higher part of myself is orchestrating my experiences in a manner that's appropriate for my current understanding. I recognize and understand the dreamlike imagery of this experience, but I question whether it is necessary.

In my mind, the experience is clear. I am striving to free my inner energy-self, my soul. The dirt represents all the negative trash that I've collected and accepted over the years—attach- .
ments, fears, limits, all the negative attributes and emotions I

am working to remove. My personal dirt is limiting, blocking, and restricting the light of my soul from shining forth. I can't help but wonder what would happen if I demanded to see the true energy source represented by the form.

Now, for the first time, I fully understand that many of the forms I see when out-of-body are created for my benefit. They are manifested for my comprehension. Our minds are obviously conditioned to react to forms, not to pure energy. Increasingly it's clear that my higher mind or soul is creating the outer forms I perceive in order to teach me what I need to know.

Now I feel ready to see the reality behind the forms. Next time, I'm going to ask to see the actual raw energy behind all the forms that I perceive.

Journal Entry, January 24, 1990

I feel the vibrations and direct myself away from my physical body. Within seconds I'm standing at my bedroom door. Out of habit I verbally request clarity and guidance. Suddenly I feel an intense inner motion, and within seconds I find myself at the entrance of a large stone building. The size and shape of the building are like nothing I've seen before; the structure extends to the horizon and appears to be extremely old. In front of me is a set of fifteen-foot-high brass-and-wood doors. Upon entering I see an open room leading to an endless series of corridors. I walk through the open area and enter the closest corridor. All around me are huge rooms filled with forms and objects that appear the same. On closer examination, though, I notice that the objects are slightly different; they appear to be a progression, or possibly an evolution, of the same object. In another room are hundreds of toys, each slightly different in form and structure.

I have no interest in the objects and proceed down a long hallway. I realize that I'm in an area that is vacant and appears unused. In front of me are timbers blocking a double door. Using all my strength, I push the timbers out of my way and open the door. Behind the door is an engine or power room of some kind. Directly in front of me is a mammoth engine, three stories tall and the size of a football field. Somewhat confused, I say aloud, "What does this represent?" A stream of vivid images appears in my mind. "This is the power source behind the forms you see. Your mind is attempting to relate to concepts it can comprehend. True power has no shape or form." The engine fades from my sight, and an overpowering sensation of pure energy radiates before me. Focusing, I see waves of light emanating from a single source.

As I stare, the light becomes blinding. A part of me wants to turn away, but I don't. It feels as if the outer layers of myself are being burned away—my old concepts, beliefs, assumptions, and conclusions are incinerated by the intensity of the light. I can take no more and scream out, "What is this?" Instantly, I'm drawn within the light. My mind is overwhelmed as I realize that I have merged with a greater, more expansive part of myself. I suddenly understand that I am the engine of my life—I'm the creative force within me. I recognize that I have separated from myself. For several moments, the light and I are one. I feel a deep peace and interconnectiveness I have never known before. For the first time I realize that I can create whatever reality I choose—my creative power is beyond my comprehension. I now know that I have limited myself by the ideas and beliefs I have accepted, and I recognize the need to release all my limits, fears, and expectations. A profound sense of empowerment sweeps through me as I scream inside, *I will remember this.*

Instantly, I snap back within my physical body. As my physical senses return, I review the experience and realize that I can remember everything in detail but feel a deep sense of separation. I miss the unity, the oneness. As I lie in bed I know that I've experienced a more expansive part of myself. Whether we call it our higher self, our creative mind, or our soul is unimportant. But I absolutely know that this is a part of me that possesses complete access to the answers.

For some reason I seem to know that this huge building was similar to a museum—possibly a living record of all forms, or even all things that will be made. I realize that my mind was interpreting the forms I witnessed in relation to my current physical surroundings. It's taken me a long time, but I'm finally learning that it's not the forms we see that are important; it's what the forms represent. This recognition appears to be a major step forward. As strange as it may sound, I strongly suspect that the same holds true for the physical world around us.

Journal Entry, February 6, 1990

I fall asleep without doing any techniques but awaken at 1:00 A.M. in the vibrational stage. I quickly sit up within my physical body and look around. I'm startled by the sight of a man next to my bed looking through my journal. He sees me sitting up and jumps back. I am extremely angered by his presence and yell at him, "Who are you?"

He steps away from my bed, appearing shocked and frightened by my appearance. He is a fat, unshaven, middle-aged man with short hair and stands about five-feet-eight-inches tall. He continues to back away from me as I shout even louder, "Who the hell are you?" A combination of anger and fear explodes from me as I yell, "Get the hell out, get the hell out!"

He turns and runs out of my bedroom and I instantly snap back within my body. I am shouting in my physical body as I return and my mumbled cries awaken my wife. Startled, I sit up and look around. Slowly, I calm down and review the experience.

I realize that I probably overreacted, but the sight of this strange man in my bedroom created an instant self-defensive response. I couldn't sleep the rest of the night, wondering who this man was. Try as I might, I couldn't place his face. He seemed to be extremely interested in my writing; perhaps he was even spying on me. In retrospect, I probably scared him more than he scared me. After some thought, I have concluded that he was probably one of the millions of inhabitants living within the first inner energy dimension. It's possible that my out-of-body experiences made him curious about what I was writing and he was simply checking it out.

I can't help but wonder how often all of us are visited by other-dimensional inhabitants. In addition, I seriously question our concepts of privacy. I suspect that there's something more to this experience than I currently understand.

Journal Entry, March 14, 1991

I feel the vibrations and will myself to the door. Out of habit I ask for "Clarity now!" My awareness is remarkably good and I instinctively say aloud, "I move inward." I feel an intense inner motion for several seconds and come to an abrupt halt.

My entire being is immersed in a wondrous liquid light. I feel completely peaceful and at home. A warm glowing feeling of total love surrounds me.

As I focus, all my questions seem to become instantly clear. A simple request fills my awareness, "I need to see my life." Instantly, crystal-clear pictures appear before me. A series of three-dimensional pictures expands and unfolds; hundreds, then thousands, then tens of thousands of pictures come into focus. I instinctively know that each picture is of me. I focus on one. The picture is alive. I'm a small boy wearing a tunic and sandals; the floors and walls are stone and marble. This is me two thousand years ago. I'm neither shocked nor surprised—I just seem to know. Like a memory of an event long forgotten, this moment in time passes briefly before me. Then I pull back my attention and look at the countless other pictures that come alive before me. Each one is my life: some on earth, others occurring in nonphysical areas of the universe.

As I observe these events they seem to make sense: each event, each life, was a necessary step; each one achieved a specific purpose. Like the pieces to a puzzle, each picture falls into place, each contributing to the whole. Each picture, each experience, was needed to create the sum of what I am today.

Suddenly, I'm overwhelmed by the magnificence and wisdom of all that I observe. I see the good and the bad, the triumphs and the defeats. I see my countless weaknesses and faults and my occasional strengths. Suddenly it hits me that I'm witnessing my evolution through thousands of years of living. Each individual life was a step, an experience of growth; each life built upon the previous one.

A sense of joy flows through me as I understand the need for hardships and adversity. Each challenge was an important learning situation, a learning environment especially created for my development. I see the wisdom of it all. I'm the student and the teacher; I'm the writer, director, and actor of my life. An inner realization floods through me: the only way to know and understand something absolutely is to experience it for yourself. Anything less is theory and speculation. The staggering truth becomes clear: physical life is an interactive school, a relentless training ground for developing souls.

In fascination I stare at my life before me. Countless years and experiences all contributed to what I am today. The expanse of time was unimportant. I recognize that I am immortal and that time is meaningless. As soul, as pure awareness, I need no artificial device like time to track change. As soul, I never age or deteriorate; I only grow in knowledge and experience. Each of my explorations into matter increased my knowledge. Each physical journey expanded my vision and my appreciation of life. Each physical experience gave me the opportunity to develop and grow, the opportunity to express my inner qualities of love, humility, patience, and strength.

I am comforted by the simplicity of it all. It makes perfect sense: experience creates wisdom. Time is irrelevant. Deep within ourselves we keep a permanent record of each experience. Each event, each moment, is recorded in our subconscious mind.

As I stare at the pictures of my life, I realize that the physical events were only a small portion of the whole. I lived in countless different forms, in countless worlds.

A feeling of compassion flows through me as I recognize the purpose. The entire universe, physical and nonphysical, is a training school for developing souls. I clearly see schools within schools, dimensions within dimensions, all serving as an interactive learning environment. Each energy level of the universe is serving a specific purpose. Each is providing specific challenges and opportunities for growth, for evolution.

A sense of purpose and order becomes clear: I'm witnessing the evolution of consciousness, the evolution of myself through eons of time. My awareness overflows with love and gratitude. For the first time in my life, everything around me makes perfect sense.

At that instant I return to my body with a warm feeling of love and knowledge radiating through every cell of my being. For the first time, I understand my purpose and reason for being.

With each out-of-body experience I continued to examine the nonphysical forms I encountered. At first they appeared to be holographic images with substance. On closer inspection, I discovered that they were every bit as real and solid as physical matter. These nonphysical objects appeared to consist of a matrix of light energy instead of molecular energy.

For years, I didn't comprehend the implications, but as my experiences continued I began to realize that all life, physical and nonphysical, is interconnected. In addition, I discovered that each physical object around us exists as a multiple-frequency object. Everything around us also exists in a parallel, nonphysical dimension of the universe. Although our eyes see only the dense molecular result of energy, matter continues in a continuum of nonphysical energy beyond our sight. Each form is independent of the physical yet is interconnected by its internal frequency, just as particles of light and waves of light are interconnected as a single unit of energy.

Matter exists as a continuum of energy extending far beyond the crude limits of our physical vision. This is an important realization because it explains the very existence of all form and substance observed throughout the nonphysical interior of the universe. It also explains the multidimensional nature of everything we observe when out-of-body. For example, when we observe physical light, we see only a tiny portion of the entire electromagnetic spectrum. Yet each of us is immersed in a sea of radiation frequencies: X rays, infrared rays, radio waves, and microwaves. Just as visible light makes up only a fraction of the electromagnetic wave spectrum, so visible matter composes only a tiny portion of the entire multidimensional (frequency) energy-universe. The vast majority of the universe is not particle based, as current science assumes, but frequency based. Physical particles of matter are simply the dense result of nonphysical energy frequencies (waves). Just as visible light is not only a particle of energy but also a wave temporarily exhibiting particle behavior, so our entire physical universe is not just molecular energy but a continuum of energy frequencies extending deep into the heart of the multidimensional universe. Simply put, all objects and life-forms are multidimensional in nature. Everything around us is multidimensional, simultaneously existing in different energy frequencies of the universe. Yet all these energy dimensions coexist in the same time and space, just as radio waves, microwaves, X rays, and visible light exist together, each within its own frequency band.

Journal Entry, April 12, 1991

I enter the vibrational state and will myself to the bedroom door. I'm slightly out of focus and say aloud, "Clarity now!" Immediately my vision improves and I step through the bedroom door. I stop my forward motion and decide to explore inward instead of walking around my house. Spontaneously I call out, "I move inward." Instantly, I feel an intense inner motion that lasts for several seconds—it's as if I'm being drawn into a vacuum of space. The sense of motion abruptly stops and I'm standing in front of an oceanfront home. The house sits about ten feet in the air, resting on twelve-inch-thick wooden pillars.

My vision is slightly foggy so I ask for clarity again. My vision snaps into focus and I think about entering the house. Almost instantly I'm inside. As I look around, everything seems familiar. I feel completely comfortable and, for some reason, am absolutely certain that this is my nonphysical home.

The wall facing the ocean is made of glass. As I move closer to the glass I notice that the corners are curved like plastic. It looks like a home of the future filled with things from the past; all the furniture, artwork, and rugs appear to be antiques. Looking around, I clearly see my lion-head rocking chair facing the ocean. As I stare, I recognize that this could be my home in the future. I don't know if it's my physical future or a possible future after my death, but I do know that it's a reality existing now.

Feeling completely at home, I walk over to the glass wall and peer out at the ocean. The sound of the ocean is magnificent. Instead of pounding surf there is a strong rhythmic harmony, like a song. I listen intently, trying to recognize the melody. Instinctively, I open the door and step out onto a huge deck overlooking the ocean. The music of the waves is almost hypnotic in its beauty. The sound seems to move through me; it resonates deep within my body and mind. It's hard to describe, but the ocean seems to radiate love. As the music flows through me, it feels as if I'm being caressed by the vibrations of the song.

As I look at the ocean, I'm amazed at the changing colors of the waves. It's like nothing I've ever seen before. Shimmering hues merge and blend to form endless swirls of vivid color. The colors are beyond description, millions of shades and tints changing and mixing to form a flowing light show of indescribable beauty.

My mind is lost in the vibrations and song of the ocean. I feel completely at peace, my entire being resonating with the music of the song. I feel a need to merge with the ocean, but inwardly I'm afraid that I could be swallowed up and drown. My indecision suddenly becomes clear and I recognize my fear; I thought that I had overcome my fears, but now it's obvious that I have considerable work ahead of me. As I try to analyze this realization, I'm snapped back to my body. The numbness and tingling sensations quickly fade as I ponder the experience.

I realize that this is the second time I've been in this house. The first time was at a meeting I attended with several people. This house feels so much like home, I wonder if it's where I lived before I was physically born. Even more, I wonder about the ocean of color and music. I suspect that the ocean is my mind's interpretation of something that's beyond my comprehension. I can only guess that it's a sea of consciousness, or maybe my mind's interpretation of God itself. Perhaps both of these are the same. I still don't know, but I'm sure I'm getting closer to the answer.

Journal Entry, October 24, 1992

I repeat my favorite affirmation aloud for five to ten minutes: "Now I'm out-of-body." As I drift off, I intensify the affirmations in my mind. I awaken to the sensations of strong vibrations surging through my body. Immediately I focus my full attention on the idea of floating to my bedroom door. Within seconds I feel myself lift and float to the door. Then, with a sense of exhilaration, I walk though the door and into the living room. As I look around, I realize that I'm in my first (densest) energy-body and have a sudden overwhelming urge to explore. Almost shouting, I verbally make a firm request, "I want to see more." Instantly, a sensation of rapid motion draws me inward. I feel as if I'm being drawn into a vacuum, and in seconds I'm in a new environment. I'm startled and blinded by the intensity of the surrounding light. When I instinctually attempt to shield myself from the radiation, I realize that my body is without form—no arms or legs, just energy. I try to comprehend that I have no shape whatsoever. I seem like light without a distinctive outer form. My vision is endless.

All around, pure energy emanates; there are no shapes or forms, just radiation of light. I'm drawn to what appears to be a column of pure white light. As I move closer to the light, the sheer power of its radiation is overpowering. I stop and try to adjust. The energy is so intense it feels like the outer parts of me are being burned away. My entire outer self—my thoughts, fears, and concepts—is being incinerated by the light. At first, I try to shield myself. I surround myself with thoughts only to realize that they too are being burned away by the intensity of the light. Unsure of what to do, I instinctively release and surrender myself to the light. At that moment, the light enters me like a warm liquid permeating my body and mind. My entire being is filled with light, and every part of me seems to resonate at a new frequency. I relax and enjoy the sensation of pure energy flowing through me.

Deep within, I realize that something of extreme importance is before me. There is something else within the column of light. No longer afraid, I have an overpowering desire to know and understand the light. I move closer and try to peer inside. The pure energy and power are beyond words; I feel like I'm standing next to a blazing white sun that radiates waves of light. Somehow I know that I'm safe, and I slowly move forward and touch the light. An intense surge of energy flows through my entire being. I'm suddenly immersed in an ocean of pure knowledge. I'm flooded with memories of all I've been, all I've done, all that I am. Everything is now. I'm overwhelmed by the absolute simplicity of it all. For the first time, everything is clear. Everything we are and need is already here. For the first time, I recognize that we have separated ourselves from our source. How foolish we are. We focus on decaying molecular forms when true reality is always here, patiently waiting for us to open our eyes and see. An overpowering feeling of love, a deep feeling of compassion for everything that is, permeates my being. I realize that we are all interconnected in an ocean of living light. The separateness we feel is but the dense illusion of molecular form. My awareness comes alive with the realization that my mind and its capabilities are but another temporary vehicle of expression. We exist beyond thought, beyond time, beyond linear cause and effect.

I'm overwhelmed by endless waves of pure knowledge. My mind is filled beyond its limits, and I realize that this is more than I can ever hope to remember. I scream out, "I will remember this." Instantly I'm snapped back to my body and attempt to open my eyes.

I'm unable to move and recognize that I'm in a cataleptic state. Slowly, I can feel a numbness and tingling spread through my physical body. After about a minute, I can move my fingers and toes. I lie still and review the experience with a feeling of awe. I absolutely know that the column of light was really me—not just another part of me, but the pure me, the very essence of all I am. Is it possible that we are really that incredible? Now I feel separated and alone; yet, at the same time, I feel connected to something far greater than I've ever imagined. My mind races with realizations, more than I can begin to comprehend.

I now recognize that we as human beings have a natural tendency to attach labels to everything we experience and to filter it according to our physical concepts and beliefs. I wonder if all shapes and forms are really our minds' interpretation of something else—something that exists beyond all form and substance; something so pure and ethereal as to be beyond our minds' ability to classify and interpret. It's possible that our recognition of this is a major step forward in and of itself. Maybe the constant infighting between different religions, faiths, and sects would finally come to an end if we only recognized that all religious beliefs are the physical interpretations of mortals. It's now absolutely clear that God does not care about our personal theology. Our physical beliefs are all rooted in temporary forms and substance; they are all but a passing moment in time. What really matters is experience, spiritual experience. It appears that the purpose of the entire universe is experience—firsthand, gut-wrenching, personal experience. Nothing can replace it. It's now clear that personal experience is the road to wisdom that we all share.

As I expanded my exploration beyond the first inner dimension, I began to notice some unusual sights. In some areas, clouds of energy dominated the environment. I was especially amazed to see some of these clouds taking specific forms. I saw what appeared to be cars, homes, even cruise ships partially created.

After years of experience, I have concluded that these items are the direct result of human thought. The environments within the nonphysical dimensions are made of thought-responsive energy. Thoughts appear to be innately capable of rearranging the subtle energies that make up the unseen dimensions.

I have found that the natural energy-substance of the inner dimensions appears as cloudlike forms of energy. In a sense, this energy is an easily manipulated radiation of light. It appears that the building blocks of the unseen dimensions are not particles (atoms and quarks) but waves or frequencies of energy and light. When I examined the energy clouds, it became apparent that they exist as clusters of raw, unformed energy—much like holograms that are slowly growing and changing in form and density.

Journal Entry, April 12, 1991

I feel the vibrations and will myself to the foot of the bed. I feel a little hazy and out of focus, so I immediately demand complete clarity. Instantly, my conscious mind seems to snap in gear; my thoughts become clear. My mind is alive and racing with excitement as I say to myself, "This is better than my physical brain."

Suddenly I feel an intense inner need to discover my past life. Spontaneously I say loudly, "I need to know my past life."

Instantly, there's a sensation of inner motion and I find myself in a completely new environment. I'm surrounded by an incredible scene of destruction. As I look down a long city street I see nothing but demolished buildings. I realize that my upper body is extending through the hatch of a tank. Then it hits me that I'm seeing through the eyes of this other man— the soldier. I am this man; I feel his thoughts and emotions.

I'm extremely arrogant and self-assured and feel strangely powerful as I look at the burning buildings and rubble around me. I'm proud of what I've done. I'm a tank commander, a German panzer commander. Somehow I know that the city is Warsaw, Poland, and that my soldiers and I have just conquered it.

My tank grinds to a halt at the center of what used to be a major city intersection. Several tanks around me fire, and entire blocks of buildings collapse before me. I am pleased with myself. Holding some kind of device, I bark orders to a tank on my right. As I look at my arm, I notice that my uniform is black and is covered with gray powder.

Suddenly, an intense sense of motion, like a vacuum, snaps me back into my physical body. I open my eyes and feel a numbness and tingling as I reunite with the physical.

I'm startled and amazed at the intensity of the experience. I was not just an observer but an active participant. For a few moments I felt what this man felt—I was this man. I feel disappointed with myself; I had envisioned myself as something more than an arrogant German officer. Maybe this explains my current antiwar sentiment and also my fascination with World War II documentaries. If this German tank commander was indeed my last physical life, I wonder just how much of him influences me now. A realization sweeps through me that he may affect me more than I would like to admit. As I look at myself as objectively as possible, a flood of new insights comes to light. I seriously wonder just how arrogant, demanding, and aloof I am now. Do I still bark orders and expect to be instantly obeyed?

I wonder just how much of me is influenced and molded by my past. How strong is this influence? It appears that an unlimited amount of self-knowledge is available if we are willing to pursue it. I can't help but be curious. How many past lives have I experienced? How deeply have they influenced me? How much could I learn from knowing the answers?

Journal Entry, December 7, 1992

I enter the vibrational state and float approximately two feet above my body. Determined to experience my finer vibratory body, I say aloud, "I experience my higher body." After a brief sensation of motion, I'm floating in a different form. I feel calm and energized and sense a smoother internal energy.

Inwardly, I know I've shifted to my inner energy-body. But I feel out of sync and my vision is hazy, so I demand complete clarity of awareness, "Clarity now!"

Immediately my thoughts are clear. I feel extremely light and overflowing with energy. At that moment, my goal flashes in my mind: "I wish to visit another system." Instantly, I'm moving through a dark void at incredible speed. At first I'm startled by the speed, but I relax and adapt to the new sensations. Within seconds I'm floating in space. I look down at myself and see that there is little to see: my form has no arms or legs; I'm like a spherical form of conscious energy. For some reason, I'm not surprised—it seems completely natural that arms and legs are unnecessary in whatever state I'm in. I slowly rotate and focus on the spectacular sights around me. In awe, I stare at things I've never even imagined before. Clusters of lights are everywhere, thousands of them, like Christmas lights strung across the heavens. I feel as if I'm floating in an ocean of lights.

My attention is diverted to something I have never seen before: a hazy foglike form is visible. The form extends as far as I can see. It looks like an immense curtain of dense fog except that it appears stable, a permanent fixture hanging in space. I ask for clarity and find myself floating at a different vantage point, several miles from the hazy form. Now I see it more clearly. It's larger than my mind can comprehend, stretching across the heavens like an endless border.

Suddenly, I sense the vibrational energy of someone close by, an intense radiation without form or substance. I am instantly aware of communication, like a series of clear pictures appearing in my mind. The following is a little disjointed but as close as words can explain the inner meaning of the pictures.

"Beautiful, is it not?"

I roll over to see who it is. My awareness is blinded by the intensity of the light. I begin to back away and shield myself from the crushing energy. The entity continues to communicate with my mind.

"I will adjust."

The radiation immediately diminishes. I can't perceive a form, only light.

"I have no form as you understand it. Form is unnecessary. Not many of your kind venture this far in."

I am unable to respond—my mind is overwhelmed, and I don't know where to begin. The energy being must sense my dilemma and begins to respond.

"What you see before you is one of many wonders of the universe. The infinity of fog you see is one of the many inner membranes dividing different frequencies of the universe. What you are witnessing is the inner structure of the universe. The stars and galaxies you see in the distance are but the outer crust of the universe. The key to true exploration is the movement through the energy membranes. As you move farther inward, toward the source, your internal energy frequency must change accordingly. You can only cross through the energy barriers that are in accordance with your inner light. What you see before you is the key to stability and structure throughout the universe."

I'm amazed at the clarity of the pictures entering my mind. This being seems to automatically know my thoughts.

"All conscious energy (souls) live within the energy frequency that is in phase with their personal vibratory rate. The membrane before you separates one wavelength of energy from another."

As I stare, I can't think of an appropriate response. I feel inadequate, like a child taking an advanced calculus class. The energy being again responds to my thoughts.

"You are ready or you would not be here. All of us are where we should be. I was once as you and you shall be as I; we are all on a great journey together. Your perception of me is inaccurate. I am but a child compared to others who dwell within the universe. The possible evolution of consciousness is unlimited.

My identity is unimportant and labels are unnecessary. Remember well what you see, for the recognition and exploration of the energy membranes will have a significant impact upon the evolution of your species."

I'm somewhat confused by the speed of the information entering my mind and ask for clarification.

"I don't understand. The purpose for the energy membranes?"

"They simply separate different frequencies of energy from each other. You are observing the convergence point of two different dimensions. Energy membranes provide the necessary substructure for each dimension to exist. They are the internal cell walls of the living universe."

"My God, that's incredible."

"There is much to see. Your adventure is just beginning."

"How do you mean?"

"You will see soon enough."

"I still don't understand."

"You will, my friend, you will."

I snap back to my physical body with a jolt. At first I'm out of sync and unable to move. After twenty seconds or so I feel my physical sensations returning.

After twenty years of out-of-body experiences, I have found that there is a natural tendency for our nonphysical bodies to become progressively less dense as the experience continues. It appears that our personal frequency rate slowly returns to its "normal" or natural vibrational state. Our nonphysical body slowly adjusts to the vibrational frequency (internal density) that is our natural state of being. This process of internal adjustment is reported by several serious out-of-body explorers. Robert Monroe refers to this change when he describes his nonphysical form becoming progressively "less humanoid" in shape as the time duration of his out-of-body experience lengthens.

This tendency for us to return to our natural internal frequency rate has another important implication. On countless occasions I've noticed that when I'm out-of-body for more than several minutes, the observed environment slowly fades and a new environment becomes visible. For years I thought my vision was simply adjusting to its expanded abilities to perceive. But now I realize that this is only part of it. When we are out-of-body our nonphysical form is not static, as it may first appear, but is actually an expansive energy system that fluctuates in its internal energy frequency. This becomes especially noticeable as we control and extend our nonphysical experiences. In other words, the nonphysical body is not a body at all but a highly sophisticated energy system that responds to our thoughts. As we prolong our nonphysical adventures, our consciousness has a natural tendency to return to its true nonphysical state. As strange as this may sound, I'm now certain that our concepts related to form, shape, and substance are all temporary conditions. It appears that, as soul, we are without form of any kind. Our true self is not humanoid as we now conceive ourselves. Soul or pure consciousness is without form but can, and does, use various shapes and forms of energy for its purposes.

In November 1993 I developed an acute case of pneumonia and was bedridden for ten days. During my illness I became extremely weak, didn't eat, and slept twelve hours a day. By the third day, I noticed a dramatic increase in my out-of-body experiences. Each time I drifted off to sleep, I would find myself floating just above or near my physical body. As my illness progressed, I experienced a coinciding increase in spontaneous out-of-body experiences. It seemed as if the connection between my physical and nonphysical body was growing progressively weaker as my illness continued. At the peak of my pneumonia and for several days thereafter, I felt a sense of freedom I had never known before. While lying in bed, I would spontaneously slip out-of-body whenever my physical body dozed off to sleep. Sometimes it felt as if I wasn't connected to my physical body at all. I began to use my physical body like a reference point or staging area to regroup between nonphysical explorations. For over a week I became so detached that I viewed my physical body as a necessary encumbrance to be endured.

During this time I experienced a dramatic increase in cluster out-of-body experiences—generally, two to five separate experiences occurring in sequence. Each experience was quite short, lasting from thirty seconds to several minutes. On a few occasions, I noticed that the sequence of events seemed to address a related topic or subject. For example, one afternoon I dozed off while reading a book about past-life regressions. Almost immediately I felt the vibrations and was floating above my body. As I floated comfortably, my thoughts turned to the possibility of past lives and I immediately felt a sensation of movement.

Journal Entry, November 29, 1993
I am standing at the ramparts of a castle as smoke rises from below. A battle has raged for several days and I'm exhausted and sick of fighting. I realize that I'm some sort of medieval soldier. We have been under siege for over two months, and for the first time in my life I question why we're fighting. It seems so meaningless. For the last five years I've been fighting and killing and I've had enough. The only things that keep me going are my pride and my sense of duty. After twenty years of loyal service to my king, I own nothing but a sword and the armor on my back. As I look around, I'm amazed at how real this is. I'm more than just an observer: I somehow feel this man's thoughts and emotions, his pain and disappointment. I feel I am this man, yet I know I'm not. I experience a great sense of sorrow and disgust, a life filled with empty victories. I realize now that duty and honor alone are not enough. I know there must be more to life, but I know only weapons

and the art of war. With a sudden jolt I feel a sharp pain and
pressure in my back and begin to lose consciousness. At that
moment I feel the familiar tingling sensations and recognize
that I'm back in my physical body. I think of floating and immediately rise above my body. I'm amazed at the clarity of my
thoughts and ponder the meaning of the soldier's experience. I
feel a shift of my awareness and a sense of rapid inner motion.
Within seconds, I'm in a completely new environment.

I'm seated on a stone floor. All around me are dozens of
bald-headed monks sitting in ceremonial meditation. Somehow
I know that I'm a Buddhist monk. I can smell burning musky
incense and hear bells and rhythmic chanting. Three dozen of
us are sitting in a circle around an altar. A thin column of white
smoke rises from the center of the altar as a bald-headed boy,
about twelve years old, walks around us chanting and swinging
a large, ornate incense holder. He appears to be in a trance. I can
feel myself rocking gently back and forth as I softly chant a
phrase that seems to be a part of me. I and all those around me
are wearing orange robes, and as I look down at my hands I realize that I'm very old—my hands and wrists are thin and frail.
I am content with my life, completely free of all needs and desires. My mind is at peace. I know I will soon die. With a slight
sense of motion I'm back in my bed. Even though I am in my
body, I feel completely out of phase with it, as if I'm floating
within it. My mind is still focused upon the meaning of the
monk experience when I again feel an inward motion.

I am incredibly cold. My body and mind are numb. It's beyond my endurance to endure. All around me are the frozen
corpses of my friends and fellow soldiers. The ground is too
frozen to bury them, so they lie where they fell. My tank has
become an icy tomb.

My mind and body are a hollow broken shell of my former
self. My will to live is gone. Thirty yards away I see two ragged

soldiers pull the boots off a dead man. Beside me, a taunt, nearly lifeless man, a friend of mine, mumbles something to me. I can't hear him so I lean closer.

"For God's sake, kill me."

I cannot. I lack the courage and the strength to move. The snow is falling again and I know I'll soon be dead. A pounding sound is heard in the distance; the Russians will be here soon. I feel no fear, no hate—I feel nothing at all. I close my eyes and slip into unconsciousness.

Whether these three experiences were past lives or not, I cannot prove. I do know, however, that they were as real and vivid as any physical experience I've ever had. It seems wise to remain nonjudgmental when we are exploring new dimensions of energy. Our minds have a natural tendency to be influenced by our physical preconceptions of reality. The key to understanding is to remain as open-minded as possible.

During the time I was ill, I also began to realize how easily out-of-body experiences can be controlled if we just remember to request clarity on a regular basis. The simple, firm request for clarity of thought and vision has a tremendous effect upon our out-of-body state of consciousness. Repeating the clarity technique, I found it possible to prolong out-of-body experiences for several hours.

During my illness I would sometimes amuse myself by moving back and forth between my physical body and my floating nonphysical body. While doing this, I discovered an odd state of consciousness that I refer to as dual consciousness. I found that sometimes I was able to shift a percentage of my awareness between my physical and my nonphysical body. It's possible to perceive with both forms simultaneously and to adjust or shift the percentage of our awareness between our bodies. In other words, for brief periods we can simultaneously experience the physical world and a nonphysical environment with varying degrees of effectiveness. I also found that it was possible to control the movement of consciousness between the first and second energy-body. By force of will, we can control this shift of awareness; the key is to remain focused and centered and mentally ask to experience the second form. Always remember, once we are no longer attached to a specific form—whether matter or energy—we are free to move beyond it.

My interest in physics increased with the number of out-of-body experiences I had. When out-of-body, I would closely observe the energy structures around me. I became fascinated with the nonphysical forms and substances I encountered. I recognized that each environment and dimension within the interior of the universe has specific similarities and differences.

The most significant difference appears to be the degree of responsiveness to thought of a given nonphysical environment. Some nonphysical environments are easily molded by thought while others are extremely resistant. I believe that all nonphysical energy is thought-responsive; however, when a group of individuals maintains the same image or beliefs, the group creates, molds, and maintains a consensus reality. In effect, group thought-energy forms, stabilizes, and actually solidifies nonphysical energy. The larger the group (some number in the millions), the more stable the immediate energy environment becomes. This is an important discovery because it explains the vast differences encountered when exploring the nonphysical dimensions. For example, the first nonphysical dimension is a parallel energy world almost identical to the physical universe. This dimension of energy existing close to the physical is molded by the consensus thoughts of the six billion inhabitants existing in the physical.

The underlying cause of this phenomenon appears to be remarkable: consciousness creates reality. All reality, including matter, is shaped and molded by thought. Creation itself is the result of conscious thought-energy influencing, arranging, and manifesting form and substance as we know it. Countless nonphysical explorations into the interior of universe confirm this observation. It's only the density of matter that obscures the truth of this from our physical senses. In the physical world, consciousness uses biological vehicles for its expression. Our physical bodies are the direct tools of our consciousness; our thoughts direct our bodies to build the reality we experience every day of our lives. This process of consciousness creating reality is more important than words can begin to express. Our recognition of this reality is the first step to true mastery of ourselves and our surroundings. Each of us possesses the creative ability and power to shape and mold his or her ideal physical, emotional, and intellectual surroundings. It is up to us, however, to recognize and implement our creative ability.

Our recognition of the creative power of consciousness will dramatically affect both our immediate future and the evolution of our species. Until we truly comprehend and consciously control the unseen energies flowing through us, we will be bound to the dense molecular forms that surround us. Our evolution from a physical creature to a multidimensional, nonphysical being is directly linked to the recognition and conscious control of our thought-energy. Once we truly comprehend our individual ability to shape and mold the energy around us, we can begin to take full responsibility for our thoughts. With every thought and deed we become aware that we are the creative artists of our lives.

The truth of this becomes apparent during an out-of-body experience. When out-of-body we are experiencing and exploring a higher-frequency environment, one that is significantly less dense than matter. This subtle energy environment is sensitive to thought. Each focused thought can and will create an immediate result: if we think of flying, we will fly; if we think of walking through a wall, we do so. Our thoughts exert complete control over our experience. For the first time, the true creative power of thought becomes clear. This realization is a major step in our personal evolution, for now we know that we must take full responsibility for our thoughts and our life.

The concept of consciousness creating or molding reality is not as far-fetched as some may believe. Many of the finest minds of modern physics consider this theory the logical basis of all reality. The eminent physicist David Bohm, Princeton physicist Eugene Wigner, Berkeley physicist Henry Pierce Stapp, and legendary physicists Walter Heitler, Fritz London, and John von Neumann are all supporters of the "consciousness creates reality" quantum theory. In increasing numbers, physicists and mathematicians around the world are arriving at the same conclusion: physical objects would have no attributes if a conscious observer were not watching them. Nobel laureate Eugene Wigner summed up this observation when he stated, "It is not possible to formulate the laws of quantum mechanics in a fully consistent way without reference to the consciousness. . . . It will remain remarkable in whatever way our future concepts may develop, that the very study of the external world led to the conclusion that the content of the consciousness is an ultimate reality."

As my nonphysical explorations continued, I came to realize that I was observing and interacting within a parallel energy dimension. My concepts of space, time, and distance no longer seemed valid. I began to recognize that the dimension I was exploring when out-of-body was extremely close to the physical; in fact, it was not separated at all by space or distance, but rather by energy frequency or density. As strange as it may sound, the other dimensions (possibly countless numbers of them) exist with us now. In addition, I observed that each physical object possessed a nonphysical counterpart or energy duplicate that appeared similar to an energy mold. For example, the closest nonphysical dimension and its energy structures coexist with the physical dimension and function as a form of energy substructure for matter itself. However, the same nonphysical structures also exist completely independent of the physical universe.

The immediate nonphysical environments I encountered appeared to be physical-like representations of matter. These nonphysical objects, though stable in structure and quite similar to matter, were often not an exact duplicate of my physical surroundings. At first this was confusing, but slowly I learned that it was my expectation of reality that often needed reappraisal.

I made several startling observations. First, we assume that our physical surroundings are the stable and firm basis of reality. We view density and form as the ultimate test of "real." But what if we are wrong in our assumptions? What if reality is completely relative to the vibratory rate of the observer? What if there are numerous, even countless, energy dimensions?

Second, after repeatedly exploring the immediate nonphysical environment, I began to question whether the physical world is a duplicate of the nonphysical or vice versa. This observation is important because it points to the fundamental structure of all energy, matter, and reality as we know it. At first I assumed that the parallel nonphysical dimension was the result of matter. But with experience I have come to recognize that this is not so. The parallel universe is indeed a separate energy-universe that functions as the unseen substructure of all physical energy form and substance. The nonphysical and the physical are inseparable elements of the same. Third, I gradually began to understand that I was actually observing a continuum of energy. Each physical object we observe around us exists in multiple dimensions of the universe. As startling as it seemed, the end result was clear: all physical objects, including all life-forms, are multidimensional in nature. Everything we see around us exists as a continuum of energy.

Matter is not the center of reality as we view it. Instead, matter appears to be the end result of a series of energy interactions occurring in the unseen dimensions. With each out-of-body experience I realized more clearly that matter is only a tiny portion of the energy environments that exist. In many respects, matter is the dense outermost result of a magnificent chain of events occurring just beyond our physical vision.

It appears that our perception of matter, the visible universe, and our place in the universe is completely inaccurate. The universe we see around us is not the center of reality; it is only the outer crust, the thin epidermis layer of the unseen universe. In time, I was further convinced that everything we believe is solid and real is only a temporary vehicle of consciousness. This solid reality around us only appears real to us because we are currently focusing on our physical senses. Once we separate from our biological body, the world of matter looks like a world of ghosts, a world of hazy, ethereal forms.

With each out-of-body experience, I've observed that the solid physical objects around me appear as vaporous forms. In several instances, physical objects such as walls and furniture appeared like holographic images possessing a defined but vaporous substance. When I tried to touch these objects, my hand just passed through them. Often, I felt a tingling sensation as my hand or body moved through the physical objects, but the objects didn't seem real anymore in relationship to my new vibratory rate. In addition, I noticed that the longer I remained separated from my body, the more my immediate physical surroundings seemed to fade from my view. It became obvious that the only reality to me was the objects or beings that were vibrating close to my new personal frequency rate. In other words, reality is relative to the vibrational density of the observer.

At first glance, this observation may sound strange; however, modern physics has provided some evidence that helps explain it. For example, scientists have shown that visible light exists simultaneously as a particle and a wave.

The dual nature of light is now a recognized fact of modern science. I believe the particle-wave nature of light provides substantial evidence that all energy is a multifrequency (dimensional) continuum extending far beyond the dense particles of matter that we observe around us. Just as light possesses a dual nature, both particle and wave, so all physical objects and lifeforms consist of both physical particles and nonphysical energy components. It is this interconnected continuum of energy that creates and sustains the entire multidimensional universe. Every physical object around us is actually the dense outer result of this continuum of energy. Just as light exists as both a particle and a wave at the same instant in time, so all physical objects exist simultaneously as dense molecular forms and nonphysical-spiritual forms. This realization opens the door to a remarkable new frontier of exploration and research.

Part 2

SOLVING OUR GREATEST MYSTERIES

CHAPTER 3

The New Frontier

The worldwide scientific community now agrees that an unseen energy structure must exist.
— David Seckel,
Cosmologist, University of California

In the last few decades science has become aware of the serious limitations of human visual perception. The human eye is sensitive to only a narrow band of radiation. We see only the wavelength between .00007 cm. and .00004 cm.; the rest of the electromagnetic wave spectrum remains invisible to us. In fact, only a few one-hundred-thousandths of a centimeter make the difference between visibility and invisibility. Yet all of us are literally swimming in a sea of energy, immersed in an ocean of electromagnetic waves: gamma rays, X rays, ultraviolet and infrared rays, microwaves, radio waves, and shortwaves, to name just a few. When we feel the heat of the sun, for example, we are feeling the result of invisible

Electromagnetic Wave Spectrum

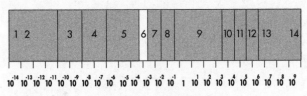

Wavelength (in centimeters)

1 Unknown	8 Heat waves
2 Cosmic rays	9 Radar
3 Gamma rays	10 Television
4 X rays	11 Short radio waves
5 Ultraviolet	12 Broadcast waves
6 Visible light	13 Long radio waves
7 Infrared	14 Unknown

infrared rays; their wavelength, .00008 cm. to .032 cm., is a little too long for our retina to detect even though our skin will register the rays as heat.

In effect, our perception of the universe is based upon only a tiny fraction of the energy around us. Even more shocking is the recognition that our current scientific technology detects only a portion of the entire energy spectrum. Most scientists believe that the electromagnetic wave spectrum continues far beyond our technological vision and possibly into infinity.

When we put this into perspective, we recognize that each of us is visually aware of only three-one-hundred-thousandths (.00003) of a centimeter of the energy radiation around us. We, who see so little of the universe, are quick to reach conclusions and judgments based upon the narrow limits of our vision. Our perspective of the universe, and of reality itself, is severely limited by the narrow range of our physical senses.

When we look around, we see a world of solid objects. On the surface, reality appears to consist of three-dimensional form and substance. Yet, as science explores deeper into the unseen heart of matter, remarkable discoveries are being made. Einstein's famous equation $E = MC^2$ tells us that matter is nothing more than a form of energy—in a sense, stored energy temporarily molded to construct the physical objects around us.

Once we recognize that all matter is actually energy, we can begin to form a new vision of ourselves and the world around us. We begin to realize that our surroundings are not what they seem.

This new vision is expanded even further when we examine the latest discoveries of quantum physics. Quantum theorists no longer consider energy to be particlelike in nature. Subatomic particles are no longer viewed as static things but as four-dimensional entities in space-time. In fact, the elemental particles of our reality (quarks and so on) are no longer considered substance at all. When physicists observe elemental particles, they describe them as dynamic patterns, constantly moving and changing into one another. Quantum mechanics has shown us that the elemental building blocks of our reality are not material but are patterns of energy interconnected to form an inseparable cosmic web.

Quantum physics has proved that our current physical concepts of form and substance are obsolete; not only is matter energy, but all energy is essentially nonphysical in nature. Physicist Werner Heisenberg clarified this new scientific viewpoint when he stated, "Atoms are not things."

After decades of remarkable discoveries, modern physics has reached an impasse. The observed motion of subatomic particles appears to follow little or no logical order. Elemental particles change their location and trajectory, appear and disappear, and move in all sorts of mysterious ways. Even more startling is the realization that they can actually be influenced by the thoughts of the scientists who are observing them.

As a new century dawns, the greatest mysteries of science remain unsolved. What are matter and energy? What are the unseen building blocks of physical reality? Increasingly, physicists and astronomers worldwide are recognizing that an immense unseen energy system must exist just beyond our technological vision. Years ago a few astronomers observed that specific areas in space existed with insufficient mass to explain their motion. In the 1980s this mysterious condition was termed "dark matter." The discovery of dark matter was first brought to light by the extensive research of astronomer Vera Rubin. In *The Astronomers* Donald Goldsmith outlines her work and its significance.

By analyzing the motions of outlying stars, Rubin's observations revealed enormous quantities of invisible matter in spiral galaxies such as our own Milky Way. Studies of the motions of galaxies in clusters, performed by other astronomers (and some by Rubin herself), showed that the *clusters* of galaxies likewise contain tremendous amounts of invisible matter. Indeed, even before Rubin's work, astronomers had found that most large galaxy clusters appear to contain far more mass than can be explained by the stars that shine in their galaxies. But it took Rubin's detailed studies of the motions of stars within our own and other galaxies to convince astronomers that nearly every galaxy, and not just those in large galaxy clusters, has far more mass in invisible form than in stars.

In short, Rubin's work established the existence of a previously unconfirmed component of the cosmos, a component that is no small addition to what we know but (broadly speaking) the universe itself. Everything we see—all the stars, star clusters, star-forming regions, and gas clouds lit by newborn stars—apparently amounts to no more than 10 percent of the total mass of a large galaxy such as our own Milky Way. Hence Rubin's research implies that all the visible matter in the universe forms only a sort of light frosting on the cosmic cake, which consists basically of invisible matter.

The discovery of dark matter (invisible mass) provides evidence of an unseen substructure to the universe. In the last two decades physicists and astronomers worldwide have arrived at the same conclusion: something unseen is interacting with matter. In 1981 the eminent theoretical physicist David Bohm proposed that the substructure of the subatomic makes sense only if we assume the existence of additional, more complex dimensions beyond our vision. This concept is growing in popularity. Many of the greatest scientific minds of the twentieth century have commented that something mysterious is occurring just beyond our technological vision. Einstein, Heisenberg, Planck, Pauli, Schrödinger, Jeans, Eddington, Bohr, and de Broglie have all expressed a belief that physics and mysticism are somehow connected. Sir James Jeans may have summed up this belief when he stated, "The universe begins to look more like a great thought than a great machine."

The Multidimensional Structure of the Universe

When we examine the evolution of science over the last few decades, we see a growing body of evidence supporting the multidimensional structure of matter and the universe. The latest discoveries of quantum physics provide numerous examples. Also significant is the growing number of physicists, astrophysicists, and astronomers who believe in the existence of parallel universes. Well-known physicist Fred Alan Wolf summarized this view when he stated, "By including quantum physics, we find strong and surprising evidence for the existence of parallel universes at the very beginning of time."

The Concept of Parallel Universes

The idea of parallel universes or dimensions is not new. Einstein's theory of relativity first predicted the existence of four-dimensional space-time and black holes. It was not until 1935, however, that Einstein and his Princeton University associate

Nathan Rosen presented their new theory concerning the function of black holes. They proposed that instead of being a simple hole or rift in space-time, as was first believed, a black hole was actually a bridge connecting one universe to another possible universe. Einstein and Rosen stated that black holes were "bridges" to anywhere and any time. In physics today this concept is known as the Einstein-Rosen Bridge.

The Einstein-Rosen Bridge was the first widely accepted scientific theory concerning the possible existence of parallel universes or dimensions. Einstein and Rosen's work set the stage for following generations of physicists to seriously study the concept of parallel universes. For example, the "many worlds interpretation" presented in 1951 by physicist Hugh Everett III was heavily influenced by the earlier work of Einstein and Rosen. Everett's theory states that many worlds or universes coexist with our own; however, they are continuously splitting into separate, distinct

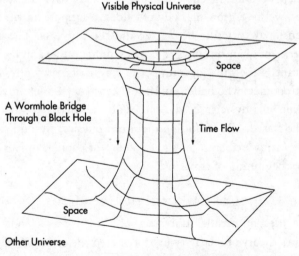

Visible Physical Universe

Space

A Wormhole Bridge
Through a Black Hole

Time Flow

Space

Other Universe

Modern Interpretation of the Einstein-Rosen Bridge

dimensions that are mutually inaccessible. According to Everett, each world or dimension contains a different version of the same people living their lives and performing various acts at the same moment in time. This theory, though highly controversial, has become well known in modern physics and is considered by some to provide a possible explanation of quantum reality.

Over the last sixty years the concept of parallel energy-universes and their interconnecting bridges has been developed by a number of well-known physicists, including Arthur Eddington, Christian Fronsdal, David Finkelstein, John Wheeler, G. Szertes, and Charles Misner. But it was another physicist, Princeton's Martin Kruskal, who first developed a written concept of it. In 1961 Kruskal presented his black hole map showing an interconnection between our physical universe and another, unseen universe.

In 1963 Australian physicist and mathematician Roy P. Kerr developed precise equations relating to the rotation of black holes. Kerr's equations indicated the existence of an infinite number of

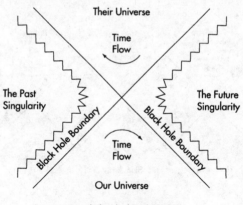

Kruskal's Black Hole Map
Showing a Parallel Universe

parallel universes, all directly connecting to black holes. He proposed that an infinite series or patchwork of universes extends toward the past and toward the future simultaneously. As strange as the concept may sound, Kerr's work is highly regarded by physicists around the world. Many consider his equations to have been one of the most important developments in theoretical astrophysics in the mid-twentieth century.

In addition, H. Reissner in Germany and G. Nordstrom in Denmark formulated a scenario of black holes connecting to other universes. Because of their work, an electrically charged black hole is sometimes called a "Reissner-Nordstrom black hole."

I believe that the existence of black holes, the Einstein-Rosen Bridge, and the equations, maps, and theories of Everett, Kruskal, Kerr, and Reissner and Nordstrom are all evidence of the multidimensional nature and structure of the universe. This growing body of evidence compiled by physicists and astronomers around the world points to the most important discovery of the twentieth century: our universe is a multidimensional continuum of interconnected energy.

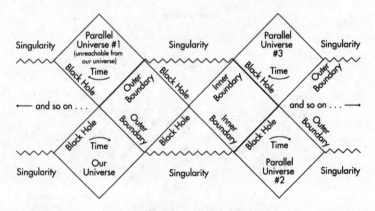

The Infinite Patchwork of Parallel Universes
in a Spinning Black Hole Found by Roy Kerr

Historical Evidence Supporting the Multidimensional Universe

When we look at history, we see that the idea of heaven or nonphysical universes is one of the oldest and most widely held beliefs of humanity. The concept of heaven appears in every culture and religion.

The Jewish and Christian religions teach the existence of three universes or dimensions: the physical world, heaven, and hell. Catholicism added a fourth with the concept of purgatory. In the Koran, Mohammed speaks of seven heavens or universes.

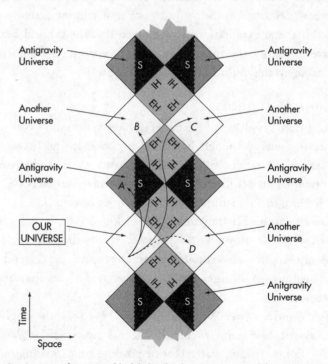

Penrose map of a rotating black hole. The diagram repeats indefinitely to the past and future. The universes outside the black hole are the white squares; the universes inside the black holes are the light and dark shaded squares.

In more recent times the theosophy view developed by Madame Blavatsky described seven dimensions. This concept of seven dimensions is also incorporated into various New Age philosophies. When we examine religions and cultures around the world, the concept of unseen heavens or universes of energy is without a doubt the most universal belief of humanity. Today practically every religion and culture has incorporated this concept. Even though this is likely the most widely held theory in human history, verifiable evidence concerning the unseen heavens continues to elude humankind. As you will discover, out-of-body exploration provides powerful personal verification that the religious "heavens" described in the scriptures of your religion actually do exist. Firsthand explorations have proved that the biblical heavens are in reality the magnificent unseen energy environments that make up the multidimensional universe.

Energy Tunnels

Additional evidence of the belief in nonphysical universes and connecting energy tunnels has been displayed in the literature and artwork of various cultures for the past two thousand years. For example, artists for centuries have portrayed tunnels of energy leading to a radiant new environment or heaven.

Dutch painter Hieronymus Bosch (1460–1516), in his well-known work *The Ascent into the Empyrean*, clearly illustrates an individual being escorted through an energy tunnel. At the end of the tunnel is a bright light indicating heaven (a higher-frequency dimension).

Two centuries later William Blake (1757–1827), the English poet, mystic, and painter, created his masterpiece titled *Jacob's Ladder*. In his striking watercolor he portrays human beings and angels moving both upward and downward toward a brilliant circle or tunnel of light.

Jacob's Ladder, William Blake

Later in the nineteenth century Gustave Doré (1832–1883) created his famous engraving of Dante and Beatrice as they experience the beatific vision. In graphic detail he portrays a nonphysical tunnel leading to a light. (See frontispiece.)

I believe a startling connection is apparent: the energy tunnels depicted by Bosch, Blake, Doré, Einstein, and Rosen and the energy conduits outlined in this book are all descriptions of the same event—an energy tunnel connecting the physical dimension with a nonphysical counterpart.

Additional evidence for this belief is provided by millions of near-death experiences reported worldwide in the last twenty years. One of the most fascinating aspects of the near-death accounts is their vivid description of a tunnel leading toward a bright light or a new environment. According to extensive studies conducted by Raymond Moody, Melvin Morse, Kenneth Ring, and other physicians, this description of an energy tunnel leading to a bright light is reported in every culture and country of the world. Notice the similarity between the Einstein-Rosen Bridge (see illustration on page 80) and the observations made by countless people who have had a near-death experience.

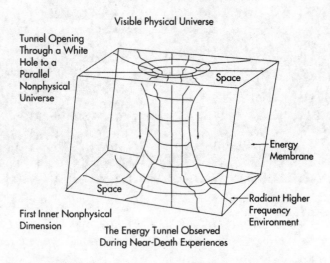

The Energy Tunnel Observed
During Near-Death Experiences

Observations obtained during controlled out-of-body explorations suggest that the tunnel of light is the opening of the nonphysical energy membrane separating the physical dimension from its parallel nonphysical neighbor. The energy tunnel commonly observed during a near-death experience is actually a highly organized temporary opening or rift in the nonphysical energy membrane and appears to open automatically to allow life-forms to pass through. After the life-form (consciousness) passes within the higher-frequency energy dimension, the tunnel opening immediately returns to its original shape and form.

The tunnel experience is much more significant than most people recognize. Not only does it provide substantial evidence of a logical transitional method for consciousness after physical death, but it directly relates to the modern physics theories concerning parallel universes and energy wormholes, as well as to my observations concerning the multidimensional universe. The time has come for modern science to investigate this reality. Millions of near-death and out-of-body experiences occurring in every culture and society of the world cannot be a coincidence. In addition, the countless reports of energy tunnels reaching back five hundred years can no longer be overlooked. The scientific investigation of the parallel nonphysical energy dimensions and their tunnel openings will be a major step forward in modern science, for it will light the way to a true comprehension of our multidimensional universe.

A Remarkable New View of the Universe

As scientists continue to focus on external matter, another group of people have fearlessly explored the very heart of the universe. Bypassing the traditional scientific methods, they have ventured far beyond the limits of our current technological evolution and expanded human explorations into undiscovered areas of the universe. This has been achieved by incorporating a revolutionary new form of investigation: self-controlled nonphysical

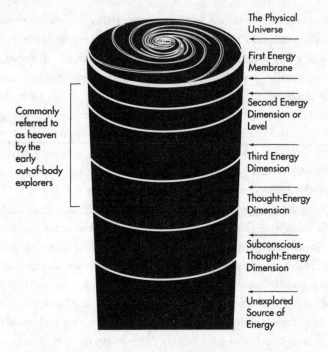

The Physical Universe

First Energy Membrane

Second Energy Dimension or Level

Third Energy Dimension

Thought-Energy Dimension

Subconscious-Thought-Energy Dimension

Unexplored Source of Energy

Commonly referred to as heaven by the early out-of-body explorers

Our universe is not what it appears to be. Visible stars, dust, gas clouds, and cosmic debris make up less than 10 percent of the mass that scientists know is present. Astronomers, astrophysicists, and physicists are currently hard at work searching for the unseen energy that supports our galaxy and our physical universe.

explorations into the unseen substructure of the universe. The discoveries made during these nonphysical explorations provide revolutionary new insights into the unseen structure of the universe, our existence, and our continuation after death.

Based on out-of-body observations, all energy dimensions exist here and now. The seen and unseen universe is a continuum of energy frequencies. Each dimension exists independently according to its individual frequency, yet they are all linked by the flow of nonphysical energy. Each dimension of energy is interconnected with its energy neighbors to form a complete system—the multidimensional universe. The eminent physicist David Bohm was absolutely correct when he observed that "Reality is an undivided whole." The entire multidimensional (frequency) universe is an inseparable whole; there exists no spatial or temporal separation. Bohm was decades ahead of his time when he said, "One is led to a new notion of unbroken wholeness which denies the classical analyzability of the world into separately and independently existing parts. . . . The inseparable quantum interconnectedness of the whole universe is a fundamental reality."

Forget all your spatial concepts of up and down, near and far. The entire multidimensional universe is here and now. The closest physical concept that describes the structure of the universe is degree of density. Each dimension encountered after we shed the physical body is progressively less dense in its vibrational substance. In effect, the universe can be compared with an energy wave spectrum of incomparable depth and beauty. Each frequency of the energy spectrum is experienced and observed by us as a separate and distinct dimension, yet all are interconnected to form a magnificent universe extending beyond space, form, and substance as we perceive it.

Out-of-body explorations provide startling new evidence that the universe is a multidimensional continuum of energy emanating from a nonphysical source; the physical galaxies we observe around us are merely the dense molecular crust of the complete universe. Comprehending the existence of this multidimensional universe is difficult because our current perceptions of space-time and reality offer inaccurate reference points.

All the energy dimensions exist simultaneously within the same space-time continuum. For example, when I'm out-of-body I can occupy the same space as a physical wall or ceiling. I'm not separated from the physical wall by distance but rather by my individual energy frequency. This recognition leads us to an exciting new adventure.

The Multidimensional Universe

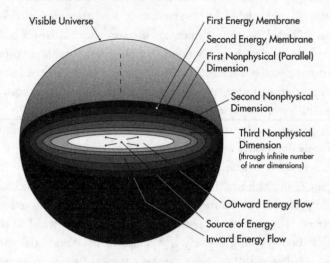

Visible Universe

First Energy Membrane

Second Energy Membrane

First Nonphysical (Parallel) Dimension

Second Nonphysical Dimension

Third Nonphysical Dimension
(through infinite number of inner dimensions)

Outward Energy Flow

Source of Energy

Inward Energy Flow

The universe is a continuum of energy frequencies emanating from a nonphysical source. The physical universe we observe is the molecular epidermis layer of the complete multidimensional universe. All energy dimensions exist within the same time-space as the visible universe.

Charting the Unseen Universe

As traditional science continues to focus upon the dense epidermis layer of the universe, the exploration and charting of the unseen dimensions have quietly begun. Through extensive trial and error, a few individuals have taken the leap beyond matter and the limits of our current physical technology. The observations made during these nonphysical explorations shed light on a multidimensional universe of incredible depth and beauty.

If we are to comprehend the structure of the unseen dimensions, we must constantly consider the natural thought-responsiveness of the subtle nonphysical energy environments. Beyond the parallel (first) nonphysical dimension, we are exploring an interactive, thought-responsive universe of energy. Once we recognize the energy interplay between thought and nonphysical energy, however, we can begin to focus on the specific energy similarities inherent in a given vibrational level or area. This is best accomplished by classifying the way a specific nonphysical environment responds to focused thought-energy. This kind of energy classification is far more practical than concentrating on the visual appearances and differences between dimensions. Two different and distinct vibrational dimensions can appear surprisingly alike even though their vibrational frequencies may be completely different. This is why traditional physical concepts are inadequate to judge nonphysical environments. To effectively chart the unseen universe, we must create a new baseline or method of comparison. The most practical method to achieve this is to classify the thought-responsiveness of a given nonphysical area.

The vast majority of nonphysical environments encountered are extremely thought-responsive. In other words, when we separate from our bodies and enter a nonphysical dimension, our thoughts, both conscious and subconscious, will immediately begin to interact with and restructure the subtle energy around us. The thought-responsiveness of the inner dimensions explains why out-of-body explorers often describe the environments they witness with such diversity. Complicating this situation is the fact that countless environments and realities exist within each individual dimension of the universe.

Even though there is an unlimited variety of possible environments within the universe, all the nonphysical environments and dimensions appear to have certain similarities and differences. Each dimension and environment consists of specific frequencies or wavelengths of nonphysical energy. In addition, each nonphysical dimension and environment appears to be the direct result of thought. The natural thought-responsiveness of the inner dimensions has created much of the confusion and mystery surrounding the inner environments. We have a natural tendency to relate nonphysical experiences directly to physical reference points—we compare everything to physical objects with which we are familiar. In effect, the molecular forms around us are not a valid baseline of reality. Physical objects and events are not the center of the universe, as many assume, but the end result of a chain of unseen energy reactions occurring deep within the unseen interior of the multidimensional universe.

To comprehend the nature of the universe, we must reappraise our current concepts of substance, energy, and time. We must be open-minded to a new viewpoint of reality. To truly understand the underlying structure of our universe, we must investigate the unseen cause of form and substance. I believe the overwhelming power of out-of-body exploration is our ability to do just that.

Information concerning the nonphysical dimensions is more valuable than most of us recognize. Not only can it help us to adapt and adjust within nonphysical environments, but it can also dramatically affect our current physical existence.

Up to now the vast majority of humanity has died without prior knowledge of its destination. Death has remained a dark void; we hope and pray for good things, but most of us approach the transition of death in absolute ignorance of our final destination. Up to now humankind has lacked firsthand, verifiable information about the mystery of life after death and the nonphysical environments that are experienced.

Controlled out-of-body experiences change all this. By pursuing nonphysical exploration, we can experience the many possible environments that will be our future home. In a very real sense we can scout ahead and become familiar with our nonphysical homeland.

Types of Energy Environments

A single nonphysical dimension can (and often does) contain three primary types of energy environments: consensus, nonconsensus, and natural.

A consensus environment is any environment or reality that is created and maintained by the thoughts of a group of individuals. For example, the heavens of each religious group are created by the thoughts and beliefs of their respective inhabitants. Like all realities, the consensus environments are molded by the group consciousness. Many of the consensus environments are extremely old and resistant to change. As unusual as it may sound, physical cities and communities are examples of consensus energy environments. Every city and town is created and developed according to the thoughts of its inhabitants. Essentially, human thought-energy uses biological vehicles to manipulate and mold the physical molecules around us. The end result is the temporary physical structures we see.

During an out-of-body or near-death experience, we transfer our conscious awareness from our physical body to our higher-frequency nonphysical body. For the sake of clarity I refer to this as "moving inward." I use the term *movement* because this energy transition is often experienced as a sensation of inner motion. Any reference to inner movement or inner exploration relates to the conscious recognition of a higher-frequency energy area of the universe.

As we explore inward away from matter, we discover that the first nonphysical dimension parallels the physical universe and is also a consensus reality. This energy environment is so physical in appearance that most people believe they are observing the physical world. In reality, they are observing the first inner energy dimension of the universe. Since this dimension is closest in frequency to matter, it is often seen and experienced during out-of-body explorations. This dimension is a classic example of a consensus reality: its structure is solid and stable within its own vibratory frequency. Our thoughts, no matter how focused, have little effect on the energy structures within this environment. However, our thoughts will exert a tremendous impact upon our personal energy-body. Thoughts of flying will enable us to fly.

94   Thoughts of walking will enable us to walk. The distinction between external and internal (personal) energy changes is critical
to understanding the inherent structure of a nonphysical dimension or environment. In a consensus environment, our thoughts
influence our personal energy but not the energy surrounding us.
The various heavens referred to by Saint John in Revelation and
Mohammed in the Koran are classic examples of consensus environments. These nonphysical cities and structures exist within
the second and third energy dimensions and continue to be
molded and maintained by the group consciousness of millions
of nonphysical inhabitants. When we enter these environments,
our thoughts will not change the structures encountered.

A nonconsensus environment is any nonphysical environment
or reality that is not firmly molded by a group. I have found that
this type of environment is the most prevalent. The appearance
can be anything we imagine: a forest, a park, a city, an ocean,
even an entire planet. Nonconsensus environments are easily de-
tected because, while often physical-like in appearance, they are
extremely sensitive to focused thoughts and will rapidly change
and restructure according to the prevailing conscious and subconscious thoughts present in the immediate area.

If you find yourself in an environment that changes often or
seems to be unstable, you are more than likely in a nonconsensus
reality. If this is the case, then it is important for you to know
that your thoughts, both conscious and subconscious, have probably influenced the reality you are experiencing. Nonconsensus
areas are often molded by our subconscious mind for our benefit.
For example, if you are experiencing a recurring problem or
block in your personal development, your subconscious mind or
higher self may mold an environment and situation that allow
you to confront this block on a very personal basis. You could
face a representation of your fears in the form of a crashing plane
or car, or confront a personal limitation or self-concept.

This personal confrontation can take any shape or form that will effectively assist us in experiencing and overcoming our limits, barriers, or fears. Many people report themselves projected into a situation that tested or tempered them in a very personal way—often through confronting their greatest fears and limits. For example, if you are deathly afraid of heights, you could experience yourself climbing a mountain or crossing a narrow bridge. A good example of this is detailed by Robert Monroe in *Journeys Out-of-the-Body,* where he describes repeated attempts to land a small plane on the top of a building while he is out-of-body.

More often, the nonconsensus environments will appear much like our normal or even idyllic physical surroundings; parks, landscaped country gardens, and peaceful green meadows are commonly reported. I believe it's probable that many of these areas were created by the thoughts of other nonphysical lifeforms who have inhabited or explored the areas in the past. Unlike in the physical world, once an energy environment is formed, it can last for centuries. Cellular and molecular decay are not an issue; it's simply a matter of thought-energy formation and stability. A single, firmly held, creative thought can mold an energy environment capable of lasting almost indefinitely; however, a stronger (more focused) thought could alter the entire environment within seconds. Remember that all environments are a form of energy, and all energy is thought-responsive to some degree.

Natural (raw) energy environments are completely unformed areas of the universe that appear without a specific shape or form of any kind. These areas are often observed as misty voids, empty space, or featureless, open areas consisting of white, silver, or golden clouds of energy.

Natural energy environments are extremely sensitive to thought. Any focused thought will instantly mold the immediate energy environment. This is why it is so important to gain some degree of control over our thoughts. Our personal evolution largely depends on the way we focus, control, and direct our thought-energy. No matter what dimension we inhabit, our personal responsibility for our thoughts and actions is absolute. All thoughts are creative; both positive and negative thoughts and action will create a corresponding restructuring of the immediate nonphysical environment. This is why spiritual leaders have always stressed themes of "do unto others" and "love for all." Once you fully recognize the power of your thoughts, you will never again create or hold a negative or destructive image in your mind. Negative and self-limiting thoughts are the real enemy we must face. Within the inner dimensions of the universe, our thoughts, both good and bad, exert a powerful creative influence upon our immediate environment. This is readily observed and experienced during an out-of-body experience.

In addition to the three most prevalent types of environments encountered when out-of-body, there are two others. The first, though rarely observed and reported, seems to consist of dimensions and environments that exist beyond thought-energy. Currently, few explorers have consciously ventured far enough within the universe to provide an accurate description or model of these dimensions. Possessing no perceivable shape or structure, these areas of the universe are postulated to exist beyond space, time, and energy as we conceive of them. It is possible that these dimensions and their inhabitants are indescribable by our linear concepts. Even so, I'm certain that nonthought and nonform energy environments exist deep within the interior of the universe.

The other observed environment is an area that appears to be a duplicate of empty space. This is an extremely low energy environment. Some believe that nonphysical space is a consensus environment. I seriously doubt this theory because no perceivable energy radiations or vibrations are emitted from empty space itself. All noticeable energy emanations appear to be located near inhabited locations. I think it is more likely that "empty" space lacks sufficient local energy to be affected by thought; as a result, it remains in a relatively constant state.

It should also be noted that empty nonphysical space appears to become increasingly prevalent as we explore inward away from the physical dimension and toward the source of all energy. The reason for this is unknown. The observations of numerous nonphysical explorers will be required before we can arrive at a conclusion.

The multidimensional universe is not just another theory; it is an observable fact. By implementing the out-of-body techniques presented in this book, you can verify this discovery for yourself. Self-initiated and controlled out-of-body experiences give us a remarkable opportunity to explore deep within the unseen interior of the universe. The current scientific focus on dense molecular activity will slowly shift to a frequency-based form of research. In the twenty-first century, science will begin to recognize that the dense forms around us are the outer vehicles of energy and that the entire physical universe is only a tiny portion of the magnificent multidimensional universe.

Solving Our Greatest Mysteries

Nonphysical exploration into the unseen substructure of the universe provides new insights into many mysteries of science and religion. The following are a few examples.

PSYCHIC PHENOMENA

The multidimensional nature of the universe logically explains the existence of present-day mysteries such as extrasensory perception, telepathy, precognition, channeling, psychokinesis, apparitions, and faith healing. In fact, all psychic and spiritual phenomena are the direct result of the subtle energy interactions between the physical dimension and its parallel energy counterpart.

For example, apparitions and poltergeist activity are simply the natural result of a nonphysical inhabitant lowering its personal vibrational frequency (density) so that it can temporarily be seen or interact within the denser physical dimension. This and all "paranormal" events are quite normal and to be expected in a multidimensional universe.

SPACE-TIME CURVATURE

According to Einstein's theory of relativity, the curvature of space is directly related to matter. In effect, space curves around massive celestial objects such as stars. To visualize this, you might think of a lead ball placed upon a tightly fitted bedsheet. The sheet (space) will curve to accommodate the ball. After decades of intense scrutiny, Einstein's theory has been validated mathematically by some of the brightest minds of modern physics. Still, the curvature of space remains a perplexing mystery.

I believe the mystery can be solved if we explore deeper into the unseen core of the universe. According to numerous out-of-body explorers, the direct energy substructure of the physical universe is a parallel dimension of subtle nonphysical energy. The outer physical dimension we observe around us is separated from its energy neighbor by an unseen membrane of energy. This membrane is often observed during near-death experiences and is reported to form a temporary tunnel-like opening allowing the individual to enter the next energy dimension.

Based on extensive nonphysical observations, I contend that the curvature of space is the direct result of the curvature of the supporting nonphysical energy membranes and dimensions that support the visible universe. The outer physical dimension (the visible universe) actually conforms to the shape of the unseen energy membrane. This nonphysical energy membrane acts as an internal cell wall, providing the support and substructure necessary for the existence of an external physical universe (dimension). Because the inner energy membrane is remarkably stable and flexible in its form, it appears likely that the energy membrane provides the necessary support required by all physical celestial bodies.

ENERGY MEMBRANES

The unseen substructure and support for the visible universe are provided by a series of unseen, nonphysical energy membranes. The outermost (densest) energy membrane exists parallel with the physical universe.

The energy membranes occur at interdimensional convergence points and serve as energy buffers. Similar in function to biological cell walls, they separate different frequencies of energy from one another. For example, the first inner energy membrane separates the outer physical dimension from its parallel but unseen energy neighbor.

Curvature of Interdimensional Space

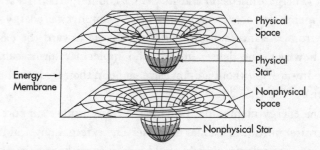

Embedding of an uncollapsed spherical star. The embedded surface shows the curvature of space around the star. All points outside the embedded surface are without physical significance. Each circle traced on the surface represents the set of points situated at the same distance from the center of the star, while the orthogonal curves pass through the bottom of the hollow that is the center of the star. At great distances from the star, the gravitational field is weak and the embedding surface loses its curvature. However, it does not become a horizontal plane as the illustration suggests, but rather a paraboloid. Near the star, the curvature is more accentuated. The shaded area indicates the region effectively occupied by the star. Adapted from the original.

All energy membranes are structured, yet extremely flexible in form and substance. When pierced or entered, they commonly take the form of an opening or tunnel large enough to accommodate the entering object. This tunnel effect is a temporary phenomenon. The membranes quickly return to their normal shape after an object or life-form has passed completely through them. This temporary tunnel effect has been observed and reported by millions of people who have had near-death experiences.

Each energy membrane provides the underlying support, stability, and substructure necessary for its energy neighbor. For example, the first membrane provides the energy support system for the physical universe. It's the invisible, internal cell wall that supports the physical universe. This unseen energy membrane and its containing energy constitute the "dark matter" theorized by astronomers and physicists.

Each membrane provides a highly organized and structured system for energy transfer between the higher-frequency (less dense) energy dimension and its denser counterparts. In a sense, each membrane acts as an energy filter. Nonphysical energy can flow from the internal areas of the universe toward the external; however, the denser atomic and molecular forms cannot move inwardly without a dramatic change in their frequency rate (death).

The energy membranes provide the unseen inner support for the entire multidimensional universe. The external physical universe and its galaxies simply could not exist without this essential energy support system.

THE EXPANDING UNIVERSE

In 1929 Edwin Hubble shocked the world's scientific community with the most important discovery in modern astronomy. He provided conclusive evidence that the universe, until then considered a static and stable environment, is actually expanding in size. Hubble proved not only that the universe is expanding but that distant galaxies are traveling away from us at even greater speeds than the galaxies near us.

Hubble's discoveries continue to perplex scientists. Over the last few decades many theories have been presented to explain this incredible expansion of our universe. Today astronomers, astrophysicists, and theoretical physicists have largely accepted the big bang as the logical explanation of this expansion. According to the big bang theory, the universe began with a massive explosion approximately fifteen billion years ago. This explosion created the expansion of space now observed. It may help clarify the idea of an expanding universe to visualize the galaxies as dots drawn on a balloon. As the balloon inflates, the galaxies move apart from one another in all directions. Note that the galaxies themselves are not flying through space; instead, it is space itself that is expanding.

Today, most scientists assume that the big bang is the cause of the current expansion of our visible universe. Based on the available scientific data, this appears to be a logical conclusion. When we explore deeper into the interior of the universe, however, we discover a far more complex energy system than our modern physical sciences are aware of.

According to observations obtained when out-of-body, the interior substructure of the universe (the inner dimensions and their supporting energy membranes) is expanding in size. This expansion appears to be extremely well controlled and systematic. Even more important, the expansion of the inner dimensions appears to be the direct result of an ongoing energy-conversion process that occurs within the unseen thought-responsive dimensions existing beyond the second nonphysical dimension. This outward expansion of nonphysical energy and space appears to be controlled by the external energy conduits (black holes) located throughout the universe.

The Expanding Multidimensional Universe

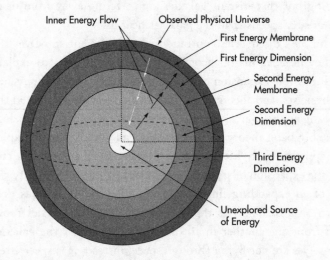

Energy expansion begins within the inner dimensions and moves progressively outward toward the physical universe. The expansion of energy creates the outer movement of galaxies observed in the universe. The inner membranes provide the substructure and support for the progressively denser outer dimensions of energy. The expanding inner membranes provide a stable but flexible energy framework for the entire multidimensional universe.

One thing is certain. Decades of nonphysical explorations and millions of near-death experiences consistently point to a single conclusion: the direct substructure of the physical universe is a subtle form of energy undetectable by our current physical technology. This unseen energy is highly organized, structured, and supportive of the outer physical universe. The incredible amount of interdependence existing between the unseen, nonphysical dimensions and the outer physical crust of the universe points to a much more complex system of energy than modern technology and science are currently able to observe.

Even though the underlying cause of the expansion of the multidimensional universe remains a mystery, it's now clear that unseen, nonphysical energy reactions do influence the current physical expansion that we observe. The big bang theory is a superficial conclusion based on incomplete physical observations. Indeed, many of our physical-based scientific theories of cosmology, evolution, and the structure of matter are seriously lacking in vision. This occurs because current scientific theorems rely entirely upon physical observations and speculation. A classic example of this shortsightedness is displayed by the long-standing scientific assumption that consciousness is the direct result of chemical and electrical reactions occurring in the brain.

When we recognize the multidimensional structure of the universe, we realize that physical observations alone are inadequate. The galaxies and matter we observe around us are not the entire universe, as we assume, but only the dense outer dimension or molecular crust of the complete universe. The volume of the visible universe amounts to perhaps less than one-tenth of 1 percent of the multidimensional universe. Clearly, any scientific conclusion or theory based entirely upon observations of matter is built upon incomplete data. Each new nonphysical exploration into the interior of the universe substantiates this observation. Ask any of the millions of people who have had a near-death or out-of-body experience and they will agree: the universe is far more expansive and complicated than current physical science can even begin to comprehend or explain. As millions of people every year have out-of-body and near-death experiences, the reality of the multidimensional universe and its energy reactions will be recognized as observable fact.

BLACK HOLES

A black hole is an area in space postulated to be so dense that its gravity attracts all surrounding matter, including light. There are several theories concerning the existence of black holes. Some scientists believe that they are "bridges" or "wormholes" to other universes. Others suggest that black holes may be pathways to the past or future, while still others contend that they collapse into nothingness.

In recent years an impressive list of physicists, mathematicians, and astronomers have expressed the belief that black holes are interdimensional tunnels leading to another energy-universe. Kruskal, Szekers, Kerr, Reissner, and Nordstrom have all created conceptual maps linking black holes to unseen parallel universes. These black hole theories are not wild speculation, but concepts taken quite seriously by modern physicists and astronomers.

Based on out-of-body observations, I believe that black holes function as energy conduits between the physical universe and the inner energy dimensions. These energy conduits are necessary to balance the energy generated between the inner energy dimensions and the outer physical universe.

In the future, science will be able to verify that black holes are not a random event of nature but a highly organized and structured energy-conversion system. This theory will be scientifically validated when it is discovered that black holes are

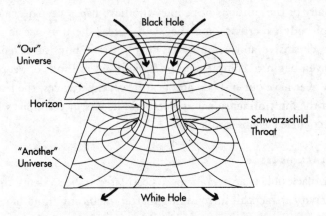

The Schwarzschild throat connects "our" universe (upper sheet) with "another" universe (lower sheet).

strategically located within the center of each galaxy. As the physical universe continues to expand, there is an increasing need for the external energy forces to be vented and balanced. Black holes provide the essential energy counterbalance for the expanding multidimensional universe. I believe that black holes are created by a massive opening in the inner-dimensional energy membrane. This opening or rift in the energy membrane creates a corresponding opening within the outer, visible universe. In the twenty-first century we will discover that black holes are an integral part of the universal energy-transference system. They not only attract all particles (including light) in their gravity field but also emit enormous amounts of energy undetectable by current technology. The unseen energy flowing from the energy conduits is essential to the overall maintenance, structure, and stability of the physical galaxies.

THE TUNNELING EFFECT

Physicists discovered years ago that primary particles such as electrons have the ability to pass through barriers that were considered impenetrable and then rematerialize on the other side. Based upon the traditional scientific knowledge of subatomic reality, this should be impossible. Physicist Heinze Pagels of Rockefeller University refers to this strange rematerialization as "right through the wall." This unexplained motion of subatomic particles is now called the tunneling effect.

I believe it's possible that the observed tunneling effect is the result of elemental particles moving within the multidimensional universe and then reemerging in a different area of the physical universe. Since each particle of matter (subatomic or molecular) already exists as a multidimensional unit of energy, this process of disappearance is to be expected, not only in physics but also in the realm of human consciousness. In a very real sense, out-of-body and near-death experiences are a result of the tunneling effect of consciousness as it moves within the unseen energy levels of the multidimensional universe and then returns to its physical form.

An unmistakable connection exists between the tunneling effect, parallel universes, dark matter, black holes, and the curvature of space-time. All five are the direct result of unseen energy interactions occurring within the interior of the multidimensional universe. In fact, all subatomic and celestial phenomena are the result of nonphysical energy waves radiating outward from the unseen interior of the universe. The entire physical universe is essentially the thin outer molecular crust of a massive energy continuum created, sustained, and supported by nonphysical energy waves. Quantum theory, the existence of black holes, the Einstein-Rosen Bridge, and the particle-wave nature of light all support this observation.

Quantum Physics and Mysticism

There exists an undeniable relationship between quantum physics and mysticism. As physics evolves in its recognition of the frequencylike nature of the universe, the connection will become even more apparent. It's only logical that first scientists will research and analyze the latest information presented in recent books on new physics and near-death and out-of-body experiences. As we absorb and become comfortable with this extensive body of knowledge, we will slowly begin to extend our awareness beyond our current physical perceptions.

The step from intellectual curiosity to firsthand experience is the all-important next step each of us will eventually take. If we ever wish to know the answers, we must follow in the footsteps of the mystic but maintain the intellectual curiosity of the physicist.

The connection between new physics and mysticism is presented with great skill in Fritjof Capra's *The Tao of Physics*, Gary

Zukav's *The Dancing Wu Li Masters*, and Michael Talbot's *Mysticism and the New Physics*. My purpose is to take this exploration to the next step. Intellectual observations and comparisons are only the preliminary step in comprehending the true significance of the new physics and the concepts of mysticism. The books mentioned have set the stage for the next major evolutionary leap of human consciousness: the movement of human awareness from the dense molecular vehicles of matter to the conscious exploration of the nonphysical parallel dimensions of the universe. Without a doubt this is the evolutionary step toward which all of us are moving. Birth, death, and our current physical existence are integral elements of our evolutionary journey. Every day we are closer to leaving our biological vehicle and entering into a new realm of higher-frequency energy and light. By pursuing the techniques and information presented in the following chapters, each of us has the opportunity to go beyond intellectual analysis and experience the truth of this for him- or herself.

Not only does controlled out-of-body exploration expand our vision of the universe; it also provides insight into new areas.

1. Reality is relative. Experienced reality is relative to the personal energy frequency of the observer. We experience the energy frequencies closest to our personal density or vibratory rate.

2. Consciousness is a form of nonphysical energy extending its influence into matter through the use of biological vehicles.

3. All biological life-forms (including plant and animal life) are temporary cellular vehicles used by conscious energy (consciousness) for expression in a dense environment.

4. Our current perception that consciousness is within the physical body is incorrect. Consciousness exists at a much

higher frequency or wavelength than matter and must interact with biological forms by the use of energy conduits or
vehicles of form. These unseen energy vehicles transfer and
step down the higher frequency of consciousness into the relatively dense physical body.

5. The biological brain is not the origin of consciousness. Instead, it functions as a temporary biological transfer-and-
storage device for consciousness.

6. Consciousness is a continuum of nonphysical energy extending its awareness through multiple frequencies (dimensions)
of the universe.

Evolution of Science

The evolution of our sciences reflects the evolution of human
consciousness. When we examine the progress of physics in the
twentieth century, we clearly see the development from particle
(physical-based) concepts and theories to nonphysical (frequency-
based) observations and discoveries. The progression is especially
evident when we recognize that the most recently discovered subatomic particles (quarks) are now known to be frequencylike in
their behavior. The growing recognition of the frequencylike nature of elemental particles is a necessary step on the evolutionary
path toward science's ultimate discovery of the multidimensional
structure of matter and the universe itself. The table below provides a brief overview of this evolution.

Evolution of Physics from a Particle (Physical) Science to a Frequency-Wave (Nonphysical) Science

1897	Electron discovered
1900	Quantum hypothesis (Max Planck)
1905	Photon theory (Einstein)

1905	Special theory of relativity (Einstein)
1908	Space-time (Hermann Minkowski)
1911	Nucleus discovered
1913	Special-orbits model of the atom (Niels Bohr)
1915	General theory of relativity (Einstein)
1924	Matter waves (Louis de Broglie)
1924	First concept of probability waves (Niels Bohr, H. A. Kramers, John Slater)
1925	Exclusion principle (Wolfgang Pauli)
1925	Matrix mechanics (Werner Heisenberg)
1926	Probability interpretation of wave function (Max Born)
1926	Schrödinger wave equation (Erwin Schrödinger)
1926	Matrix mechanics equated with wave mechanics (Schrödinger)
1927	Copenhagen interpretation of quantum mechanics: there is no deep reality—observation affects reality
1927	Uncertainty principle (Werner Heisenberg)
1927	Davisson-Germer experiment (Clinton Davisson, Lester Germer)
1928	Antimatter (Paul Dirac)
1932	Neutron discovered
1932	Positron discovered
1932	Quantum logic (John von Neumann)
1935	Einstein-Rosen Bridge paper (Albert Einstein, Boris Podolsky, Nathan Rosen)

1935	Meson predicted (Hideki Yukawa)
1947	Meson discovered
1949	Feynman diagrams (Richard Feynman)
1947–1954	Sixteen new wavelike particles discovered
1957	Many worlds interpretation of quantum mechanics (Hugh Everett)
1958	One-way membrane hypothesis (David Finkelstein)
1961	Black hole map to parallel universe (Martin Kruskal)
1962	Quasars discovered
1963	Spinning black hole connecting an infinite series of parallel universes (Roy P. Kerr)
1964	Quarks hypothesized
1964	Bell's theorem (J. S. Bell)
1970	Implicate order (David Bohm)
1971	Nonlocal connections (Bell theorem) (Henry Stapp)
1972	Freedman-Clauser experiment (Stuart Freedman, John Clauser)
1974–1977	Twelve new wavelike particles discovered
1982	Aspect experiment (Alain Aspect)
1993	Gravitational waves (Huise and Taylor)

In the twenty-first century, science will recognize that the substructure of the universe is indeed a nonphysical continuum of energy. This recognition will initiate a renaissance of scientific discoveries relating to the unseen structure of matter and the universe itself.

Scientific nonphysical exploration will open the door to a new world of opportunities and knowledge. From astrophysics to philosophy, the established scientific observations and conclusions will begin to be reexamined and reappraised. The new knowledge obtained from scientific out-of-body exploration will empower each science to see beyond the dense molecular forms and peer within the very heart of matter.

Our current scientific data are largely the result of molecular observations. The subtle underlying structures and energy systems remain undiscovered. The traditional scientific method and its dependence upon physical technology will eventually evolve into a cooperative merger of physical and nonphysical research techniques. In the twenty-first century, the interaction between physical technology and human consciousness will become a science in and of itself.

Just imagine what could be gained if a team of respected scientists and researchers were trained to explore out-of-body. Physicists could personally observe the undiscovered building blocks of matter. Medical researchers could explore the unseen energy forces that cause cancers, AIDS, cellular decay and disorders. Chemists could document the invisible energy that influences and controls molecular change. Biologists could investigate the very essence of physical life, and psychologists could explore the invisible inner realms of the mind.

Thousands of bright, curious researchers today are hungry to discover and explore the unseen structure of matter. Many of them have a burning desire to observe beyond the current limits of technology and are looking for an opportunity to expand their vision beyond the maze of quantum theories. Only consciousness can observe and record the multiple complexities of space-time and thought-created realities. The door is now open for those who have the courage to step away from their physical preconceptions and explore the quantum realms of energy. The well-known physicist and author Fred Alan Wolf concludes his *Parallel Universes* by stating:

> The human mind is the laboratory of the new physics. It already is tuned to the past and the future, making existential certainties out of probable realities. It does this by simply observing. Observing oneself in a dream. Observing oneself in this world when awake. Observing the action of observing. If we are brave enough to venture into this world with consciousness as our ally, through our dreams and altered states of awareness, we may be able to alter the hologram by bringing more conscious "light" to the hell worlds that also exist side-by-side with our own.
>
> It is time to speed up the process of illuminating the hologram, time to bring in the big laser of consciousness. It is time to know this universe place for the first time ever.

Continuum of Consciousness

The non-mathematician is seized by a mysterious shuddering when he hears of "four dimensional" things, by a feeling not unlike that awakened by thoughts of the occult. And yet there is no more commonplace statement than that the world in which we live is a four-dimensional continuum.

—Albert Einstein

Consciousness is a continuum extending from physical wakefulness through progressive states of awareness into nonphysical areas of the universe existing far beyond our current scientific vision. This continuum of consciousness is as large and diverse as the universe itself; each time we "fall" to sleep we are shifting our awareness inwardly within the continuum. Each dream, meditation, and hypnosis session is a partial glimpse into our personal continuum of consciousness. Our recognition of this is a major step forward in our evolution. It's only natural that first we must explore the different states of consciousness experienced during sleep, meditation, and lucid dreams before we can begin to recognize that these states of awareness are linked by a common flow of consciousness.

All states of awareness are connected; even death is the movement of consciousness from one area of the continuum to another. The continuum of consciousness is not just another theory, but a fact that each of us can observe and verify for ourselves. Controlled out-of-body experiences give us the unique opportunity to explore the continuum of energy firsthand. In a sense, our awareness is like a light that has the natural ability to illuminate any portion of the universe. Wherever we focus our light, that area of the universe (in the physical body or out) becomes conscious and real to us.

All movement of consciousness is inward within the nonphysical interior of the universe. The states of awareness we currently perceive are only a tiny fraction of the whole. The continuum extends deep into nonphysical areas of the universe far beyond our current physical comprehension.

Continuum of Consciousness (Modes of Perception)

1 2 3 4 5 6 7 8

1 Physical waking consciousness
2 Hypnagogic state/meditative states/creative visualization/hypnotic states/numerous altered states of consciousness
3 Dreams
4 Lucid dreams
5 Spontaneous out-of-body experiences
6 Near-death experiences
7 Controlled out-of-body exploration within various nonphysical dimensions of the universe
8 Continues within the nonphysical dimensions of the universe into infinity

The states of consciousness illustrated above are not the continuum itself but our modes or methods of perceiving this continuum of consciousness. The various states of consciousness, such as meditative, hypnagogic, and hypnotic, obviously overlap and exist differently for different people. Meditative states, for example, can extend over the entire spectrum of the consciousness continuum, but most people experience only a peaceful state of relaxation occurring in the light alpha range. The vast majority of those who practice meditation are not highly trained yogic masters who can control and extend their awareness at will.

It is important to recognize that our individual states of consciousness exist as perceptions or segments of a whole. This recognition is the first major step in understanding the nonphysical essence and function of consciousness. Such an understanding is critically important because all the mysteries of our existence and the universe itself are related to consciousness. This will be confirmed in the near future when it is discovered that our individual consciousness is a microcosm of the universe itself. Dreams, out-of-body experiences, and near-death experiences are the recognition of our awareness as we move beyond the physical viewpoint and explore the nonphysical continuum of consciousness. This concept of human consciousness moving through an unseen universe is gaining support. Physicist and author Fred Alan Wolf postulates that lucid dreams are actually visits to parallel universes. He has repeatedly stated that lucid dreams might better be called "parallel universe awareness."

The states of consciousness that we are currently aware of are, I contend, but a tiny fraction of the continuum that we will experience after we permanently shed our physical bodies. Each year millions of near-death and out-of-body experiences provide convincing evidence that this is true. Observations obtained when out-of-body show that our current concepts of consciousness and awareness are severely limited. Physical-based states of consciousness are relatively crude and encumbered when compared with the nonphysical states. Once we transcend our biological vehicles, we are free to experience the unlimited essence of our consciousness. This essence exists and extends far beyond our imagination.

The continuum of consciousness extends inwardly to the very heart of the universe; unending levels and frequencies of nonphysical life and realities exist just beyond the dense limits of our sight. Each of us has much to look forward to: incredible worlds of beauty and light patiently waiting for us to explore. To experience this ourselves, we must simply extend our awareness beyond our physical body and explore our individual continuum of consciousness.

Evolution of Consciousness

Our current concept of evolution derives from the Darwinian theory that biological organisms adapt and change in response to the physical conditions around them. This theory, built entirely upon the observed changes of biological organisms, has remained the scientific basis of evolution for over one hundred years.

Millions of reported out-of-body experiences provide convincing evidence that our evolution is far more complex than the biological changes we observe around us. In fact, out-of-body experiences point to an entire new vision of evolution, one that is more comprehensive than any previous theory in human history. On the basis of nonphysical explorations, we can say that evolution is the progressive development of conscious energy (soul) through the use of temporary biological vehicles of expression. Biological birth and death are simply the entrance and exit of consciousness within this dense outer dimension of energy. The observed changes of biological organisms are actually a secondary effect, created by the unseen development of consciousness.

Currently, evolutionists observe and record only the outer physical changes occurring around us, while the truly important changes remain unseen. Every day we encounter new situations that psychologically stretch and mold us. Every physical problem is a new opportunity to grow; each hardship helps us to develop our inner qualities of courage, love, and compassion; each new challenge is an opportunity to learn. In a sense, each of us uses matter as a tool of transformation. Our biological bodies are temporary vehicles for expression and experience in this dense realm of matter. The very act of assuming physical form and being human is an integral element of our development. Each of us is currently experiencing the most effective system of growth ever devised: evolution by direct personal experience, by the very act of being.

It doesn't matter what we believe or don't believe; each of us will shed our temporary biological vehicle and continue to evolve. We are all active participants in a magnificent evolutionary system that extends far beyond the narrow limits of our physical vision. Birth and death themselves are essential elements of our progress—the entrance and exit of consciousness upon the molecular playing field of evolution.

Over the last twenty years, new insights concerning our spiritual existence have emerged. Two decades ago, subjects such as near-death experiences, out-of-body experiences, parallel universes, multiple dimensions, and energy tunnels between universes were unknown to the vast majority of our species. Today, these topics are debated in households around the world. In a single generation, our concepts of reality have dramatically changed. This shift will continue as people open their minds to a new vision of themselves and their existence.

Throughout history the evolution of human consciousness has been molded by countless people worldwide. The following are a few examples of individuals who have influenced the group consciousness and evolution of our species in the last few decades. This process of human evolution will accelerate in the next millennium as we expand our search for answers beyond the dense limits of matter.

In 1975 Dr. Raymond Moody's book *Life After Life* created an international explosion of interest in the topic of life after death and possible nonphysical realities. Moody's groundbreaking work on near-death and altered states of perception continues to influence millions of people around the world. Since 1975 the overwhelming acceptance of his many books has opened up an entirely new field of study and research. Moody's work has especially affected the medical community, setting the stage for hundreds of medical researchers—among them Drs. Melvin Morse and Brian Weiss—to delve into the many mysteries of nonphysical experiences. To a great extent his work has legitimized the entire subject of nonphysical research and the exploration of the unseen universe. Moody's work has helped to initiate a dramatic shift of thought, both conscious and unconscious.

Kenneth Ring, Stuart Twemlow, Bruce Greyson, and other visionary physicians have assisted the evolution of human consciousness by investigating the worldwide reports of out-of-body and near-death experiences. Their research and insights have helped legitimize the subject of nonphysical experiences, thus setting the stage for innovative new explorations.

Brian Weiss has been instrumental in the growing worldwide acceptance of past-life regression therapy as a valuable healing tool. Increasingly, psychologists and psychiatrists are incorporating regression techniques into their daily practices. Weiss's work is a major step forward in the recognition of the relationship between nonphysical states of consciousness and our current physical existence. In addition, his books point out the importance and potential of obtaining self-knowledge.

John Stewart Bell, the Irish physicist who developed the interconnectedness theorem, proved that all particles of matter are connected by an invisible (nonlocal) force. His work has dramatically influenced the direction of modern physics. Many physicists believe that the interconnectedness theorem is one of the most important discoveries of the twentieth century.

Hugh Everett, Roy Kerr, Martin Kruskal, and other physicists and mathematicians have developed theories and conceptual maps that assume the existence of innumerable parallel universes as real as our own. This idea of parallel energy worlds has influenced quantum theorists, astrophysicists, and astronomers worldwide.

Filmmakers such as Steven Spielberg, through movies such as *E.T.* and *Close Encounters of the Third Kind,* reduce our fears of the unknown and open us to new possibilities existing beyond our physical perceptions.

Gary Zukav's clear insights into the relationship of physics and consciousness and his search for the meaning and purpose of life have influenced millions.

Shakti Gawain's clear message of the importance of creative visualization has affected millions of people around the world.

Physicist and writer Fred Alan Wolf has presented and clarified the concepts of parallel universes and consciousness-created reality to both the scientific community and the general population.

Drs. Wayne Dyer, Bernie Siegel, Deepak Chopra, and many others have shown us through thought and deed how important the connection is between body, mind, and spirit.

Bruce Joel Rubin's vivid, thought-provoking portrayals of life, death, and unseen energy dimensions (*Jacob's Ladder*, *Ghost*, *My Life*) have been seen by over a half-billion people.

Norman Vincent Peale's uplifting message of positive thinking and its effect upon matter and life has affected us all.

Albert Einstein moved scientific thought and theory beyond Newtonian physics into expansive new realms of curved space-time and energy bridges to other universes. In doing so, he set the stage for the emergence of modern quantum physics, the concept of parallel universes, and the many worlds interpretation.

David Bohm, another visionary physicist, has originated numerous ideas concerning consciousness-created reality and unseen energy substructures. His concepts have influenced modern physics and are a major intellectual step toward the recognition of the multidimensional nature of the universe. His piercing intellect has inspired an entire new generation of physicists to look beyond the particles of matter for the answers to reality.

Four excellent writers, Nick Herbert, Michael Talbot, Heinze Pagels, and Fritjof Capra, have influenced the evolution of human consciousness by clearly portraying the connection between new physics, metaphysics, religion, and consciousness.

Robert Monroe, a modern pioneer, has been instrumental in presenting the subject of out-of-body exploration to millions of people around the world. His books and research organization, the Monroe Institute, provide ongoing training, information, support, and classes related to expanded awareness and nonphysical exploration.

Paul Twitchell is the modern founder of ECKANKAR. His many books (more than thirty) introduced and detailed the historical influence of out-of-body exploration upon the evolution of the human race. Considered by some to have been a modern master of out-of-body travel, he was instrumental in introducing the subject of nonphysical explorations to people throughout the world.

Movie producers such as George Lucas and Gene Rodenberry have helped to expand human imagination beyond earthbound visions of reality. Their images of the future encourage all of us to see beyond the dense limits we now experience.

Science fiction writers, as a group, are some of our most talented visionaries. For those who may doubt, remember the far-fetched stories of Jules Verne; his nineteenth-century submarines, spaceships, airships, and lunar explorations were considered outrageous ideas in his day.

Betty Eadie, the author of *Embraced by the Light,* and others who have come forward to share their near-death experiences will continue to have an impact on the collective unconscious of humankind. Their uplifting accounts of personal journeys within the magnificent unseen dimensions of the universe have sparked worldwide debate and interest in the concepts of nonphysical realities and our place in the universe. These personal accounts of nonphysical explorations within the inner dimensions of the universe provide more than just comforting evidence of our immortality. Millions of people are awakening to the realization that answers to the mysteries of our existence are available. An important question is emerging: if a few of us can experience and explore the nonphysical realms of the universe, then why can't all of us? This realization is a major step in the growth of the human race. This process of change is inevitable, since all of us are approaching a time where we will shed our biological vehicles and enter the nonphysical dimensions of the universe. The significance of these nonphysical explorations into the interior of the universe is not the stories themselves, but the realization that such explorations are possible and even obtainable by all of us.

As the evolution of consciousness continues, more individuals will step forward to offer new and daring insights into the nature of reality and the purpose of our existence. Our evolution will continue to be influenced by people from many walks of life: writers, musicians, inventors, healers, movie producers and directors. Often they will be unaware of their impact on society. Their ideas and images go out into the world like ripples on the surface of a pond, creating a slight movement of thought and consciousness for millions of people. For example, the movies *E.T., Cocoon,* and *Ghost* appear on the surface to be lighthearted adventure fantasies; however, the nearly two billion people who watched these movies came away with a new viewpoint about areas of life unknown and unexplored by modern science. For many, their fears of the unknown were replaced by a sense of wonder and positive anticipation. The collective unconscious of our entire species was influenced by the ideas conveyed. Our fears of the unknown both consciously and subconsciously were slightly reduced by the positive and uplifting images communicated.

In the twenty-first century, a new form of entertainment and imagery will escort us into the nonphysical levels of the universe. This will be a gradual evolution from traditional movies to increasingly interactive adventures implementing virtual-reality technology. In the twenty-first century, virtual-reality programming will become a popular springboard for self-controlled out-of-body explorations into the interior of the universe. As we progress, it will become evident that the evolution of technology and the evolution of human consciousness are interrelated in ways beyond our current comprehension. Eventually, each of us will evolve beyond the chrysalis of matter and explore within the nonphysical dimensions of the universe.

Future Evolution

In the last few years of my nonphysical explorations, I've come to realize that the more experienced and familiar we are with the nonphysical dimensions of the universe, the more expansive are our choices after our physical death. The nonphysical (spiritual) options available to us increase exponentially with our ability to explore the source of all energy and life. This is more important than I can begin to express. The vast majority of humanity dies in complete ignorance of its spiritual existence. Even though many people possess firm religious beliefs, their firsthand knowledge of their spiritual identity and their continuing existence after death is zero. At the moment of death, they transfer their consciousness from their physical body to their higher-frequency nonphysical form and are immediately met by their passed-on loved ones and friends. Of course they're thrilled to discover that they continue to exist, and are overjoyed to be reunited with their loved ones. Over the next few days and weeks they are reintegrated into a new vibrational reality and begin to adapt and conform within their respective social groups. This collective feeling of togetherness brings and holds millions of people together in magnificent nonphysical consensus environments.

Different groups of people hold different concepts of heaven. For example, the Islamic perspective differs from the Christian viewpoint. Keep in mind that the nonphysical environments are thought-responsive; each major religion and social group has created its own concept of heaven according to that group's beliefs and convictions. Many of these energy environments are extremely old and well established by the collective consciousness of their inhabitants. As a result, the heaven that each of us experiences after death is molded by the group consciousness of its nonphysical inhabitants. Much as in the physical world, most people are content to adapt to the consensus reality inhabited and created by their friends and loved ones. And why not? It's incredibly pleasant when compared to matter. There are magnificent landscapes and environments to discover and explore. All the most beautiful and inspiring sights of earth are available, plus much more. Every tree and blade of grass radiate a vibrant spectrum of color that's beyond our imagination. Everything—plants, animals, the earth itself—is composed of light. A matrix of thought-responsive energy manifests whatever the inhabitants focus upon. It's only natural that the inhabitants would conclude that this must be the ultimate reality—heaven.

These magnificent nonphysical environments are assumed to be heaven, and compared with physical existence, these consensus environments *are* heaven—they are free of death, disease, decay, crime, and so on. There's only one problem: the vast majority of the nonphysical inhabitants (billions of them) are unaware that other, even more magnificent energy dimensions exist just beyond the limits of their nonphysical perception. These spectacular energy dimensions consist of endless frequencies of pure energy and light, each more radiant than the last—a progression of living light existing far beyond our frail concepts of form and substance and continuing into the very heart of the multidimensional universe.

This information is important because the first step to expanding our awareness is to recognize the various limits we place upon ourselves, both physically and spiritually. This knowledge points out the need for all of us to extend our perception and experience beyond the dense limits around us. Once we develop an ability to explore beyond the boundaries of our bodies, we can implement the same ability in our future existence within our nonphysical home.

Developing our ability to explore beyond the body has profound implications for all of us. Our ability to experience the various nonphysical frequency levels of the universe depends upon our personal ability to transcend our current energy limits. In effect, once we learn to transcend our physical limits, we can use the same ability after death to experience even greater regions of the universe.

Currently there are those who can raise their personal vibratory rate and explore multiple dimensions of the universe. These unique individuals are not limited to a single dimension or environment. The ability to explore beyond our current physical limits is an essential element of our evolution from physically immersed creatures to unlimited spiritual beings. Only by transcending our dense limits can we ever hope to consciously express ourselves throughout the multidimensional universe. It is our destiny to evolve to the point where all of us will have the ability to extend ourselves, our consciousness, through the entire length and breadth of the universe.

All of us are interdimensional beings currently focusing our attention upon a single dimension of energy-matter. Out-of-body and near-death experiences, dreams, altered states of consciousness, even death itself are evidence of our multidimensional nature. Consciously recognizing and personally experiencing our nonphysical nature is a major step in our individual evolution. Eventually all of us will evolve to the point where we are able to consciously experience and explore the entire universe. This will occur when our species grows to recognize that we and the universe are the same—multidimensional.

After twenty years of personal out-of-body exploration, I am certain that we are evolving through matter. We are using biological life-forms as instruments of expression. Our physical bodies are the tools we use for experience and growth. Each birth (exploration) into matter furthers our progress by increasing our experience. Every physical life-form is using and controlling a temporary biological vehicle for its evolution. Like the proverbial butterfly, each living organism sheds its temporary biological vehicle in order to continue its journey within the refined energy levels of the multidimensional universe.

Evolution is much more than our eyes can see. It is the movement and change of consciousness from the simpler, biological life-forms to the progressively more complex and organized, nonphysical life-forms. Each life-form continues its evolutionary journey within the multidimensional universe. Each continues to grow and change, slowly learning and adapting to its new challenges and adventures, to its new forms of expression. To truly comprehend evolution, we must explore and observe the sub-structure of the universe: the nonmolecular energy structures and systems that cause the physical changes we perceive around us.

Einstein's Dream

The dream of Einstein and every other physicist has been to understand and explain the structure of the universe. For many decades, physicists have hoped to discover a single theory that explains and unites all energy, space, and time concepts. This single unified theory is often referred to as grand unification.

Most physicists now believe that undiscovered energy reactions are occurring just beyond our current technological vision. As modern science explored into the heart of matter, an incredible discovery was made: elemental physical particles possess no inherent material attributes or properties. The primary building blocks of matter become progressively frequencylike. This discovery has far-reaching implications.

When we recognize the frequencylike nature of physical particles, the concepts of multiple dimensions of energy are not as far-fetched as they may first appear. For example, Newton's classic experiment with the prism showed that visible light contains different frequencies that appear as colors. The various light frequencies exist together within the same space-time that we observe, yet each frequency of light also exists completely separate from the others.

The electromagnetic wave spectrum displays an incredible array of radiation, from gamma rays to long radio waves. Since different frequencies of energy coexist within the same space-time that we occupy, why couldn't entire energy environments and possibly even worlds coexist with our visible physical universe? This question is taken seriously by modern physicists around the world. Physicists are now convinced that something

126   of substantial proportion exists just beyond our technological vision. This unseen and unexplored energy is thought to be the key to understanding the structure of matter and the universe.

I believe that Einstein's ultimate dream of grand unification can be realized by developing new methods to explore and verify the reality of the multidimensional universe. The scientific recognition of the multidimensional universe and the continuum of consciousness is the primary missing element in our comprehension of the unseen nature and structure of all energy throughout the universe. Grand unification can be realized if modern physicists are willing to refocus their attention from elementary particles to nonphysical wave function. This is not a dream but a reality patiently waiting for our scientific perceptions to evolve beyond their current obsession with physical particles.

The New Frontier of Science

In the twenty-first century, science will recognize that the answers to the elusive physical mysteries of our existence—the cosmology of the universe, the unseen nature and structure of matter, the evolution of our species, and even the existence of life after death—can be found only by exploring the unseen substructure of the universe. This recognition will be a major evolutionary step of science and a turning point in human evolution. Slowly we will move from being an externally focused, biological species to being an increasingly multidimensional species. This process of change has already begun. Astrophysicists, quantum physicists, and particle physicists are even now conducting extensive experiments that support the concept of a multidimensional universe. This trend will continue throughout the twenty-first century.

Once we begin to explore the interior of the universe, a new age of scientific research and discovery will emerge. Modern science will expand its current observations of matter and reality beyond all current concepts. Science will begin to explore the unseen source of physical energy and matter.

As we evolve, we will begin to chart the unseen universe much as astronomers are now charting the visible universe. The exploration of the interior of the universe is a massive endeavor reaching far beyond our current intellectual concepts of time, space, and energy. The exploration of the unseen dimensions is a task that all of us will eventually confront, for it is our birthright and our destiny to explore beyond our primitive biological vehicles and experience the magnificence of our true home within the multidimensional universe.

CHAPTER 4

Transformative Qualities

Knowledge is the antidote for fear.
—Ralph Waldo Emerson

The benefits of out-of-body exploration extend far beyond the limits of our physical senses and our intellect. After an out-of-body experience, many people report an inner awakening of their spiritual identity, a transformation of their self-concept. They see themselves as more than matter—more aware and alive. They express a profound inner wisdom based on personal spiritual experience.

Many report being connected to something greater than themselves, connected to the very source of life itself. They describe a powerful feeling of breaking through a dense barrier of ignorance, fear, and limitation.

During my workshops, I often hear reports of an increase in personal knowledge and an inner connection to spirit. Many describe a dramatic expansion of their ability to perceive—a new capability extending far beyond their physical limits; an overwhelming sense of knowing based on direct personal experience. Perhaps the most important benefit of out-of-body experiences is that we recognize our personal ability to discover the answers for ourselves.

When I am asked, "Why out-of-body exploration?" my response is simple: I need to know the answers for myself. I find little comfort in beliefs, especially since they are the most abundant commodity available today. Every society, every culture is overflowing with its version of the truth—a man-made collection of solid convictions. These beliefs change with time, evolving and decaying, while the truth of our existence remains the same, hidden under the ever-growing mountain of doctrines, dogmas, assumptions, and conclusions.

I believe that the purpose of life is experience. We must experience and explore for ourselves. We must discover and know, or be a slave to other people's opinions. As the twenty-first century approaches, the time has come for us to recognize our true potential and to explore beyond the prevailing beliefs and convictions. The time has come for us to discover and see the truth for ourselves.

We have this opportunity today. Controlled out-of-body experiences open the door to an incredible new frontier of human potential and discovery. They allow us to explore beyond the narrow limits of our physical senses and discover the answers to the oldest mysteries of our existence.

Transformative Qualities of Out-of-Body Experiences

According to research and studies conducted by many highly respected physicians—among them, Raymond Moody, Melvin Morse, Ken Ring, Bruce Greyson, and Stuart Twemlow—the transformative qualities of out-of-body experiences are limitless.

Each year new studies point to additional psychological and physical benefits derived from out-of-body experiences. As I research this topic, I realize that the number of reported benefits is absolutely staggering.

As reported out-of-body experiences increase, the evidence is overwhelming that life-changing benefits are regularly obtained during these out-of-body adventures. The following is presented as an overview of the many benefits reported worldwide in the last twenty years.

1. *Greater awareness of reality.* According to an in-depth study conducted by Stuart Twemlow, M.D., Glen Cabbard, M.D., and Fowler Jones, Ed.D., and presented at the 1980 annual meeting of the American Psychiatric Association, 86 percent of their 339 out-of-body participants reported a greater awareness of reality. In the same survey, 78 percent believed that they received a lasting benefit.

2. *Personal verification of our immortality.* Without a doubt, out-of-body experiences provide firsthand, verifiable evidence of our ability to exist independent of our physical bodies. This is a powerful, life-changing event for millions of people each year.

3. *Accelerated personal development.* Recognizing that we are more than physical beings opens entirely new levels of personal development. I strongly believe that self-initiated and controlled out-of-body experiences are the cutting edge of accelerated personal development. Once we consciously access and control our nonphysical self, we can unlock the unlimited knowledge of our subconscious mind and harness our ability to explore the universe. The entire subject of human potential is dramatically expanded beyond all current concepts and comprehension.

4. *Decreased fear of death.* When we experience ourselves consciously separated from and independent of our physical bodies, our fear of death is noticeably reduced. Fear of death is
fear of the unknown. Once you separate from your body, you
absolutely know that you continue. I have found that the
more out-of-body experiences we have, the less we harbor
fears and anxiety about death.

5. *Increased psychic abilities.* Precognition, telepathy, premoni-
tions, prophecy, the ability to see auras, and many other psychic abilities are often enhanced by out-of-body experiences.
The reason for this is currently unknown, but many believe
that it is simply a natural result of our becoming more at-
tuned to our internal energy systems.

6. *Increased desire for answers.* Once they recognize that answers
are available, many people begin a personal spiritual quest
to solve the mysteries they have pondered since childhood.

7. *Realizations concerning death.* Out-of-body experiences provide
evidence that the process of dying may not be a painful or
scary experience but rather a wondrous, spiritual adventure.

8. *Accelerated human evolution.* True evolution of our species is
not the biological change around us but the evolution of consciousness. As our world becomes progressively more complex, there is an inner need to discover the unseen reason
behind the rapid physical changes we perceive around us.
This need to know the answers to the many mysteries that
surround us will take our species into the next level of human
evolution.

When we look back at human evolution, we see a transition from physical labor-based (agricultural) societies to
increasingly intellectual-based (technological) societies. Eventually our species will be ready for the next major evolution-

ary step—the recognition and experience of our nonphysical self and the exploration of the nonphysical dimensions.

9. *Spontaneous healing.* There are numerous reports of people healing themselves and others when out-of-body. Often this healing is initiated by a focused thought directed to a specific area of the body.

10. *More expansive self-concept.* Instead of viewing themselves as physical beings possessing souls, many recognize themselves as souls (consciousness) temporarily possessing biological bodies.

11. *Increased spirituality.* According to the previously mentioned study conducted by Dr. Stuart Twemlow, 55 percent of the participants referred to their out-of-body experience as a spiritual experience. Many people report a deeper connection to their spiritual essence, profound insights into their spiritual nature, or a definite sense of being connected to something far greater than themselves. Whether we call it spirit or the universal mind of God, there are consistent reports of a powerful inner connection.

12. *Past-life influences recognized and experienced.* The work of Brian Weiss and other respected physicians and hypnotherapists has provided convincing evidence that past-life influences are an important element of our current psychological makeup. These subconscious memories can be effectively accessed and explored through personal out-of-body experiences.

13. *Accelerated psychological change.* Out-of-body experiences help us break free of old mental ruts and habits. On many occasions, individuals have told me that the shock of experiencing themselves independent of their physical body gave

them a more enlightened perspective of their current existence. This expansive vision of themselves has been instrumental in awakening new levels of personal growth and understanding.

14. *Obtaining personal answers.* Each of us has questions relating to his or her existence. What am I? What is my purpose? Do I continue? What is the meaning of life? These questions and many more can be answered only through personal experience. Out-of-body exploration provides a powerful method for all of us to obtain the answers we seek. Why settle for beliefs when the answers are available?

15. *Encountering a being of light, an angel, or another nonphysical resident.* Many people report face-to-face meetings with some form of nonphysical inhabitant. Thirty-seven percent of Twemlow's study group were aware of the presence of a nonphysical being, while 30 percent reported the presence of guides or helpers.

16. *Increased respect for life.* A pronounced aversion to violence and killing seems to appear. For example, the idea of hunting and killing an animal becomes repugnant. I believe this change owes to the personal knowledge we obtain concerning our spiritual interconnectiveness.

17. *Increased self-respect, self-responsibility, and inner dependence.* Many people recognize for the first time that they are the creative center of their physical existence. They often experience the vast potential and power of their inner, nonphysical self and tap into their creative essence. Many people have told me that they realize more than ever that they are completely responsible for all their actions, both thoughts and deeds.

18. *Reduced hostility, violence, and crime.* Those who experience themselves as more than just their bodies often realize the self-destructiveness of stealing or harming another person. Owing to their personal recognition that they truly do continue after death, they realize that their personal responsibility also continues.

19. *Increased knowledge and wisdom.* Only experience creates wisdom, and out-of-body experiences have the unique ability to provide knowledge and wisdom far beyond the limits of our physical perceptions.

20. *Profound sense of knowing instead of believing.* Personal knowledge is powerful and life-changing, especially when compared with beliefs. Out-of-body experiences provide first-hand, verifiable knowledge of our immortality and our spiritual identity. This knowledge cannot be adequately explained; it must be experienced.

21. *Inner calm.* A feeling of peace comes from knowing instead of hoping that we are immortal.

22. *Increased zest for living.* There is a certain difficult-to-describe excitement inherent in out-of-body exploration—an exhilaration that reaches deep into the very core of our being. When we separate from our physical body and actively explore our surroundings, we know deep down that we have become the ultimate explorer. We realize that we are much greater than our current physical personality or ego. Life itself becomes an adventure, an exciting journey of discovery. The inner excitement we feel is unmistakable; it comes from an inner knowing that we are blazing a path far ahead of our time.

23. *Increased intelligence and memory recall; enhanced imagination.* Many people report that their out-of-body experiences have somehow enhanced their awareness and intelligence. Some believe that out-of-body experiences may stimulate areas of the brain previously untapped during normal physical life. From a biological point of view, this could be a stimulation of the right temporal lobe or the pineal gland. The medical reason for the reported result is unknown, but according to extensive research conducted by Wilder Penfield, a Canadian neurosurgeon, when the right temporal lobe is stimulated by a mild electrical charge, patients consistently report out-of-body experiences. In addition, there is substantial evidence that the right temporal lobe is mysteriously activated during death and near-death experiences. There is also research supporting the existence of a connection between the biological brain and our nonphysical energy system. If this is so, then maybe there are interactions both electrical and chemical of which we are still unaware. This entire subject requires additional research.

24. *Sense of adventure.* Every day and night is an opportunity to experience a new adventure. The author Tom Robbins may have said it best, "Our great human adventure is the evolution of consciousness. We are in this life to enlarge the soul and light up the brain."

The transformative qualities of out-of-body experiences are a reality that each of us can experience. All we need is an open mind and the proper guidance to access our unlimited personal potential. The ability to explore unseen areas of the universe is now available, but it is up to us to take the step from being a curious observer to becoming an active explorer.

I believe this step is an important turning point in our lives and our personal evolution. Exploring beyond the limits of our physical bodies can be an effective way of obtaining the answers and insights so many of us seek. This journey of consciousness from the physical to the nonphysical is a reality we cannot escape; our only real decision is when we are going to begin.

Physically Challenged

Out-of-body exploration offers tremendous benefits for millions of physically challenged people around the world. For those who endure a lifetime of physical limitation, out-of-body exploration provides an incredible rebirth of hope, joy, and perception—an opportunity to experience themselves temporarily free of their physical pain, disease, or disability.

Just imagine the crippled girl who will never walk being able to move effortlessly past the confines of her disabled physical body, or the blind man who will never see his own face suddenly able to perceive beyond the limits of physical sight. The potential is staggering.

The benefits of out-of-body exploration extend far beyond our current medical and scientific comprehension. The medical profession has a long-standing history of focusing primarily on the physical aspects of disease and disability. Because of this physical emphasis and indoctrination, the exploration of expanded human potential and perception to benefit the physically challenged is sadly lacking in our society.

Our natural ability to transcend our physical bodies allows us to temporarily step away from any physical limitation we may currently experience. With the proper guidance, preparation, and techniques, almost anyone can become proficient at out-of-body exploration and experience the incredible joy of unrestricted freedom.

The startling reality of this unique form of exploration must be experienced for its unlimited potential to be comprehended and fully appreciated. Intellectual reasoning and analysis cannot give us this perception—we simply must experience the truth of it for ourselves. My fondest hope is that we will open our hearts and minds to this new potential of human growth and development. We have nothing to lose but the most widespread disability of all—ignorance.

When attempting out-of-body exploration, physically challenged individuals often possess a significant advantage over the general population. Their burning desire to escape their physical limitations often creates a powerful incentive for change. This desire and motivation is the single most important aspect of out-of-body exploration.

The following is an out-of-body experience reported by a man who has been paralyzed from the waist down for the last twenty years.

Sitting in my wheelchair, I am reading a book about out-of-body experiences. Being a sixty-three-year-old man with traditional upbringing, I seriously doubt that this kind of thing is real. It sounds too strange to be true.

In the book is a visualization exercise that appears pretty simple. I decide, What the hell—it doesn't hurt to try it. I begin to picture my daughter's home in my mind. I pretend I am at her home and opening her front door. I mentally step into the living room and begin to picture the furniture, carpet, windows, pictures, and even the plants. I'm kind of surprised how easy and fun it is to do this. I pretend to walk over to the coffee table and try to feel it. I sit down in a chair and try to feel the texture of the upholstery.

The next thing I remember is a dream in which I am flying across a beautiful meadow.

Then I feel a strange vibration all through me. The noise becomes louder and louder until I realize that I'm floating just above my wheelchair. At first I'm startled, but completely awake and aware. The floating sensation is wonderful. I think about moving to the door and I instantly float to it. A feeling of joy flows through me as I float through the door and around my house. I seem to glide wherever I wish.

Gaining my courage, I decide to try flying. As I think about it my body turns in midair. I spread my arms and picture myself flying like a bird. Instantly I'm gliding like an eagle in the sky. I fly over my neighborhood and can see the homes below me. For the first time in my life I know what true freedom really is. I think of my physical body and I'm suddenly back in my wheelchair again.

My heart is pounding with excitement as I write this. The exhilaration of this experience is beyond words. I only wish I had learned about this twenty years earlier.

Benefits of Out-of-Body Exploration

- Discover and know for yourself the answer to humankind's oldest mysteries: Do we continue after death? What is the meaning of life?

- Answer the basic questions of your existence: What am I? Why am I here? What is my purpose?

- Solve the mystery of your final destination: Where do we go at death? Does "heaven" exist? What does it look like? Why is it a mystery?

- Observe and solve current physical problems from a "higher perspective."

- Gain a greater understanding of the challenges and lessons you experience daily.

- Observe and understand the incredible, unseen power of thought-energy at work.

• Step beyond the labyrinth of beliefs and discover the truth yourself.

• Accelerate your personal evolution beyond the dense limits of matter.

• Confront and remove your personal fears.

• Gain a far clearer understanding of your life, your relationships, and your world.

• See and experience the magnificent beauty of our multi-dimensional universe.

• Realize your unlimited personal potential and power.

• Recognize and understand the unseen reasons for the past and present events in your life.

• Enjoy absolute freedom of movement without limits.

• Gain a far greater understanding of modern religions.

• Discover and experience absolute, firsthand verification of your personal immortality.

• Observe and comprehend the subtle energy currents that shape your life and your world.

• Receive the knowledge and wisdom that comes only with experience.

• Recognize and free yourself from inaccurate opinions, conclusions, and belief systems.

• See a clearer vision of the universal plan.

• Observe and understand the natural process of birth and death.

• See, experience, and explore the biblical "heaven" for yourself.

Joys of Out-of-Body Exploration

- The thrill of an exciting new adventure.

- The absolute joy of experiencing your personal immortality.

- The exhilaration of experiences and explorations beyond the ordinary.

- The overwhelming sense of personal accomplishment.

- The pure joy of exploring an uncharted, undiscovered terrain.

- The excitement of being a pioneer in a new field of exploration.

- The delight of discovering the truth of your existence beyond all beliefs and assumptions.

- The intense, personal satisfaction of knowing firsthand the purpose and meaning of your existence.

- The incredible feelings of knowing, instead of hoping.

- The joy of discovering new levels of personal growth and development.

- The overwhelming feelings of accelerated personal evolution.

- The intense, inner joy of solving ancient mysteries and discovering the answers for yourself.

These benefits and much more await you; however, it's up to you to explore and experience the reality of this for yourself. Out-of-body exploration gives you the rare opportunity to know and see, instead of hope and believe. This opportunity is yours today.

CHAPTER 5

Developing Your Natural Ability

Sit down before fact like a small child, and be prepared to give up every preconceived notion, follow humbly wherever and to whatever abyss nature lead, or you will learn nothing.
—T. H. Huxley

Keep your mind open to change all the time. Welcome it. Court it. It is only by examining and reexamining your opinions and ideas that you can progress.
—Dale Carnegie

Reappraising Our Concepts of Reality

Many psychological issues affect our ability to have an out-of-body experience. Our self-concept and the way we view this subject have a tremendous influence on the results we obtain. It's quite common for personal limits, fears, and beliefs to inhibit our ability to experience and enjoy our full potential. This is especially true when we are embarking upon a new form of exploration.

144   The self-evaluation in the table below briefly reviews topics and issues that may influence your ability to have an out-of-body experience. Your responses can offer useful insights into your personal beliefs, assumptions, and conclusions concerning this unique form of exploration.

As objectively as possible, examine your emotional and intellectual responses to each question. If you discover an area that holds a potential limitation or conflict, take your time and delve into it; look for the underlying reason for your current beliefs.

Belief reappraisal is one of the most important aspects of out-of-body preparation. I have found that conscious and subconscious fears, limits, and misconceptions are the most common obstacles we confront in out-of-body exploration. Recognition of our personal limits and fears is a major step forward in reducing or eliminating any blocks we may experience. Take all the time you need and feel free to expand upon any subject you believe is relevant. I recommend that you write your responses, in as much detail as needed.

Self-Evaluation

1. Self-Concept

What do you believe you are? How do you view yourself? Describe your self-concept in detail.

2. Personal Viewpoints

What are your perceptions and feelings concerning out-of-body experiences? Do you consider them an adventure?

3. Motivation

Is your personal motivation to obtain answers? To solve a mystery or a problem? Is it curiosity? Is it to obtain personal verification of some kind? Be specific.

4. Safety	Do you feel that it is completely safe to have an out-of-body experience? Do you have any concerns, such as that you might become lost or die? Be specific.
5. Special Ability or Talent	Do you believe that some kind of special ability or talent is required to have an out-of-body experience?
6. Importance	Do you consider this exploration important to your personal development? On a scale from 1–10, how important is it?
7. Desire	Do you possess the inner desire and drive to follow through? What benefits or information do you want from this experience? How strong is your desire?
8. Commitment	Are you willing to devote the time and effort needed to achieve your goal? Are you willing to commit thirty minutes a day for a month?
9. Fears	Are you anxious or fearful about this kind of exploration? Do you fear the unknown, the dark, or new challenges? Are your fears logical or the result of a lack of information?
10. Religious Beliefs	How does out-of-body exploration fit into your religious beliefs and concepts? Do you consider this a spiritual experience?
11. Degree of Difficulty	Do you believe that this experience is natural and easy or difficult to achieve? Why do you feel this way?

12. Confidence	Are you confident that you can achieve your desired goals?
13. Expectations	Do you expect positive results? What are your personal expectations?
14. Personal Issues or Limits	Are you aware of any personal issues that may limit your ability to have an out-of-body experience? If so, write them down.
15. Goals	Have you made this exploration a firm personal goal? Is it a written goal? Is it an important goal? Is it a priority?

Many subjects covered in this self-evaluation do not require an explanation. A few areas, though, may need further clarification.

COMMITMENT AND GOALS

Your positive attitude toward and commitment to out-of-body exploration are essential to your success. If you pursue this exploration with halfhearted interest, your results will reflect your desire. On the other hand, if you are passionate, determined, and committed, your success is practically assured.

It's important to make this exploration a personal priority for a specified time. In my workshops I recommend a minimum thirty-day total commitment. I instruct each student to set aside the time necessary to do at least one out-of-body technique daily. For thirty days, focus as much mental and emotional energy as you can muster upon your goal of a conscious out-of-body experience. For many people, writing out the goal daily helps to crystallize it within their minds and emphasizes its importance. For example, before bed each night write twenty times, "Now I have an out-of-body experience," "Now I have a fully conscious out-of-body experience," or "Now I'm out-of-body."

When you make this exploration a personal priority and incorporate written goals, the intensity of your commitment is magnified. In effect, you begin an almost mystical chain of events—your inner commitment and desire begin to mold your subconscious mind. Often your dreams become more memorable, and increasingly lucid. Dreams involving movement, such as flying, are often reported. These dreams are an indication that your subconscious mind is responding to your commitment to an out-of-body experience. These dreams and the inner signals associated with them are often an effective springboard to a fully conscious experience.

Write your goals today and make a firm personal commitment to follow through.

WRITTEN GOALS

In a class I recently conducted, a woman asked me what single event or experience had most influenced my ability to have out-of-body experiences. After some thought, I realized that more than any other thing, my decision to make a written list of personal spiritual goals had had a dramatic effect. For example, "I easily separate from my physical body" and "I now experience my higher self."

As strange as this may sound, committing my goals to paper had a powerful effect on the results I experienced. During each out-of-body experience, my personal goals seemed to flash in my mind at just the right moment for me to act on them. As I progressed, my goals evolved. Often, after returning from an out-of-body adventure, I would write my experience and realize that now I had several more goals and questions. It's as if each experience compounded itself. The power of setting firm, written goals

148 is evident; they focus our thoughts, both conscious and subconscious. All things physical and nonphysical begin as a thought, and the more specific our thoughts, the greater the probability of their manifestation.

During the first seconds of an out-of-body experience, our thoughts are critical to the immediate results we experience. It's quite common for our first focused thought to propel us into a nonphysical environment or situation that is directly related to that thought.

Specific written goals create a strong imprint on the subconscious mind and are more likely to be implemented by our nonphysical state of consciousness. If they are used properly, it's possible to program our out-of-body adventures toward a specific purpose or goal. The importance of this should not be overlooked: it is the first step to effective, conscious control of the out-of-body state. This is the underlying reason why affirmations and visualization are so effective.

FEARS AND LIMITS

Fears and limits exert an amazing control over our lives. Personal beliefs, limits, and fears create invisible walls of anxiety around us. These feelings of anxiety manifest themselves as the limits we experience in our daily lives.

Fear, anxiety, and the resulting limits are the number-one obstacle to success that we must face. Each day we are confronted with decisions and choices that we must act upon. These decisions determine the course of our lives and the results we experience.

If you look at the lives of successful people, you will notice that they share one overriding attribute. All of them had to confront and overcome their fears and limitations to reach their desired goals. Examples are the introverted actors, musicians, and public speakers who have conquered their intense stage fright, pilots who were once afraid of heights, and even the child who fears the dark.

Each fear and anxiety in our lives is a personal obstacle for us to overcome, a personal barrier separating us from our desired goals. Life itself can be viewed as a series of challenges and obstacles we must eventually confront and overcome. How we react to each challenge will determine the personal accomplishments we experience during our lives.

The fears and limits in our physical lives will many times affect our out-of-body explorations as well. In effect, our fears will manifest as nonphysical walls and barriers that restrict our freedom and mobility.

For example, during the third year of my out-of-body explorations, I experienced a large, heavy object pressing down on me immediately after separation. I perceived the object to be an ornate, gold-leaf mirror; it was so massive that I was pinned under its crushing weight. I began to push against the mirror with all my strength, trying again and again to remove it. An intense despair flowed through me as the weight of the mirror continued to crush me. In desperation, I focused all my attention, all my energy and strength, on moving this pressing weight and screamed out, "I have the power." Instantly, I felt a surge of strength and easily lifted the mirror and tossed it aside.

At that moment, I experienced a powerful new sensation of freedom and mobility. I was as light as a feather and able to go wherever I pleased. For the first time in my life, I felt completely free, completely in control. I was able to move, perceive, and comprehend at an accelerated rate. I somehow knew that I had opened the door to new levels of personal possibilities and growth.

Each fear and limit we experience is an opportunity for us to learn and grow. Our recognition of this can assist us in confronting each new challenge.

As surprising as it may sound, you don't have to believe in out-of-body experiences to have one. Countless individuals worldwide have reported spontaneous out-of-body experiences. Most of these people possessed no previous knowledge of or belief in out-of-body travel. Several books are currently available by Raymond Moody and other authors detailing such near-death and out-of-body experiences and their dramatic results.

Over twenty years ago when I first heard of this strange phenomenon, I didn't believe out-of-body experiences really existed. I had concluded that so-called out-of-body travel was probably a weird hoax, a drug-induced experience, or some kind of extremely lucid dream. Out of halfhearted curiosity, I decided to investigate these strange reports for myself. Looking back, I realize that belief was unnecessary. Instead, curiosity was my greatest asset when investigating this unique form of exploration.

PHYSICAL CONDITIONING AND INDOCTRINATION

Since birth each of us has received the most extensive conditioning that our society and culture can muster. We have been conditioned to accept the assumption that we are physical creatures—mammals with a mind.

This physical indoctrination is largely the result of a single undisputed conclusion passed down generation after generation: since we experience and observe ourselves as physical beings, it's only natural to conclude that we are our bodies. Based on physical perceptions, this appears to be a rational conclusion. What else could we be?

As we grow, we are repeatedly told that we are physical creatures. Every day of our lives this conclusion is reinforced by family, friends, the mass media, and society in general. Eventually we are taught a few nonphysical concepts, usually in the form of religious beliefs. These nonphysical concepts are normally passed to us in a very ambiguous manner. Most religions teach that we possess a soul or spirit of some kind—an invisible, indescribable form of energy. We are told to believe this mysterious concept without question, but are offered nothing as evidence—no facts, no logic. We are told to have faith, for the answers are in God's hands. Many religious leaders would have us believe that we are practically powerless to obtain the answers to the mysteries of our existence and of life.

The end result is a massive, double indoctrination. First we are taught that we are mammals with a mind; then we are taught that we are powerless creatures of God, unable to obtain the answers for ourselves.

There's only one problem with these conclusions—they're built entirely upon the limited range of our physical senses. As any physicist will tell you, we see only a tiny fraction of the energy around us. Basing our entire concept of reality on physical perceptions alone is a formula destined to create incomplete conclusions, not only about ourselves but about everything around us. A classic example is the early perception that the earth was the center of the universe. For thousands of years it was obvious to everyone that the sun revolved around the earth. In more recent times, we were taught in science that the atom was constructed of tiny particles spinning in harmony around a solid, stable nucleus. Today, according to quantum mechanics, this neat, orderly picture of subatomic reality is inaccurate and incomplete.

One of the current universal conclusions taught in schools around the world is the scientific assumption that the biological brain is the origin of consciousness. Medical science concluded long ago that the brain is the obvious source of all consciousness. What else could it be? Yet today, tens of millions of out-of-body and near-death experiences provide clear evidence that our state of consciousness continues even when we are separated from our physical body.

The first step in breaking free from our physical conditioning is to recognize its existence. From now on, begin to pay attention to the many assumptions and conclusions that make up your life. Notice all the subtle things that are built into our society and everyday life. For example, listen for all the statements referring to you and those around you as physical creatures: my hair, my skin, his arms, her legs. This may sound trivial, but we hear these kinds of statements countless times every day. Each statement referring to us as a physical body acts to condition us to this self-concept. In hypnosis this is called a suggestion. It is proven that when suggestions are repeated daily over a period of time, they will generate an extremely effective conditioning of our minds.

Every year millions of people are conditioned by hypnotic suggestions to alter their daily habits or behavior patterns—often in one or two sessions. For decades, suggestions have been used successfully to stop smoking or alter eating habits. If the human mind can be conditioned in one hour to change a lifelong habit such as smoking or overeating, just imagine how powerful a lifetime of social conditioning can be.

In effect, the constant reference to us as physical creatures molds our self-image to accept this assumption as reality. This is especially powerful when modern scientific and medical experts repeatedly reinforce the same assumptions. The result is clear: we accept the self-image that we are indeed physical creatures. This is without a doubt the greatest single falsehood dominating our species. In truth, the physical body is simply a temporary biological vehicle that we are using for expression in a dense environment. This is the primary reason that millions of people who have had near-death and out-of-body experiences are so profoundly changed by their experience. Often for the first time, they personally discover (not believe or hope) that they are a spiritual being inhabiting a temporary physical vehicle. This is a powerful, life-changing realization that is difficult to convey with words alone. Just think for a moment of your entire self-concept being radically and instantaneously changed forever. Many people don't talk about such experiences at all because they simply go far beyond current physical concepts of reality.

I believe that the underlying purpose of near-death and out-of-body experiences is to give each of us a personal glimpse into our spiritual nature. Only by experiencing our nonphysical-spiritual self can we completely overcome the restrictive influence of our physical and social indoctrination. Only by stepping free from our dense, physical limits can we know the truth of ourselves and our universe.

Anatomy of an Out-of-Body Experience

Just as specific elements are often present in near-death experiences, so the out-of-body experience has several commonly reported stages. The following are the most often mentioned.

1. *Vibrational Stage.* At this stage, energy vibrations flow throughout the body. Buzzing, humming, or roaring sounds, along with occasional numbness and catalepsy (inability to move), often accompany the vibrations. The variation and intensity of reported vibrations and sounds are immense; they can range from mild and soothing to intense and startling. During the vibrational stage, our consciousness is shifted to our nonphysical energy-body. The vibrations and sounds (inner signals) are not physical events, as some believe, but the conscious recognition of our higher-frequency body as it separates from (moves out of phase with) our physical body.

2. *Separation Stage.* When the subtle energy-body separates from the physical body, there is generally a distinct feeling of lifting, floating, or rolling out of the physical. After separation is complete, the vibrations and sounds immediately diminish.

3. *Exploration Stage.* Once we move away from and consciously
exist independent of the physical body, we can begin to explore the nonphysical environment. The energy-body is often
experienced as a duplicate of the physical body but consisting
of a higher-frequency form of energy. Because of its subtle
structure, the energy-body is extremely thought-responsive.
The method of mobility we use is completely unlimited; we
can walk, run, fly, float. To maintain our exploration, we must
continue to focus our attention within the new environment
and energy-body we are experiencing.

4. *Reentry Stage.* Reentry—the reintegration of the subtle
energy-body and the physical body—automatically occurs
by simply thinking about the physical body. On occasion,
during reentry the integration of the two bodies is accompanied by temporary vibrations, numbness, and catalepsy.
These sensations quickly fade as we become reunited and
in phase with our physical body.

Four Steps to Success

The first step to a successful, self-controlled out-of-body experience is to remain mentally and emotionally calm as you begin
to recognize any form of movement or shift in your awareness.
Your ability to remain calm is essential for achieving and maintaining any degree of control when out-of-body. The initial sensations associated with out-of-body experiences can be startling
to the beginner. This is especially true if you are unprepared for
the experience. Many times this excitement is caused by the intense sensations and sounds that may occur just before and during separation. Some people become so excited or startled by
these inner sounds and sensations that they immediately think of
their physical body. This causes an instant "snap back" into the

physical. The key is to welcome the unusual vibrations and sounds and to remain as calm as possible.

The second step is to incorporate the habit of automatic self-control. Whenever you experience any sensations or sounds associated with out-of-body exploration, immediately begin to encourage these feelings or sounds to expand throughout your being. For example, if you experience an intense buzzing sound or unusual vibrational feeling, immediately begin to encourage the sensation or sound to spread. Focus your complete attention on the enjoyment of your new, higher vibratory rate. Then, mentally encourage the vibratory sensations or sounds to immerse your entire being.

The third step is to direct yourself away from your physical body. This is easily accomplished by a verbal or mental internal dialogue that directs and maintains you away from your physical body. For example, "I'm floating up, up . . ." or "I'm becoming lighter and lighter . . ." or "I'm now moving to my living room [or backyard, or any other location away from your body]." Any phrase that directs and separates you from your physical body will be effective. Remember not to think of, or mention, your physical body in any way, shape, or form. Even random thoughts directed to your physical body can cause an abrupt return.

The fourth step is to maintain your focus entirely away from your physical body. The easiest way to achieve this is to temporarily forget about your body and become completely involved in the new environment you are experiencing. The success and duration of your out-of-body experience will depend utterly upon your focus of attention. Thoughts or feelings related to your physical body will instantly snap you back into it.

Always remember, we are powerful, nonphysical beings currently inhabiting a temporary vehicle of flesh. Our ability to control our out-of-body experiences is a natural part of our personal development. Each experience is an exciting adventure of

156 discovery. In effect, we are exploring and rediscovering our true identity and home.

Recognizing and Responding to the Vibrational State

Internal vibrations and sounds often indicate an approaching nonphysical experience. I refer to the inner sounds and vibrations as the vibrational state. These vibrations commonly begin at the back of the neck and then spread rapidly through the entire body. They are often accompanied by numbness and a buzzing or humming sound.

According to an extensive national out-of-body study conducted by Dr. Stuart Twemlow in 1979, 55 percent of the 339 participants reported "a sense of energy" during their out-of-body experiences. In addition, 50 percent stated that they felt vibrations in their bodies and 38 percent that they heard noises in the early stages of their experience. The most commonly reported noises were buzzing (29 percent), roaring (19 percent), and music or singing (16 percent).

In the beginning it's helpful to notice any inner signals you experience during sleep or dreams and as you are waking. Pay close attention to any unusual vibratory feelings or sounds, even if they are subtle. Many people routinely experience vibrational sensations and sounds but disregard them as dream-related or as unexplained physical phenomena.

Your recognition of and response to these sensations and sounds will, many times, determine how successful your separation process becomes. Some people are so startled by the sensations and sounds that they think of their physical body. This causes an instant return to the physical.

Your positive reaction to the initial sensations and sounds associated with out-of-body exploration will help you take advantage of every opportunity to separate from your physical body and experience the ultimate adventure. The more knowledgeable and prepared you are, the more successful you are likely to be. Recognizing and responding to the vibrational state is an important step in your preparation. The following list may help you identify the inner signals associated with the initial phases of an out-of-body experience.

- Buzzing, humming, or roaring sounds.

- Unusual tingling or energy sensations.

- Voices, laughter, or your name being called out.

- Heaviness or sinking.

- Numbness or paralysis in any part of your body.

- Weightlessness or spreading lightness.

- Any internal vibrations out of the norm.

- Electrical-like sense of energy.

- Footsteps or other sounds of a person's presence.

- Internal rocking, spinning, or movement of any kind.

- Arms or legs lifting while you are asleep.

- Surge of energy flowing through your body.

- Any noise out of the norm: wind, engine, music, bells, and so on.

Currently, several theories address the cause and nature of the vibrations associated with out-of-body experiences. Based on my experience, I believe that the vibrations are the direct result of the higher-frequency, nonphysical body separating from (moving out of phase with) the physical body. I've reached this conclusion because the intensity of the vibrations diminishes immediately

158 after complete separation is achieved. The way we respond to these initial vibrations will often determine how effectively we separate from the physical body. The following are some basic guidelines for responding to the vibrational state.

1. Remain calm. The vibrations, sounds, numbness, and catalepsy are a normal experience.

2. Allow and encourage the vibrations to spread through your entire body. Remember not to move or think about your physical body; any physical movement will shut down the vibrational process.

3. As you allow the vibrations to expand, visualize yourself moving away from your physical body toward another area in your home. This visualization can be enhanced by mentally directing yourself with a repeated thought: "Now I move to the door [or any other location away from your body]."

4. After complete separation is obtained, the vibrations will immediately diminish. At this point, it's important to focus and maintain your complete attention away from your physical body.

I have found that being knowledgeable about the vibrational state, recognizing it and responding positively to it, is one of the keys to controlling out-of-body exploration. During the first year of my out-of-body experiences, I was often startled and sometimes even scared by the intensity of the vibrational state. As I look back, I realize that I learned the hard way. In the seventies little information was available on this subject, and what was written scarcely mentioned the topic of vibrations and sounds.

After repeatedly experiencing vibrations and buzzing sounds while sleeping, dreaming, and doing out-of-body techniques, I began to realize that these strange vibrations were a natural prelude to the out-of-body experience. These unusual vibrations and sounds were one of the best early indications that I was ready to separate from my body. After several experiences, I started to enjoy the vibrations and even began looking forward to them. In retrospect, I realize that my attitude toward the vibrational state had a major impact on my ability to initiate and control my out-of-body experiences. As my anxiety concerning the vibrations and sounds slowly turned to anticipation, my personal abilities increased substantially. Eventually, I got to the point where the vibrational state was a welcome friend that heralded the beginning of an exciting adventure.

After more than a year of struggle, I finally felt comfortable with the entire process. From that moment, whenever I felt or heard internal sounds, vibrations, voices, or any form of energy sensation out of the norm, I would immediately encourage the vibrations or sounds to expand. Then I would visualize myself moving away from my physical body and toward the bedroom door.

This combination was remarkably successful. I began to recognize vibrations and sounds during sleep, in dreams, and during meditation. The intensity of the vibrations and sounds varied; sometimes they were subtle, at other times overpowering. I also found that if I experienced mild vibrations, I could focus on them and encourage them to expand and spread throughout my body. For example, on one occasion I woke in the middle of the night with a slight vibration at the back of my neck. I closed my eyes, completely relaxed, and focused on the vibration, encouraging the sensations to grow and move from the back of my neck to my entire body. Slowly, the vibrations seemed to travel down my spine and then outward, enveloping my trunk and limbs. After what seemed to be several minutes, the vibrations hit their peak and I simply willed myself out-of-body by picturing myself moving to my bedroom door. Within seconds I was standing at the bedroom door and ready to explore.

This process is completely natural and extremely enjoyable when you become accustomed to it. In addition, your newfound control and understanding of the vibrational state give you an expanded ability to take advantage of every possible opportunity to explore out-of-body. Always remember, the sensations and sounds of the vibrational state are an important reference point that can go a long way toward enhancing your abilities to have controlled out-of-body experiences.

The Hypnagogic State

Every day we experience a state of consciousness similar to a twilight between sleep and full waking awareness. This transition is often referred to as the hypnagogic state. As we drift off to sleep, we normally experience this as a brief but conscious dreamlike state.

Similar to hypnosis, the hypnagogic state is a highly creative state of awareness in which our mental imagery is clear and present, much like a changing movie in our mind. While in this state, we have the ability to exert a degree of conscious control and can actually use our internal imagery for specific purposes. For many people, this state is an excellent springboard for out-of-body experiences.

Creative artists and inventors have used the hypnagogic state to further their work. For example, Thomas Edison was well known for his daily catnaps. He developed a technique for maintaining his hypnagogic state while working on his many inventions. Sitting in a favorite chair, he would use a form of meditation and relaxation to enter the hypnagogic state. To control this delicate state between sleep and wakefulness, Edison would hold some ball bearings in his closed hand, palm down, as his hand rested on the arm of the chair. Directly beneath his hand he placed a metal bowl. If he drifted off to sleep, his hand would open and the ball bearings would fall into the metal bowl and awaken him. It's reported that he would repeat this technique

over and over until he received the inspiration or information he
sought.

Since the hypnagogic state is very similar to deep hypnosis, it
can be used effectively to program ourselves for an immediate or
future out-of-body experience. From now on, as you fall asleep
and awaken, begin to notice the transitional state you pass
through every night. For many people, this is especially evident
in the last minutes of waking awareness as they drift into sleep.
The following technique can be used both when going to sleep
and when just awakening.

Consciously begin to recognize the hypnagogic state immediately before drifting off to sleep. To increase your awareness of
the state, it may help to make a verbal or written request or goal:
"I remain aware as I drift to sleep."

As you drift into sleep, focus your complete attention on the
mental imagery that seems to flow in your mind.

As much as possible, begin to consciously arrange and control
the changing mental images and scenes that appear. Picture yourself floating up and out of your body. This could be visualized as
a hot-air balloon, an airplane, or an elevator moving up, or you
could picture yourself as a floating cloud. Whatever is comfortable and easy to picture in your mind will work. Flow with the
sensations and pictures in your mind; have fun with the visualization and allow your imagination to take off.

As you remain focused upon the internal imagery, repeat to
yourself, "Now I'm out-of-body."

The result of this technique is identical to other out-of-body
methods. You will either fall asleep, awaken in the vibrational
state, or awaken floating above or near your body. The key is to
remain calm and direct; maintain complete attention away from
your physical body.

At first glance this technique may appear difficult, but in practice it's simply a matter of remaining aware as long as possible as
we slowly drift into sleep. Our natural ability to recognize and

162 direct our consciousness is limited only by our preconceptions. Many of us have never attempted to extend our awareness beyond waking consciousness; as sleep approaches, we simply surrender to its sensations and slowly lose consciousness. I hope that from now on, as you drift off to sleep, you will view the process of "falling to sleep" in a different light. As you experiment with the hypnagogic state, you'll find that it becomes preferable to direct your attention instead of just allowing your mind to fade into unconsciousness. In addition, as you begin to pay close attention to the imagery you see, you will gain some interesting new perceptions into yourself: your motivations, passions, fears, and abilities. When recognized and used properly, the hypnagogic state can be a powerful and creative tool for extending our perceptions beyond our physical limits. Just as Edison used this state of consciousness to obtain inspiration for his many inventions, we can use it to expand our awareness beyond the physical.

The following visualization can be effective for individuals or groups. In my classes, it is often used as a relaxation and preparation before an out-of-body technique.

PREPARATION TECHNIQUE

Take several deep breaths and completely relax. Close your eyes and begin to visualize the top of your head opening and a stream of shimmering white, liquid energy flowing into the top of your head. The liquid feels warm and soothing as it slowly flows through the top of your head and past your forehead, eyes, and mouth. Completely relax and feel all your tensions release into the warm shimmering liquid. Feel the liquid absorb your tensions and your fears. Feel the warm liquid slowly flow through your head and down your throat. Feel this warm energy flow through your heart and spread throughout your body. Feel its warmth and energy as it flows down your back. Feel it absorbing your tension, your pain, your fears, and your limits as it fills every part of your arms and legs. Feel your entire body filled with this wonderful, white liquid energy. Feel every cell, every tissue, organ, and muscle bathe in this warm white liquid.

Now feel the liquid energy become even warmer. Feel it vibrate and become a liquid sponge, a liquid magnet. Feel it begin to attract and absorb your negative vibrations. Feel it absorb your feelings of fear and anger; feel it absorb all the attachments to your body. Vividly feel all your fears, anxieties, limits, and anger being absorbed into this warm, vibrating liquid energy. Feel the flow; feel it draw your negative vibrations from your body, your emotions, your mind. Feel it at every level of your being.

See and feel the glowing, warm liquid begin to darken as it absorbs all your negative vibrations. Feel every cell, every tissue and organ, every energy system in your body releasing its impurities, releasing its negative programming, releasing its limits and fear. Vividly feel all your negative vibrations let go and release their energy into the warm white liquid flowing through you. Feel this at every level of your being. Feel your emotional walls dissolve. Feel your attachments to your ego and your body begin to release to the warm liquid energy.

As your negative energies are released into the warm liquid, see the liquid become darker and darker. Feel it draw the impurities from your body, your emotions, and your mind. Feel all your impurities released to the liquid.

Now visualize valves at the base of your heels and the palms of your hands. Slowly open the valves and let the warm brown liquid begin to flow out of your body. Feel all your negative emotions—your fears and your limits—draining out and away from your body. Vividly see and feel your negative emotions and vibrations completely drain from your body.

Feel every part of your inner being, your inner self, become cleaner and clearer as your negative energies and thoughts flow from your body. As clearly as possible, see and feel your individual

164 fears, limits, and negative energies release from your physical, your emotional, and your intellectual body. Feel all your negative energies flowing out through your heels and hands.

Clearly see all your anxieties, limits, and attachments flowing from your body. Feel how good it is to be purified of your negative energies. You have never had a complete inner cleansing before, and you feel totally fresh and pure. You feel light as a feather, free from the dense negative limits and thoughts that hold you to matter.

Inwardly acknowledge that all your negative energies are flushed forever from your body, flushed forever from your physical, emotional, and intellectual body. Feel the pure power of this cleansing as your body and mind are reenergized and completely purified of all negative programming, limits, and fears. Absolutely know that all of your negative energies are washed away forever.

Deep down, feel your vibration rate increase; feel how light and airy you are. Feel the joy as you experience your new, higher vibration, your higher self. Relax and enjoy your higher, finer vibrations as you grow lighter and lighter and lighter. Feel yourself becoming light as a feather, just floating, floating effortlessly, as light as a cloud, floating up and away from your body.

Separation

Much of the current literature on out-of-body experiences indicates that we automatically float or lift out of our bodies like some form of magic. Based on my experience and information obtained from more than two hundred people, I believe this perception is inaccurate. It's quite common to enter the vibrational state but not separate from the body. This occasionally happens even to experienced out-of-body explorers. It's unclear why, during the vibrational phase, we sometimes cannot or will not separate from the physical body. Any number of reasons could be mentioned: energy or psychological attachments to the physical;

fears; vibrational misalignment; or simply lack of information concerning how to react to the experience. I believe that the last-named is by far the most common reason.

There are a number of things you can do to resolve this situation. First, focus and maintain your thoughts and imagination upon the sensation of moving away from your body. Visualize or will yourself away from your body. Second, if necessary, ask to detach completely from the physical; for example, "Now I move to the door." Third, if this fails, simply ask for assistance: "I request help to leave my body." When requesting assistance, it's important that you be completely open to receive what you request.

The subject of separation and the vibrational state is of critical importance and deserving of more emphasis than parapsychologists and writers have given it up to now. And considering its importance, it should not be overlooked.

Separation Methods

1. *Floating out.* Since the inner energy-body is weightless by physical standards, it's normally quite easy to just float away from your physical body. This separation method appears to be the most widely used. The key is to focus on the sensations of floating and allow yourself to drift up and away from your body.

2. *Sit up and out.* This method is similar to the floating technique, except that we simply sit up and then step away from our physical body. It is the primary method I used during the first ten years of my out-of-body experiences. Because of the method's physical-like qualities, it is generally easier to control than the floating or direct method. This type of separation is often heralded by the vibrational state. I believe the relatively slow withdrawal from the physical body

experienced with this method creates the intense vibrations and sounds so often reported.

3. *Rolling out.* This method is extremely effective. After you recognize the vibrational state, you simply do a sideways roll. As weird as this may sound, it gets to be fun. Several people have told me that they rolled off the physical bed and fell to the floor laughing to themselves. This method is used effectively by many people; author Robert Monroe states in his book *Far Journeys* that he often uses a rolling technique when separating from his first energy-body and moving to his second energy form.

4. *Requesting separation.* When you enter the vibrational state, simply ask to separate: "I separate now" or "I move to the next room." Any firm request that directs you away from your physical body will be effective. As in all nonphysical requests, make it a firm demand for immediate action. Always remember to maintain your complete attention away from your physical body; any thought or word relating to your body will instantly return you to it.

5. *Pulling yourself out.* This can be achieved by reaching out your nonphysical arm and grabbing any large object, then literally pulling the rest of your energy-self out of your physical body. This method can get interesting because you quickly learn that your inner energy-body does not share the limits of your physical body. In other words, our energy-body has the ability to conform to our thoughts. I accidentally discovered this about ten years ago when I entered the vibrational state while sleeping in a canopy bed. Stretching my energy arm out in front of me, I spontaneously decided to try an experiment and attempted to grab the top of the bed. To my surprise my arm stretched over five feet and I took hold of the

top of the bed. At that point, I pulled my entire nonphysical body out of my physical body. After standing, I stared at
my hand; it had returned to its normal physical size. Amazed,
I recognized that my nonphysical arm's shape and form completely depended on my thoughts. This realization is important because it allows us to expand our abilities in several
creative ways.

6. *Direct method.* Commonly called direct or instantaneous projection, this technique is more advanced than the others—
   often you find yourself fully conscious in a completely new
   environment. The sudden transition from lying in bed to
   standing or floating in a different location can be startling if
   you are unprepared. Generally, there is little or no sense of
   movement, just an instant realization of awakening in a completely new location or environment. This type of separation
   is often reported during dream conversions. It is the preferred method of many experienced out-of-body explorers.

7. *Requesting assistance.* Sometimes, for reasons unknown, separation can become more difficult. Several years ago when I was
   experiencing some difficulty, I found a simple way to resolve
   it. I entered the vibrational state and was ready to lift out,
   but for some reason my energy-body felt attached and heavy.
   Out of desperation I reached out my arm and verbally asked
   for help. Within seconds I felt the grasp of a hand pulling
   me out of my body. The feel of the hand was surprisingly
   solid and real. When I left my physical body, I eagerly looked
   around but could see no one.

During my workshops, several people have related similar
stories of assistance. Because of this and other evidence, I believe
that it's likely that every time we have a fully conscious out-of-
body experience, someone close to us is observing our progress.

168   This observer, whether it be a guide, friend, or loved one, is ready to assist if needed. I'm certain that help is available to us at all times, but it is up to us to request the assistance. Without such a request, a spiritual friend or guide is normally not going to interfere with our developmental experiences. I also think that guides stay out of sight because they know that their visible presence would disrupt our natural progress. Looking back, I wish I had asked for assistance more often. I probably would have progressed faster, but more important, I think I would have appreciated the fact that we're not alone during our explorations. An unmistakable feeling of comfort and security comes from knowing that we have assistance available any time we ask for it. This knowledge helps us to successfully confront any fear or anxiety we may experience when exploring a new energy environment.

Action

When you look back on your life, has procrastination ever carried you closer to a goal or an achievement? Has inaction ever brought you increased success, accomplishment, or personal development?

We are all creatures of habit. We repeat the same familiar thoughts and actions because they are familiar, unchallenging, and considered safe. We simply follow our individual path of least resistance. For many of us, our tendency to remain the same has become a central element of our personal habits and our life.

Many of us consider change—any change—a negative experience. It is clouded with suspicion and treated as a threat to our established thought patterns and beliefs. The end result is often a continuation of our personal habit of inaction.

We must eventually ask ourselves whether we are completely content to live our entire life following the same habits of thought and action. Are you content to accept blindly, without verification, the prevailing ideas and convictions of your society? Are you truly satisfied to settle for beliefs, hope, and faith instead of personal experience and knowledge?

Ask yourself, what would you believe in today if you had been born in Iran or Iraq. What religious and social convictions and conclusions would you hold dear? What beliefs would you die for?

If you want answers to the mysteries of your life, then the time for action is now, and out-of-body exploration can provide the answers you seek.

CHAPTER 6

Exploration Techniques

Genius means little more than the faculty of perceiving in an unhabitual way.
—William James

Today millions of people are discovering the techniques used to achieve out-of-body exploration. The variety of methods available is staggering. Throughout history, practically every religious group and mystic order has developed a system or method to explore beyond the limits of matter. Many of these gems of wisdom have remained shrouded in mystery for thousands of years, covered by the trappings of religious ritual. For example, the Tibetan Book of the Dead provides preparation and guidance for an ancient out-of-body method, but because the technique was incorporated in lengthy religious ceremonies performed over a period of days, it, like many other ancient techniques, has remained hidden for centuries.

To simplify this confusing and often misunderstood body of information, I have divided out-of-body techniques into five categories: visualization, dream conversion, affirmations, hypnosis, and sound. The methods I discuss here have proved to be extremely effective and easy to learn.

The visualization techniques are presented first because of their ease and popularity. Many people have discovered that the visualization techniques are a natural way to initiate their first out-of-body experience. After you select a technique, repeat it daily for at least thirty days. Your commitment, desire, and effort will determine the results you experience.

Always remember, the best way to approach out-of-body exploration is to maintain a playful attitude. Have fun with the techniques and enjoy the results.

Choosing Your Technique

One of the most important decisions you face in out-of-body exploration is the selection of the technique on which to focus. In general, if you can visualize well, concentrate on the visualization techniques. Select the technique that is most comfortable for you and stick with it.

If you have difficulty visualizing, then you may want to concentrate on the affirmation techniques. Keep in mind, though, that the target technique (a form of visualization) has proved effective for many people who claim poor visualization skills. I believe its effectiveness owes to the physical "walk-through," which can be repeated until the internal imagery begins to appear. Many people find it easier to visualize an object or location in their home than anywhere else.

Don't underestimate your abilities; when you are open-minded to new experiences and perceptions, they will occur. On many occasions during my workshops, people have told me that they can't visualize at all. I have found that when people verbally request the ability and begin to practice with an open mind, they experience a rapid enhancement of their natural abilities. When choosing your technique, remember to be both flexible and patient.

Visualization

One of the easiest and most effective methods of experiencing out-of-body exploration is to use your creative visualization ability. Each of us possesses the natural ability to picture an object or place in our minds. We do it every day in a thousand different ways. Most of us have little difficulty imagining our favorite vacation spot, automobile, home, or person. Using our visualization ability is easy once we recognize how natural it is.

To learn just how easy visualization can be, try the following.

Close your eyes and begin to picture your favorite vacation spot. Select a place you have visited and know well. Just relax and begin to visualize this vacation area as clearly as possible. Begin to picture the trees, the buildings, the people—all the small details associated with your vacation. Become involved in the scene as much as possible, vividly seeing and hearing all the sensations associated with your favorite vacation. You can add people, colors, and sounds as you see fit.

Now take this scene a step farther and picture yourself entering your favorite vacation paradise. Clearly see and feel yourself within a specific physical location. Imagine all the colors, sounds, and sensations associated with the location. Begin to interact with the people and environment you see. As much as possible, use all your senses; immerse yourself in the sounds, sights, and sensations of your vacation. Take your time and enjoy the experience.

Visualization techniques are easy and enjoyable when you relax and select a pleasurable place, person, or object on which to focus. Whatever you select as the focus of your attention, it should be an actual physical object or location. The key to all out-of-body visualization methods is to become mentally immersed in a real physical environment. The more focused your attention, the more success you will experience.

IMAGINATION

Your imagination is your preview of life's coming attractions.

—Albert Einstein

One of the most powerful tools we possess in out-of-body exploration is our natural ability to use our imagination. When used creatively, the imagination can help us achieve any goal or desire on which we focus. This is graphically displayed all around us. When we look at our physical possessions, we discover an amazing thing: everything we possess—our car, furniture, home, stereo, TV, even our relationships—was once imagined in our mind. For example, when you see a house being built, just think of the many imaginations that were busy creating the structure. First, some people begin to imagine a new home for themselves; then they share their ideas with others. Next an architect is called upon to put the imagined ideas on paper. Then a builder imagines the construction of the home. Slowly, the collaboration of several imaginations and thoughts comes together to form an idea, a plan, a structure, and, finally, a physical home. Of course, we take this for granted, seeing only the physical results of these busy thoughts around us.

When we explore the nonphysical interior of the universe, however, an amazing thing occurs: we begin to recognize that our imagination and thoughts have a dramatic impact upon the finer energy frequencies of the inner dimensions. We begin to understand that our imagination is a powerful creative force that shapes the unseen energy around us. When we are out-of-body, our thoughts and imagination are forming our immediate energy environment with incredible speed and precision. In a very real sense, our thoughts are building the unseen energy substructure of our external physical existence.

While living in the physical world we see only a tiny fraction of reality. We observe only the dense results of our thoughts and deeds. The pure power of our imagination and thoughts is often not recognized as we focus upon daily survival and the acquisition of physical objects. For many people, the time span between the imagined idea and the physical results is a long, hard road. They seldom see or understand that they have formed the subtle energy molds and structures that have eventually manifested within their physical environment.

Whether we realize it or not, our imagination is molding the subtle energy around us. With every thought, we are building our future. This is why creative visualization and positive thinking work so effectively. The greater the focus of our imagination, the faster the results we experience.

I cannot emphasize enough how important this creative process is to our existence. It is not some hypothetical belief or theory but an absolute, observable energy reaction constantly occurring around us. We can personally verify this by practicing the techniques presented in this book. This creative energy reaction is constantly at work shaping the subtle energy around us. For example, an accurate psychic reading is nothing more than the psychic being sensitive to the unseen energy forms around another person. This process is not some strange or mystical event, as some believe, but a simple recognition of the subtle energy forms close to a person. In fact, the entire phenomenon of extrasensory perception is actually the natural process of people being sensitive to nonphysical thought-energy and forms.

As we evolve, our recognition of this energy reaction becomes more important. Our innate ability to structure our energy environment and our life carries us beyond the animal instincts into new realms of personal creativity and responsibility. The end result is that each of us becomes the creative artist of his or her life. Each focused thought and mental image becomes the creative mold of our personal reality. At this point we can begin to consciously build the reality we wish to experience by the thought forms we visualize and hold in our mind. Instead of being the powerless result of our environment, we begin to take charge of our life and our destiny. Finally, we come to recognize that our ability to create is limited only by our ability to imagine.

One of the advantages of the visualization method is the variety of possibilities it generates. There are no limitations, so feel free to develop and use your own technique. Generally, whatever holds your interest and attention away from your physical body can be effective. For many people, visualizing their favorite friend, lover, or physical location as they fall asleep produces impressive results. For example, I know a housepainter who induces out-of-body experiences by visualizing himself climbing a ladder and painting his home. The key, he states, is to picture himself at a specific physical location as he drifts off to sleep. In as much detail as possible, he actually feels the hand-over-hand of climbing up a ladder to the roof. He feels the grip and texture of the ladder with his hands and can even feel the ladder slightly shake with each step. He then imagines himself painting his house with as much vivid detail as possible. As with all visualizations, his technique is most effective when he surrounds himself in the sensations and sounds associated with the activity.

VISUALIZATION MADE EASY

The key to out-of-body exploration is to focus and maintain your complete attention outside your physical body as you fall to sleep. One of the easiest ways to accomplish this is to focus your complete attention upon a person, place, or object located some distance from you. This can be a loved one from whom you are separated, your favorite vacation spot, or a gift that holds special meaning for you. Whatever you select, it should be an actual physical object you know, not an imaginary place or person. Select the object or place that is easiest to visualize and holds the most interest for you.

For many, visualizing a loved one is effective. Just picture the person you wish to be with as vividly as possible. It helps to be emotionally involved, so select a person you would love to be with. Choose someone you know, not a fantasy relationship. Become completely absorbed in that person's presence and actually feel yourself with him or her. If you like, role-play some kind of interaction to keep you involved.

Continue your visualization of this person for as long as possible as you allow your physical body to completely relax and fall to sleep. It's important to maintain a detailed picture of the person and your interaction as you go to sleep. As you doze off, attempt to boost your emotional and visual connection with this person as much as possible.

This method is an excellent bedtime visualization. Keep in mind, the more emotionally involved you are, the more effective this technique is. Have fun with it and let your imagination go wild.

THE TARGET TECHNIQUE

Your ability to focus and maintain your awareness away from your physical body is enhanced if you direct your full attention to a specific object or place. The target technique is an excellent exercise to help you develop this ability.

Select three targets in your home. All three targets should be physical items that you can visualize with relative ease. Your targets should not be in the room that you normally use for your out-of-body techniques.

For example, you could select your favorite chair for your first target. For your second, select a gift that holds a special meaning for you. Third, select the most visually stimulating object available, such as your favorite painting, sculpture, or crystal. All three targets should be in the same room.

After selecting your targets, physically walk to each one and examine every detail. Study each object from different perspectives, noticing any imperfections or irregularities. Take your time with the objects, memorizing the sight and texture associated with each target. Become aware of all your senses during your walk, especially your senses of sight and touch. Repeat your walk several times until you can easily recall the smallest details of each target area. Pay close attention to everything, including colors, weight, densities, reflections of light, coolness, and heat. Also feel and memorize the sensations associated with your walk from one target to another. In other words, *get into it!* Enjoy all the sensory input that you receive.

This technique helps you focus and maintain your attention away from your physical body as you drift off to sleep. If you are persistent, the results will be dramatic. To enhance this exercise, take your time and repeat your physical and visual walk-through daily for thirty days. Get interested and involved in each target. This technique is a great way to increase your concentration and visualization skill, and it only takes about twenty minutes to perform.

It's important to select targets that are easy for you to visualize. Many people select personal items that possess a sentimental attraction. Once you make a selection, stay with it; the repetition of your visualization dramatically increases its effectiveness.

This technique has been my personal favorite ever since I stumbled upon it over twenty years ago when I began to visualize objects in my mother's home. I strongly believe that the technique can work for anyone who is willing to invest the time and effort. The key is to select target objects that are easy to visualize but interesting enough to hold your attention. Items that you have made, such as a painting, a sculpture, a silk flower arrangement, or even a set of curtains, can be extremely effective targets. As you progress with this technique, you can increase the number and variety of the targets you select. After you become comfortable with a few objects, you can expand your visualization to include an entire room. This technique is extremely effective, but it is up to you to take the steps. The time you invest will be richly rewarded.

In addition to the targets mentioned above, you may want to consider some of the following objects to focus on during your visualizations.

Sense of Sight

A favorite chair, sofa, or other piece of furniture

Any object that you can visualize well

A gift or personal item that holds a special meaning

Any object or artwork that you have created yourself

A special picture, painting, or portrait

Sense of Touch

Textured fabric or cloth of any kind

An item of furniture

A door, carpet, light switch, sculpture, or wooden banister

Jewelry, ashtray, candle

Any object that has a unique or distinctive shape or texture

Sense of Smell

Air freshener

Fresh flowers

Soaps or lotions

Favorite perfume or cologne

Cedar chest or closet

Incense

THE MIRROR TECHNIQUE

The mirror technique is an effective way to enhance your visualization skills and prepare yourself for out-of-body exploration.

Begin by placing a full-length mirror in the room you have selected for out-of-body exploration. The mirror should be positioned so that you can easily see your entire reflection without having to move physically.

As you look into the mirror, begin to study and memorize your image. Become as objective as possible: view your reflection as an object you are about to paint in your mind. Pay close attention to the small details of your body and clothing. Take your time, memorizing everything you see.

Close your eyes and begin to visualize yourself in as much detail as possible. Continue to repeat this procedure until you can clearly visualize yourself on the other side of the room.

With your eyes closed, visualize yourself standing on the opposite side of the room. Then begin to picture your imaginary self. Take your time, slowly moving your image's fingers and hands, then slowly beginning to move its arms. Visualize your reflection moving its toes, feet, and legs. As much as possible, become mentally and emotionally involved in your reflection. Begin to feel the sensations of movement you are experiencing. Feel the enjoyment of movement without a physical body. Become completely involved and immersed in the movements.

As you become more deeply involved in your image's movements, feel yourself stand up and slowly begin to walk around the room. As you are walking, feel all the sensations associated with your movement.

Begin to feel and picture yourself opening your imaginary eyes. As clearly as possible, feel your image looking around the room. At first, this may feel as if you're pretending to see your room from a new perspective. That's fine; just allow yourself to flow with all the visual sensations you receive. After some practice you will begin to notice an enhancement in your ability to see beyond the limits of your body.

Take your time and enjoy the various parts of this technique. If you find it difficult to transfer your sense of sight, focus on your other senses, such as touch, as much as possible. As you transfer the majority of your perceptions to your imaginary self, completely forget about your physical body by focusing all your attention on your new sensations and sight. Completely relax and allow your physical body to fall asleep. As your body slowly goes to sleep, you will experience a transition or shift of awareness from your physical to your nonphysical body. As this occurs, remember to remain calm and enjoy your new ability to perceive.

This technique is excellent for improving visualization skills. Many people are surprised at how easily they can visualize after a short period of practice. Take your time and enjoy the results.

Dream Conversion

Dreams are an effective doorway to out-of-body exploration. For many people dreaming is a natural way to ease their awareness away from their physical state of consciousness and begin to recognize and experience other states of consciousness.

Since the dawn of civilization, societies and cultures around the world have viewed dreams as an entryway to a different world. The significance of dreams is portrayed in humanity's oldest recorded writings, including the Upanishads, the Bible, the Egyptian Book of the Dead, and the Koran. From the lavish dream temples of ancient Greece to the dream therapy techniques of modern psychologists and psychiatrists, dreams continue to provide valuable insights into our subconscious mind.

If used properly, dreams can act as an effective trigger or signal for out-of-body exploration. Some of the most common signals are listed later in this chapter. One of the best ways to initiate an out-of-body experience is to become aware or lucid within a dream. This can be accomplished by changing our attitudes toward our dreams.

First, begin to acknowledge the importance of your dreams in your daily life. Treat your dreams as valuable insights and messages from your subconscious mind. In effect, think of them as an actual form of communication, as real as your physical experiences.

Second, begin a daily dream log. Record every dream you can, even the small fragments. This should be done immediately upon waking, either by writing or using a tape recorder. Pay close attention to the feelings, emotions, and sensations that you experienced during the dreams.

Third, firmly express your desire for increased clarity and awareness within your dreams. As you drift to sleep, strongly request that your complete conscious awareness be present in your dreams. Make a firm, verbal commitment to yourself as you fall asleep that you will recognize, recall, and consciously experience every single dream.

Fourth, repeat a strong affirmation to yourself as you fall asleep each night. For example, "As I fall to sleep, I remain aware," or "Now I have a fully conscious out-of-body experience," or "I become aware in my dreams."

When doing your affirmations, make them firm and positive, fully expecting your request to be granted. As with all out-of-body affirmations, concentrate your full emotional and intellectual energy into each one. It's important to focus and maintain your affirmations as your last conscious thoughts as you drift to sleep.

The transfer of your awareness can occur quickly, so it's essential to remain calm and enjoy any changes in your personal perspective, environment, energy, or location.

The following is a dream conversion that I experienced some years ago.

In my dream I was in a pet store. Looking around, I noticed a small hermit crab on the floor near my feet. As I watched the crab, it jumped five feet straight up in the air. At first, I was startled and stepped back; then as I watched, it became obvious that the crab was attempting to get my attention. Again the crab jumped and I realized that I had to be dreaming. At that moment I said aloud, "I must be dreaming." Immediately, I felt a strange tingling sensation in my body and realized that I'd entered the vibrational state while dreaming. Out of habit I focused my complete attention on the idea of floating up and out of my physical body. Within seconds I could feel myself lift from my body and move toward the living room.

This type of dream conversion is easy to achieve if we are willing to recognize and accept the entire process. The most important element is how we respond at the moment we become consciously aware within our dream.

Vivid or lucid dreams are not necessarily unconscious out-of-body experiences; they can be psychological manifestations similar to internal projections. The unusual or outrageous events in our dreams are creations of our subconscious mind specifically designed to grab and hold our attention. I have found that once we make a firm commitment to explore out-of-body, this type of lucid dream becomes a regular event. In effect, our subconscious mind is doing its best to assist us in achieving our goal of a conscious out-of-body experience. This, of course, is another reason why written goals are so vital. The more focused our goals, the more our subconscious mind is willing and able to assist us.

This type of lucid dream can be literally anything out of the ordinary: unusual surroundings or people; outlandish colors or shapes; strange buildings, pets, or other animals. I have found that lucid dreams often manifest as a single strange event in an otherwise relatively normal dream—any strange, illogical, or inappropriate person, place, or thing that is obviously out of the norm. For example, a typical family sedan may become a bright red sports car. A regular home may become a castle. A household pet may become a lion or an eagle. A single object or event in a dream may become completely out of place and outrageous: a jumping crab, a talking cat, a flying dog. Whatever it is, it's something so psychologically outlandish that it captures and holds our complete attention.

The key to a successful dream conversion is our conscious recognition and knowledgeable response to our lucid dream occurrences. Once you recognize a strange or illogical event, situation, or object within your dream, focus your attention as much as possible upon the unusual occurrence. Verbally pinpoint the illogical event within the dream: "I can't fly," or "I don't live in a castle," or "That's strange, my car isn't red."

As you become increasingly conscious (lucid) within the dream, verbally acknowledge that you know you are dreaming. Say aloud anything that will consciously acknowledge your awareness: "I know I'm dreaming," "I am awake in my dream," or "I'm now aware."

The next step is to be ready for the transition or movement of your consciousness from your dream state to your nonphysical body. Be prepared for a rapid shift of your awareness. It's possible that you will wake up in the vibrational state while still within your physical body or that you will experience yourself out of sync with your physical body. Remain calm and direct your inner self, your awareness, away from your physical body.

Allow the inner sensations to develop as you continue to direct your full attention away from your physical body. Focus all your thoughts upon the idea of moving to another area of your home. It's essential to maintain your awareness fully directed away from your physical body; any thoughts of your body will snap you back within it.

Request clarity anytime your awareness or vision is less than ideal. "I request complete clarity now" or "Clarity now!" Always make your request a firm, specific demand for immediate action.

This entire process is very natural. Now, more than ever, I believe that dreams are created and designed to assist us in our personal development. It is our choice to recognize and use them or to ignore them. Whatever we decide, our subconscious mind will continue to send its dream messages to our conscious mind. Maybe the time has come to listen and learn from the imagery we receive every night in our dreams.

Dream Signals

- Feeling or seeing yourself in or near a vehicle of any kind—an automobile, boat, or plane, for example. Also, any dream experience involving a vehicle, such as a space flight or a boating adventure.

- Recognizing a change in your day-to-day environment, such as your home becoming a castle, palace, or log cabin. Also, any change in the location, construction, or color of the surroundings.

- Having feelings, sensations, or experiences such as numbness, paralysis, energy surges, or sounds out of the norm.

- Recognizing any event, situation, or ability that is out of the norm, such as the ability to fly, float, or move in other unconventional ways.

- Experiencing yourself as falling or sinking. This includes movement up and down stairs, elevators, and escalators.

- Having any experience in which you and your out-of-body partner are together.

- Being in any environment that changes rapidly (that is, things appear or disappear quickly).

- Finding yourself in an environment that you can easily manipulate or control. Exploring a new environment such as a desert, forest, or snow-covered landscape.

- Recognizing a problem or conflict—for example, driving a car down a mountain and the brakes are useless.

- Recognizing a bridge, tunnel, or opening of any kind. In your dream this opening may enable you to overcome an obstacle or barrier—a wall or a river, for example.

- Being taught or guided in any way or being with a companion who seems to act as a guide. Often this companion is next to you but remains out of your vision.

- Meeting with small groups of people in a classroom or conference-room atmosphere.

- Encountering multiple levels or floors of any kind: parking garages, office buildings, ships, and so forth.

- Reading a book or computer program that contains unusual or advanced information.

The following is an example of a conscious dream conversion that one of my workshop students experienced. It occurred the day after a six-hour workshop.

I lay in bed this morning deciding whether to start my morning or stay there and relax for a little while longer. It was not long before I drifted off to sleep.

I found myself dreaming I was in a classroom sitting at a desk. There were other students in the room. There was a teacher walking around at the front of the room. She had blonde hair and seemed to be very nice. I was in the room briefly, then found myself at my parents' house. At this point, the dream became lucid.

I was lying on the couch in my parents' living room thinking about out-of-body experiences and made it my intention to have one. At first I felt some tingling, then some movement. I went with the flow of it. Suddenly I found that the upper half of my body was sitting up and away from the part still lying down. From my waist down, I was still inside my body. I asked for help to complete the experience; then the rest of me slipped out of my body and onto the floor. I felt very heavy and could not get up. Everything seemed clouded and unclear around me. I remembered what Bill said in class, and I called all my energy back to me. As soon as I did, I felt light and was able to get up and move around.

I was very excited about my accomplishment. I remember saying: "I did it! I can't believe it! This is great!" I wanted to tell someone who would understand. My brother was in the room lying on the other couch nearby. I went to my parents' bedroom to tell my mom what I had done and saw my dad walking out of the room. He seemed to see me but did not say anything. I entered the room and stood by my mother's bedside. I was excited to tell her, but she was still sleeping. I was deciding whether to wake her when someone appeared alongside her in the bed and told me not to wake her. I agreed. When I opened my eyes, I was back in my body and the clock said 9:20.

Affirmations

Affirmations have proved their effectiveness over the past twenty years. Today they are a regular part of self-improvement courses worldwide. An affirmation is essentially a strong, positive statement about yourself framed in the present tense. The root word *affirm* means to "make firm"; it is a method of solidifying a

188 thought or idea within ourselves. Affirmations should always be formed as a positive statement; for example, "I am a positive person," "I deserve love," or "I am getting better and better every minute, every day" are commonly used affirmations.

Every moment of our lives, our minds are flowing with a constant stream of thoughts. Our thoughts are continuously influencing our physical and nonphysical reality. Our intellectual, our emotional, and, finally, our physical state of consciousness is the direct result of our thoughts.

Affirmations allow us to focus our thoughts and counteract some of the negative ideas we have accepted. The practice of doing affirmations enables us to begin the process of replacing negative or limiting thoughts with fresh, positive ones. It is a powerful method for reprogramming ourselves for positive change and personal success.

Affirmations can be repeated silently, aloud, or in writing; they can even be expressed in the form of a song or rhyme. In out-of-body exploration they are generally repeated silently, with increasing emphasis on the last few moments before the onset of sleep. The goal is to be completely focused upon your desire for an immediate out-of-body experience as you drift to sleep.

For maximum effectiveness, when using affirmations during any out-of-body technique, it's important that you do four things. First, as much as possible, progressively increase the emotional and intellectual intensity of your last affirmations as you drift to sleep. Second, continuously repeat the affirmations until you go to sleep. Make your final thoughts before sleep your most focused out-of-body affirmations. Third, think of your affirmations as firm personal commitments that you fully expect to experience, *now!* And fourth, as much as possible, feel completely open to receive the immediate results of your affirmations.

There are an infinite number and variety of possible affirmations; here are a few examples.

- Now I'm out-of-body!

- I consciously experience an out-of-body journey. Now!

- I enjoy out-of-body consciousness now!

- I remain aware as my body goes to sleep.

- I remain consciously aware as my body falls to sleep.

- I consciously separate from my physical body after it is asleep.

- As my body goes to sleep, I am completely aware of my out-of-body experience.

- Now I have an out-of-body experience.

- Now I separate from my body!

  Affirmations can be used to:

- Affirm your clarity of perception when out-of-body. The clarity technique is basically a strong affirmation for enhanced perception.

- Declare your immediate intentions to experience an out-of-body journey.

- Reduce fear and increase control.

- Enhance the dream-conversion process and memory recall.

- Enhance and reinforce any of the other out-of-body techniques.

- Control thought, both before and during an out-of-body experience.

- Help remove negative or limiting self-concepts and beliefs related to out-of-body exploration.

• Reprogram your subconscious for success.

   • Help you expand your self-concept beyond the physical body.

   • Enhance your ability to move away from your physical body during the initial seconds of a separation. "I move to the other room" or "I float up and away."

VISUALIZATION WITH AFFIRMATIONS

Affirmations can be combined with other techniques to enhance their overall effectiveness. They can also be helpful in focusing and maintaining your conscious attention upon your goal of an out-of-body experience as your body drifts off to sleep. The following is an example.

Lie on your back and become as comfortable as possible. Close your eyes, completely relax, and breathe deeply, slowly, and naturally. As you relax, repeat an affirmation such as "Now I'm out-of-body" or "I now separate from my body in full awareness." Continue this affirmation until you begin to get sleepy.

As you mentally repeat this affirmation, begin to visualize a familiar place: a room in your home or any other place you know well and can imagine with absolute clarity. Now begin to picture the room in your mind. As vividly as possible, see the details of the room—feel the carpet under your feet, the fabric of the curtains and furniture. See the patterns in the wallpaper and feel the texture of the furniture. Notice and explore the paintings, the books, all the small details. Become absorbed in the details of the room. Feel yourself walking around the room. Notice how good it feels, how comfortable it is. As much as possible, use all your senses.

Select one item in the room. Pick it up and feel its texture, its weight. See and feel this object as clearly as possible. Become completely absorbed in it. Continue your affirmations as you drift off.

The key to this exercise is to maintain your interest outside your body until your body falls asleep. The combination of affirmations with this visualization is extremely effective.

EARLY MORNING TECHNIQUE

One of the best times to induce an out-of-body experience is early in the morning after two or three REM periods (three to five hours) have passed.

During sleep, every ninety to one hundred minutes we begin a dream period called rapid eye movement (REM) sleep. Our eye movement during sleep is physical evidence that we are entering a dream or, in some cases, another altered state of awareness. The scientific correlation between REM periods and out-of-body experiences is yet to be confirmed; however, reports linking the two are commonplace.

The following technique is highly effective, but it does require a degree of self-discipline. Many have found the additional effort worthwhile.

Set your alarm for approximately three to four hours of sleep. After you awaken, move to another area of your home—a recliner or a sofa, for example.

As you become comfortable in your new location, select your favorite out-of-body technique. Completely relax and begin to do your affirmations, alone or in combination with your visualization technique. Repeat your affirmations, first verbally, then silently to yourself.

As you become more relaxed, focus your complete attention upon your affirmations and away from your physical body. As you drift to sleep, attempt to boost the emotional and intellectual impact of your affirmations as much as possible. With increasing intensity, make your last affirmations before sleep a firm personal commitment to have an immediate out-of-body experience. It's important that your last thought before drifting into sleep be your out-of-body affirmations. As you do this, feel completely open to receive your request immediately.

Remember to focus all your thoughts and emotions into the affirmations. Your intensity and personal commitment are most important.

Using this technique, many people report an out-of-body experience immediately after they drift to sleep. If you have the time, this technique can be repeated several times before morning. During the first few attempts, you may just go back to sleep; however, with repeated practice, the technique can provide dramatic results.

If you are having difficulty developing your visualization ability, I highly recommend this technique as your best alternative. It is one of the most powerful methods available and does not require visualization skills.

I believe the effectiveness of this technique has little to do with the time of day. What's really important is your mental state: after three or four hours of sleep, your body and mind are partially refreshed and completely relaxed. This mind-awake/body-relaxed state of awareness is the ideal starting point for any technique used in out-of-body exploration.

I discovered this technique by accident several years after beginning out-of-body exploration. One night, after sleeping about four hours, I awakened unexpectedly and decided to get up and read. On an impulse I started to write some out-of-body affirmations. After fifteen minutes of writing, I began to feel extremely tired. Selecting two affirmations, I continued to repeat them to myself as I relaxed on the sofa. I continuously repeated these affirmations as I drifted to sleep: "Now I have a fully conscious out-of-body experience. Now I'm out of my body!" I focused all my energy into each affirmation, exerting every effort to make the affirmations my last conscious thoughts as I drifted to sleep. The following experience occurred at 3:15 A.M., immediately after my physical body dozed off to sleep.

Journal Entry, March 7, 1984

I feel intense waves of energy flowing through me. A sense of movement begins—extreme, building movement. Instantly, I am at an oceanfront home. All I can hear is pounding surf. Everything in the large house appears white and fuzzy, so I say aloud, "Clarity now!"

As I look around, forms come into focus. I am standing in front of a huge oblong table, eighteen feet long. The room is filled with shining people. They seem to radiate light from every pore of their bodies.

Seven men and one woman come forward to greet me. As the woman approaches, I can see her smile. When she looks at me, vivid pictures begin to appear within my mind. The meaning of each picture becomes instantly clear. "It's good to see you again. You have been busy." I can clearly feel the warmth of her thoughts.

The group gathers around the table, and I know it's time to sit down. As I look around the room, it seems to expand with my vision. I can still hear the waves crashing and I wish to see the ocean. A clear picture appears in my mind, "You will experience the ocean soon enough. Let's begin."

I respond automatically, "The ocean sounds beautiful today."

Soon another thought appears in my mind, "Yes, the ocean is wonderful. We take it for granted. Our visitors are normally unconscious. We will adapt." There is a brief pause, then a continuation of thought-energy from the other end of the room: "There is much energy being directed into the dense regions. Those who live in the hard bodies are beginning to respond. There is much to be done. Those who are awakening from their sleep are searching for answers—searching on the outside. No wonder there is so much confusion. We know how tough the physical vehicles can be; we have all been there. The ultimate test is to recognize the truth while surrounded by dense illusions."

Spontaneously I respond with a thought, "There is too much expected and too little guidance provided. Why must it be so hard?"

Another picture appears in my mind. I somehow know it's female. "The school is firm, but fair. Each creates the lessons they need."

I look toward her and my thoughts just seem to flow. "But why so much ignorance and pain?"

Another voice enters my mind, "School is painful for some, enlightening for others. Only experience creates wisdom. The end result is always effective."

I respond, "Even so, too little guidance is provided. Five billion people, and all are hoping and praying that what they believe is true. It seems like an ineffective school to me—all these people living in the dark."

Another voice appears, "You don't see the whole picture, my friend. Time is an illusion. There is no rush. All are immortal. The very act of being is experience, and experience creates wisdom. Time is not the issue."

As I look around the room, the reality of the experience is overpowering. I can feel the table and see the room with absolute clarity. Distracted by the sound of the waves, I begin to feel an intense tugging sensation. I am being pulled back. In seconds I am within my physical body. As I slowly open my eyes, feelings of numbness, tingling, and disorientation quickly fade.

Hypnosis

Hypnosis is becoming an increasingly popular self-improvement tool. It is regularly used in behavior-modification therapy for such things as weight control, sports improvement, stress release, memory enhancement, and the treatment of fears and phobias. Recently, some powerful new uses for hypnosis have come to light. One of the most publicized and popular is past-life regression. Regressing patients to a previous physical life can help them uncover, experience, and resolve a present problem, fear, or phobia by going to the source of the dilemma. An impressive number of recently published hypnotic regressions have reported obtaining verifiable information from past centuries, including names, dates, places, and events.

During several of the past-life regressions I've conducted, I have noticed a tendency for some of my clients to experience a brief out-of-body state of awareness, generally during the transition experienced between physical lives. Additional investigation made it clear that hypnosis could be used to induce a controlled out-of-body adventure. With minor modifications, the induction techniques normally used in past-life regression are generally effective in out-of-body exploration. The basic hypnotic induction can remain the same; only the directions after the induction are changed.

Hypnosis has provided dramatic benefits for millions of people in the past decade. Now modern hypnosis can be used to initiate a self-controlled, out-of-body experience. Its benefits are especially evident in four major areas. First, hypnosis can effectively induce the ideal mental state for out-of-body exploration (mind alert/body relaxed). Second, it can assist in the control, reduction, and elimination of subconscious and conscious blocks, fears, and limits relating to out-of-body experiences. Third, hypnosis can be used to improve visualization, concentration, and meditative skills. And finally, hypnotic suggestions can be effective in triggering a fully conscious out-of-body experience. For example, the hypnotic suggestions "I become consciously aware during my dreams" and "My dreams trigger a conscious out-of-body experience" can substantially assist the dream-conversion process. Suggestions such as "After I enter sleep, I recognize and experience a fully conscious out-of-body adventure" and "Sleep

196 triggers my out-of-body experiences" can be used to reinforce and enhance an individual's ability to respond positively to his or her out-of-body techniques.

When selecting a trained hypnotherapist, first check qualifications. Many states require a certification or license. Next, inquire into areas of expertise. (Many hypnotherapists are specialists in areas such as weight control and eating disorders.) The ideal choice is someone with an extensive background in past-life regression, someone knowledgeable about metaphysics and out-of-body exploration. Such individuals are generally more familiar with the nonphysical (thought-responsive) environments encountered when out-of-body. They are also more adept at dealing with the perceptions and experiences unique to out-of-body exploration. Often their awareness of metaphysics gives them a greater understanding of the motivations and goals of people seeking out-of-body adventure.

SELF-HYPNOSIS

Self-hypnosis is another powerful new tool for self-improvement. Often our fears and limits are subconsciously programmed within us. Internally we have accepted a rigid concept of ourselves and placed limits on our abilities. These subconscious limits are the walls that hold us from our unlimited potential. In a sense we have built walls around ourselves.

One of the most effective ways to dissolve our self-accepted limits and fears is to confront them directly. Hypnosis gives us the unique ability to access our subconscious mind and resolve our fears and limits. In addition, we can reprogram our subconscious mind for success in any endeavor, including nonphysical exploration.

The following is a self-hypnosis script that you can tape and use at home. As you record this hypnosis script, take your time and speak in a relaxed tone. At each break between phrases, pause for approximately two seconds. Attempt to be consistent throughout the taping. Many people have a tendency to speed up as they record, so take your time and relax. Pauses that are longer than a couple of seconds will be indicated.

For the best results, use an auto-reverse tape recorder and a long-play (ninety minutes or more), high-quality tape.

When doing this self-hypnosis technique, become as comfortable as possible in your designated out-of-body exploration area. If possible, use a recliner or a comfortable sofa. Select a time and place that will allow you an hour and a half of solitude. If needed, temporarily unplug the phone. NEVER USE A HYPNOSIS TAPE WHEN DRIVING A CAR!

OUT-OF-BODY SELF-HYPNOSIS SCRIPT

Take several deep breaths, allow your eyes to close, and completely relax. Just allow your body and mind to completely relax. . . . As you feel yourself becoming comfortable and relaxed . . . release yourself to a special kind of experience. . . . Let go and relax. . . . Take a deep breath . . . and completely relax, completely relax. . . . Now, relax even more. . . . Take another slow, deep breath . . . letting go of all stress . . . all tension. . . . With each breath feel all your tension flowing out of you. . . . Just relax . . . completely relax. . . .

Visualize, imagine, or feel your head bathed in a soft healing light . . . a light that quiets all thoughts . . . a light that quiets all worries. . . . Your mind is at peace. . . . This soft, healing light releases your physical senses from their work. . . . Just feel your head and its senses enveloped in this light. . . . Now, allow this healing light to expand slightly . . . feel the light as it slowly moves down your neck and shoulders. . . . Each muscle and cell that it touches is made more relaxed . . . more centered . . . more harmonized. . . . No other sounds will disturb you. . . . They will only cause you to go deeper . . . and deeper. . . . You are more peaceful and relaxed.... As this quiet, soft, healing light envelops your neck and shoulders ... every nerve cell ... every muscle is completely relaxed.... Every cell and tissue of your body is completely relaxed.... Now, allow this light to flow even farther.... Feel it as it flows down through your arms ... your hands ... your fingers ... bringing greater relaxation.... Feel the light envelop your chest and your upper back ... your ribs ... your internal organs ... your lungs ... and heart.... Any tension ... any stress that is a part of your body is released as this soft healing light fills you.... Now let the light expand even more until it fills your stomach and lower back.... Feel every muscle and cell relax and release.... The warm, relaxing light surrounds and envelops your hips ... your legs.... As you completely relax, no other sounds will disturb you.... All sounds will only cause you to go deeper ... and deeper ... down ... down ... into a more peaceful and relaxed state of being.... You are fully relaxed ... fully at peace.... You feel completely safe ... completely protected.... You can feel the relaxing power flow into your feet.... All the muscles throughout your body are now completely relaxed.... They are so relaxed, you can't move them.... Every muscle is so relaxed ... so very relaxed.... Feel yourself go ... deeper and deeper ... down ... down ... deeply relaxed....

Now you can feel the soft, relaxing power of the light shining upon you.... This warm feeling of the light is radiating through your entire body.... You can feel its warmth ... feel its protection.... You are surrounded by the relaxing, warm energy of the light.... As you completely and pleasantly relax your entire body ... you can slow down a little bit.... Just allow yourself to slow down a little bit, and later, as we go, you can slow down a little bit more and let go.... I am going to count downward from ten to one; with each descending number, allow yourself to slow down and relax ... and when I reach the number

one, you will enter your own level of deep, deep relaxation. Ten
. . . down, down, nine . . . deeper, deeper, down, eight . . . down,
down, deeper, deeper, seven . . . down, six . . . down, five . . .
deeper, four . . . deeper, down, three . . . deeper, down, two . . .
deeper, down, and . . . one. You are now at a very deep level of
natural relaxation. . . . Remember . . . you are in complete control and are completely aware at every level of your mind. This
journey is something you want, because you are eager to explore,
eager to learn. . . . In a moment we will begin a series of exercises
into your perception, your ability to see and feel and be completely free from your physical body . . . from your temporary
physical vehicle.

Now, feel the part of yourself that longs for something
more. . . . There is a part of you that longs to see more . . . longs
for movement. As this longing grows within you . . . feel this
longing grow into a desire . . . a passion to know your true self
. . . to know and experience yourself completely independent of
your physical body . . . to know and experience your spiritual
self. . . . Feel this desire. . . . I want you to look on the horizon
and see or imagine a soft light . . . a doorway of light. . . . You
feel and know this light to be good. . . . This light is full of love
and protection. . . . Now begin moving toward this doorway of
light. . . . Feel yourself moving toward the doorway of light. . . .
As you see this doorway get closer and closer . . . you can feel
yourself totally enveloped in the light . . . you are totally enveloped and protected by the light . . . you can feel the warmth
and protection of the light. . . . The light surrounds you and flows
throughout your body . . . throughout your entire being. . . .

Now visualize, imagine, or feel yourself moving through the
doorway. . . . And as you move through the doorway of light, I
want you to know that you are moving away from your physical
shell. . . . As you step through this doorway of light . . . you will
view and observe your body objectively . . . knowing at all times

200 that you are always surrounded in the white light of protection; . . . as soul, you choose to step from the limits of matter. . . . So, I want you to observe every detail. . . . Now feel
yourself becoming lighter. . . . You are becoming lighter and
lighter . . . you are as light as a feather . . . light as a balloon as
you slowly lift and float up, up, up. . . . Now you can feel yourself floating free. . . .

As you float, enjoy all the warm sensations of floating free . . .
floating completely free from your physical body. . . . You are
floating above your body. . . . As you enjoy the floating sensations, you can feel your awareness increase. . . . You are more
aware . . . more aware of your new, lighter energy-body . . . more
aware of your light energy-self. . . . Now you are completely
aware of your energy-self . . . your floating energy-self. . . . Your
entire awareness is moving into your light energy-self. . . . Joy-
fully, you can feel yourself floating free, floating completely free
of all limits . . . all dense limits. . . . Now you are completely
aware within your light self. . . . You can see and feel with all
your awareness . . . all your consciousness is within your light
energy-self. . . . You can feel the joy of being free from your
physical body, completely free from all limits. . . .

Now, what do you see? . . . What do you observe?. . . [Pause
for fifteen seconds.]

You can feel and see an increase in your new perception. . . .
Your vision is becoming better and better . . . clearer and
clearer. . . . Your vision is sharper, clearer than ever before. . . .
Your lighter self now has perfect vision . . . your lighter self possesses crystal-clear vision . . . perfect perceptions. . . . You can
feel your entire awareness. . . . Your entire consciousness is completely within your lighter energy-self. . . . You focus all your energy within your light energy-self. . . . What do you see? . . .
What does it feel like? . . . Can you see your body? . . . Describe
what you see in detail. . . . Enjoy all the sensations and sights. . . .
Take all the time you need. . . . [Pause for three minutes.]

Now, slowly return to your physical body. . . . Take your time and slowly return. . . . As you return, you absolutely know that you can separate from your physical body with ease. . . . With complete confidence, you can step from your physical body whenever you wish. . . . You now know that your physical body is only a vehicle for your awareness . . . only one vehicle of many that you possess. . . . It feels good to be able to go beyond your body to see and know for yourself. . . . From now on, you can and will leave your physical body with complete ease . . . complete safety, whenever you wish.

Now, breathe deeply, relaxed and comfortable. . . . In a few moments I am going to count from one to three, so that by the time I say number three, you will be able to open your eyes and feel wide awake. . . . You will remember all that you have experienced. . . . You will awaken to even further insight. . . . You will feel invigorated and revitalized. . . . You will be rejuvenated and rested . . . as though you have taken a peaceful nap. . . . You will be in complete harmony. . . . You will feel fitter . . . better . . . and maintain a conscious connection with your inner self. . . . Because you have been able to relax so deeply and soundly, your mind will be sharp and alert. . . . You will be able to think more clearly and creatively. . . . We'll begin. . . . One. . . . You are feeling very rested now. . . . Your entire body is very much at peace. . . . You have been able to relax deeply and soundly, and this ability has enabled you to transcend your physical body. . . . In the future you will find that each session will be even more relaxing and even more rewarding. . . . Two. . . . You begin to feel energy and life flowing to every part of your body now. . . . You feel full of energy and vigor. . . . You remember all that you have experienced . . . and even more insight will reveal itself in the days ahead. . . . You feel alert and awake. . . . You have a deep feeling of well-being and knowledge. . . . You feel sound . . . healthier . . . ready to take on whatever may come your way. . . . You feel refreshed and rested as though awakening from a long

nap.... Three.... Your entire body, mind, and soul are refreshed.... Now open your eyes feeling completely refreshed
and full of energy and joy.

Sound

The use of sound to induce out-of-body experiences dates
back thousands of years. The Tibetan monks are famous for their
use of chants, chimes, and bells to enhance their meditative
states. In the last two decades, chanting and mantras have become a well-established part of meditation classes in the West.
The repetition of certain sounds is an ancient practice widely
known and accepted today as an effective method of enhancing
an individual's focus of attention.

SOUND-FREQUENCY TECHNIQUES

The practice of using sound frequencies to induce out-of-
body experiences has not been widely investigated by the scientific community. Currently, the most extensive research is being
conducted by the Monroe Institute of Applied Sciences, located
in Nelson County, Virginia. For over twenty years, the institute's
founder and executive director, Robert Monroe, has experimented
with the potential of sound-induced altered states of awareness.
In recent years, the Monroe Institute has developed some practical methods to accelerate learning through enhanced states of
consciousness. These methods incorporate a system of audio
pulses that create a frequency-following response in the human
brain. The result is a synchronization of the brain's left and right
hemispheres.

One of the institute's goals is to provide practical assistance
for individuals who are interested in exploring the nonphysical
dimensions of the universe. Toward this end it has created a series of audiotapes called Hemi-sync. The tapes are designed to
feed a 100-hertz frequency signal into one ear and a 104-hertz

frequency into the other ear; the 4-hertz difference represents the predominant brain frequency at the moment of an out-of-body experience.

Even though sound-frequency techniques are still relatively new, I'm certain that with continuing research and development, this revolutionary form of out-of-body induction will become commonplace in the near future. To introduce you to sound-frequency techniques I have included an ancient method used by Tibetan monks. This is one of the oldest out-of-body techniques, dating back a thousand years before the birth of Christ.

SOUND TECHNIQUE

Take several deep breaths and completely relax. Become comfortable in your designated out-of-body area. Close your eyes and begin to focus your attention just above the crown of your head. Concentrate all your awareness above your head until the sensations of your body begin to disappear.

As your physical sensations begin to fade, softly intone the sound OM seven times. Let the sound resonate through the top of your head.

Repeat the OM sound in your mind seven times. Be completely aware of the sound resonating in your mind. Let the sound rise through the top of your head.

Focusing all your attention on the very core of the resonance, allow the sound to slowly ascend toward the ceiling. Feel your awareness merging with the sound. As much as possible, become one with the rising sound, as your body becomes increasingly relaxed.

Feel your awareness rising with the sound. Become one with the OM resonance. Enjoy the sound, and flow with it. Feel yourself become lighter and lighter as you float with the sound. Allow your physical body to rest and sleep as you focus all your attention on the rising sound. Maintain all your attention on the

204 rising sound as your body falls to sleep. As you begin to fall asleep, concentrate all your awareness on the rising sound.

This technique can be effectively used with an out-of-body induction sound tape. When using any external sound system, remember to focus on your internal sounds. The external sound's only purpose is to reinforce and enhance your own voice.

Repetition (Ceremonial Technique)

On numerous occasions people have told me of creating a repetitive system or ritual for their out-of-body preparation. Essentially, they have created a personal series of repetitive events that lead up to their out-of-body experiences. For example, they may take a long relaxing bath, then wear a special white robe and place lighted candles around their bed or sofa as they prepare to relax and begin their out-of-body technique. Throughout this process, they constantly focus upon their desire for an immediate out-of-body experience. Many people report impressive results with this kind of approach.

I believe the success of the ritual technique owes to the special emphasis given to the goal during the entire preparation procedure. The mind registers the rather lengthy, repetitive process as something special and focuses additional subconscious attention upon the specified goal—an out-of-body experience. Moreover, the very act of repeating the same procedure for a period of weeks has an impact on the subconscious mind. There's an old saying that any act or thought repeated daily for twenty-one days becomes a habit. This idea is based on the premise that our subconscious mind takes note of the daily repetition and accepts it as a new behavior norm. I believe the same principle explains why daily repetition and the ritual technique are so effective.

Looking back over the years, I now recognize that I created my own ritual-like procedure. In the early seventies for a period of two years I woke up at 7:00 A.M., went to a morning college class at 8:30, then returned around 11:30 and relaxed. Every day at noon I would lie in bed on my back and do an out-of-body technique. This process was extremely effective. After several weeks of daily repetition, I had programmed myself to have out-of-body experiences. After several months, I didn't need to do a technique of any kind; I would just take a nap at noon and automatically lift up and away from my physical body. In retrospect, I believe that this was a form of self-conditioning. Success builds upon success, and once my conscious and subconscious mind accepted the process of out-of-body experiences, it became a very natural state of being. After I had had several successful and enjoyable experiences, my subconscious mind began to fully cooperate with my desires.

This is important because it points the way to a deeper understanding of the entire process of out-of-body exploration. To obtain the knowledge and wisdom available to us within the nonphysical dimensions of the universe, we must go beyond our superficial desires. To become proficient at nonphysical exploration, we must be willing to program ourselves for success. Halfhearted attempts at out-of-body techniques will produce halfhearted results. For real success and control, we must be willing to make a full emotional and intellectual commitment to this exploration. The easiest way to do this is to create a daily repetition or ritual of preparation and technique. The key is to do it daily and, if at all possible, at the same time and place. The combination of repetition and determination creates a powerful system of success that can be used to achieve whatever you may desire out of life.

Results Commonly Reported

The initial results reported during out-of-body experiences vary from person to person. Over the past twenty years, however, I have noticed some remarkable similarities. How we react to the initial changes we experience will many times control our success.

The rapid transfer of your personal awareness from your physical body to your nonphysical self can be a startling leap if you are unprepared. Having some idea of what to expect will greatly assist your initial explorations. The more prepared you are for the experience, the greater the control you will be able to exercise. Your positive response to the sudden change of your personal location, perception, and viewpoint is absolutely essential to a successful controlled experience.

As you focus all your attention upon your out-of-body technique, your physical body will become increasingly relaxed. Eventually your body will begin its transition into sleep. As this sleep transition occurs, you may experience a dramatic change in your normal sleep cycle. This change may occur immediately after your body goes to sleep or during a REM period. It is during this transition that the inner signals are reported most often, so pay attention to any unusual internal sounds or sensations you may experience.

The following are the most commonly reported results experienced immediately after an out-of-body technique.

1. Floating, standing, or lying just outside your physical body.

2. Experiencing your energy-self either lying or sitting within your physical body. This may be accompanied by an intense vibration circulating through your entire energy-body. You may feel out of sync with your physical body and ready to simply "lift out" of the physical. This is completely natural; just focus your attention on your new vibration rate and direct yourself to move away from your physical vehicle.

3. Standing or sitting at one of your target areas observing your new environment. This shift of awareness is rapid, so remain calm and enjoy your new vibration rate.

4. Experiencing a lucid dream (a dream in which you become consciously aware of your environment). During this dream, you may experience one or more of your inner signals. Focus your attention on the vibration or sound and will yourself away from your body.

5. Experiencing a nonphysical environment that differs from your daily surroundings. Remain calm and enjoy your new environment.

An Overview of the Ideal Mind-Set

- Begin with a clean slate. As much as possible, release your preconceptions, limits, beliefs, and convictions. Picture yourself starting your life again, completely free of self-conceptions and limits.

- Trust yourself and your abilities. You are a spiritual being possessing creative abilities and can easily separate from your temporary physical body.

- Be open to receive. Completely open to a new perception of yourself, an expanded vision of yourself possessing unlimited capabilities.

- Be open to recognize and release any personal barriers, blocks, or perceptions that limit your growth and development.

- Be open to recognize and release the intensive indoctrination and conditioning that you have received.

- Be open and receptive to a change in your awareness. Welcome a fully aware shift of your consciousness from your dense vehicle and limits to your higher energy-self.

- Strongly feel your inner self urging you to explore and experience beyond your dense physical vehicle.

- Focus all your energy, attention, and desire on your personal commitment to recognize and experience yourself independent of your physical vehicle.

- Throughout every cell, every tissue, every part of your being, absolutely know, absolutely feel that you are a high-energy, nonphysical being. Because you are more than matter, you consciously separate from your dense physical vehicle with ease.

- Feel totally safe, secure, and protected to step from your physical vehicle now.

- Fully recognize and acknowledge that the ideal environment and time for your out-of-body exploration is today. Now!

- Release and detach yourself from the earth. Vividly see yourself unhook from your body, setting you free from your physical limits.

- As you practice your favorite out-of-body technique, repeat the following affirmation: "I am more than a physical body. Because I am more than matter, I now separate from my physical body with full awareness."

Techniques Review

1. Remain calm. Internal vibrations, sounds, and motion are normal experiences.

2. Be fearless, for you are protected and immortal.

3. Demand complete clarity of your awareness, "Clarity now!" as often as necessary.

4. Focus and maintain your thoughts away from your physical body at all times.

5. Focus upon a specific desired objective: a person, place, or state of consciousness that you would like to experience.

6. Be prepared for a sense of motion after making a request.

7. Enjoy your new explorations. The unseen universe is your birthright and destiny.

Basics of Out-of-Body Exploration

1. We are spiritual (nonphysical energy) beings temporarily using biological bodies (vehicles) for experience and expression.

2. Since the physical body is a temporary vehicle, it is only natural for us to be able to separate from it and experience our true nonphysical self.

3. We are currently experiencing a biological vehicle so that we can explore, interact, and learn within the physical dimension.

4. Out-of-body experiences are the normal shift or transfer of awareness from our physical vehicle to our higher-frequency nonphysical body.

5. We are simultaneously using and controlling multiple energy (frequency) vehicles. Each of these energy vehicles exists at a distinctly different density and vibrational frequency. Ideally, all our energy vehicles work in harmony to assist in our personal development.

6. Each individual vehicle of consciousness perceives within its unique frequency of the universe. To perceive and experience matter, we must have a vehicle of matter. To consciously perceive and experience the higher (less dense) vibratory dimensions, we must consciously be using the appropriate energy vehicle.

· 7. We are the creative source of our reality and our experience. We create our individual reality by the way we focus and manage our personal thought-energy. This principle applies to all energy levels of the universe. What we experience has been influenced, arranged, and manifested by our conscious and subconscious thoughts.

Mastering the Experience

Every man takes the limits of his own field of vision for the limits of the world.
—Schopenhauer

If we are to obtain the maximum benefits available during an out-of-body experience, control is an absolute necessity. The key to effective nonphysical exploration is the conscious control of our nonphysical state of awareness. Once a degree of control is achieved, the potential of out-of-body exploration becomes absolutely unlimited. In fact, our imagination is inadequate to conceive of all the available possibilities. Experience has taught me that the more prepared we are for our explorations, the more effectively we can maneuver and adapt within the nonphysical environments. After proper preparation, many people report a high degree of control even during their first experiences.

Physical concepts and energy laws have little bearing within the nonphysical dimensions of the universe. To be truly effective when out-of-body, we must learn the nonphysical "rules of the road." To prepare and assist you, I have compiled an overview of situations, events, and challenges that you may encounter in your out-of-body explorations (see table below). This information is the result of my personal experience and feedback I've received from hundreds of people who have had out-of-body experiences over the last twenty years. I have found that much of the published information currently available is inadequate; it is either limited to a single viewpoint or slanted by religious beliefs and interpretations. With that in mind, I have presented this overview with as little cultural bias as possible.

In a world overflowing with beliefs and theories, there is a tremendous need for practical information obtained from first-hand experience. I have come to realize that the answers to the mysteries of our existence are not hidden; they are patiently waiting for us to extend our vision beyond the dense limits of matter. The keys to control will assist you in this quest.

Keys to Control

Situation	*Key to Control*
Inner vibrations (sometimes intense) accompanied by loud buzzing, humming, or roaring sounds.	You are experiencing the vibrational state. Immediately direct your full attention away from your physical body.
Catalepsy (inability to move your physical body).	This is a normal, temporary phenomenon that may occur immediately before or after an out-of-body experience. Your higher-frequency energy-body is temporarily out of sync with your physical body.

Situation	*Key to Control*
Unintentional return to your physical body.	Normally caused by random thoughts directed toward your physical body. You must maintain your full attention within the nonphysical environment and energy-body that you are experiencing.
Blurred vision; unclear or dreamlike awareness.	Firmly request clarity until your vision or awareness is clear: "Clarity now!" Then focus on a specific item or area in the environment you are exploring.
Feeling of fear or anxiety; panic attack.	Repeat to yourself that you are safe and secure. Surround yourself with an impenetrable wall or globe of protective white light. (Refer to text for additional information.)
Tunnel experience.	This occurs when the energy membrane dividing two major frequency levels (nonphysical energy dimensions) opens. Movement through a tunnel is often experienced as an intense inward motion. Remain calm; the sense of rapid movement will normally cease in seconds. The end result will be your entrance into a different energy dimension or environment.

Situation	*Key to Control*
Sensation of rapid inner movement; experience of being drawn deep within unknown areas of yourself.	This motion is often intense and can be startling if you are unprepared. Remain calm; this is a normal shift of consciousness from your denser energy-body to a higher-frequency form.
Heaviness or inability to move freely just after separation.	This is caused by insufficient consciousness in your nonphysical body. Firmly request that your complete awareness be present in the energy-body you are experiencing. Ask for "Awareness now!" and/or demand lightness and mobility.
Lack of vivid recall after an experience.	Firmly request enhanced recall of your out-of-body experience: "I remember all." This is especially effective if done when out-of-body.
Experience of being formless or shapeless conscious energy.	This is the normal recognition of our true nonphysical self (soul).
Extremely loud pop or bang (like a gunshot) close to your head, heard at the moment of separation from the body.	This sometimes startling sound is likely the result of a sudden disconnect from a point located somewhere in the head (the pineal gland, according to many).

Situation	*Key to Control*
Sensation of looking through your closed physical eyelids.	This occurs when your consciousness is transferred within your energy-body but you have not separated from your physical body. Simply direct yourself away from your physical body: "I move to the door."
Entering the vibrational state but being unable to separate from your body.	Direct your complete attention on moving away from your physical body and toward another area of your home. It's critically important to maintain the focus of your attention away from your physical body at all times.
Strange or unusual sounds during sleep (voices, buzzing, bells, humming, music, footsteps, any sound inappropriate to your current physical surroundings).	Unusual sounds are indications that your awareness has already transferred from your physical to your nonphysical body. I refer to these sounds as inner signals (see text).
Entering a nonphysical environment containing cloudlike forms (sometimes appearing as holographic images with varying degrees of density).	You are observing nonphysical thought-energy forms. They are the direct result of focused thought upon a nonconsensus or natural nonphysical energy environment.

Situation	Key to Control
Your immediate surroundings appear to duplicate your physical environment.	You are currently experiencing your slowest frequency (densest) nonphysical energy-body and observing the parallel energy dimension closest to the physical universe.
Sensation of being touched while out-of-body (sometimes occurs just before or after separation).	This can be caused by at least three things: (1) your mind's interpretation of nonphysical energy currents; (2) an energy adjustment of your nonphysical body; or (3) a nonphysical inhabitant or loved one touching you. Generally we are subconsciously inviting this to occur.
Vivid thoughts or pictures entering your mind.	Someone is communicating with you. The universal method of nonphysical communication is direct thought-transference. This could also be a form of communication with a higher aspect of yourself.
Perceiving or sensing an approaching form of energy or light.	You are recognizing an energy being near you. This could be any high-frequency being: a guide, friend, angel, or any interdimensional inhabitant.
Becoming lost or disoriented.	Stop all forward motion and request assistance and/or clarity. Select an item in your immediate environment and focus upon it.

Situation	*Key to Control*
Entering a new room only to find that the entire environment has changed.	A common occurrence. Entranceways, doors, and windows often represent the beginning of a different energy environment.
Encountering a vehicle of any kind.	This is your mind's representation of a nonphysical (formless) energy-body or vehicle of consciousness. Often this is an image of your own inner or higher-frequency energy-body.
Experiencing a barrier or blockade (a wall, a river, any kind of energy barrier).	A barrier is usually an energy representation of a possible limitation you have accepted or created yourself; it is an opportunity to confront a personal energy block and overcome it. A barrier can also represent a border to a consensus environment or reality.
Observing or confronting a strange or frightening form, creature, or being of any kind.	Generally, frightening forms are energy representations of inner fears—subconsciously created opportunities for you to confront and conquer personal fears, blocks, or limitations. The most effective way to eliminate a problem or fear is to face it. Sending love to fears is one of the best ways to dissipate their energy.

Situation	Key to Control
Rapidly changing or shifting scenes or environments.	This situation usually reflects a lack of focus. To control it, simply focus on a single environment or object. Rapidly changing scenes may also indicate that you are in a nonconsensus reality.
Tugging sensation at the center of your back.	This is generally an inner signal to return to the physical.
Entering an extremely bright or high-energy environment (may manifest as a high-energy crushing sensation accompanied by intense light).	You have entered an energy environment with a higher frequency than you are accustomed to. Firmly request an adjustment of your personal vibratory rate: "I adjust now!" "I adapt now!" Or, return to your physical body.
Inability to move through selective structures.	This could represent either a personal limitation or the boundary of a consensus environment. Your personal energy frequency may be too dense to penetrate the structure. (Refer to text.)
Sudden or gradual feeling of heaviness when flying or floating.	An inadequate percentage of your consciousness is located within your energy-body. Firmly request your full or increased awareness to be present.

Situation	*Key to Control*
Losing conscious control in the middle of an out-of-body experience.	Verbally demand that your full awareness be immediately present: "I am completely aware now!" or "Awareness now!" (Never mention or think about your physical body or you will immediately return to it.)
Becoming tangled in a nonphysical item, structure, or environment (bedclothes are the most commonly reported item).	All physical objects have finer-frequency energy duplicates. Remain calm and untangle yourself, or simply float away from the problem. This could represent an attachment to your physical surroundings.
Dual consciousness (awareness simultaneously in your physical body and your nonphysical energy-body).	This occurs occasionally. Since consciousness is not physical in nature, it has the innate ability to be aware of multiple energy areas at the same time. Our consciousness can be compared to a continuum of energy that possesses the ability to move inwardly within the nonphysical interior of the universe.

Harnessing Thought-Energy

Thought has a powerful effect on our nonphysical experience and environment, especially thought focused in the form of a firm request. Focused thought-energy will immediately begin to restructure and mold the surrounding nonphysical energy. In effect, our thoughts, both conscious and subconscious, create an energy mold or blueprint. Our thoughts interact with the subtle energy of the nonphysical environment and begin to restructure it according to the content of our thought patterns. You will soon discover that only specific kinds of environments will immediately respond to your thought-energy; densely formed and established environments will be resistant to change.

The power of thought can also be harnessed for personal mobility. Feel free to experiment with different methods of movement when out-of-body. You can easily move by whatever method is most natural and comfortable—flying, walking, gliding—encountering no limits except those that you impose upon yourself. When you have adapted to your new abilities, out-of-body travel becomes an adventure that is absolutely exhilarating.

Your knowledge of the basic thought-energy principles is essential in adapting to and controlling your nonphysical experience. Any doubts you may have about their validity will quickly disappear after your first out-of-body adventures.

Thought-Energy Principles

1. Thought is a form of energy.

2. Focused thought possesses the innate ability to influence, restructure, and ultimately mold energy.

3. The less dense the energy structure or environment, the faster the restructuring may occur.

4. The effectiveness and speed with which thought-energy restructures an energy environment are determined by the intensity of the thought and the density of the energy upon which it is acting.

Adapting to the Nonphysical Environment

To effectively maneuver within the nonphysical environments we encounter when out-of-body, it is essential to understand each new nonphysical environment and its energy principles. Successfully interacting within the subtle thought-responsive realities requires that we recognize the creative power of our thoughts and completely understand that we are the driving force of our experience. There is much to learn about the unseen dimensions, but for now the following principles will assist in guiding our steps.

Basic Energy Mechanics

1. The nonphysical universe becomes progressively less dense in substance and increasingly thought-responsive as we explore away from matter and toward the source of energy.

2. As a form of creative energy, our thoughts have a natural tendency to interact with and mold the nonphysical environments we encounter. In general, the farther within the multidimensional universe we explore, the more rapid and pronounced this thought reaction is upon the energy environment.

3. Our thoughts, both conscious and subconscious, will influence the nonphysical energy that we observe. The degree of influence is in direct proportion to the intensity of our thoughts and the density of our surroundings.

4. The reality perceived in a thought-responsive environment (nonconsensus or natural) is determined by the personal energy frequency (density) of the observer and the observer's prevailing conscious and subconscious thoughts.

Because these principles have an overwhelming impact upon what we observe when out-of-body, they should not be underestimated. What we see and experience will be greatly influenced by how we interpret each nonphysical environment and react within it.

The early out-of-body explorers exemplify these principles in action. In the Book of Revelation, Saint John describes encounters

222 with magnificent cities, angels, and entities on horseback. Five centuries later, Mohammed describes himself as riding a magnificent white stallion through what he called "the seven heavens." It's logical that these explorers' first- and fifth-century perceptions of reality influenced what they saw when out-of-body. In other words, our religious history and beliefs were influenced by the way the early prophets perceived and interpreted the nonphysical environments that they experienced.

The early observations of all mystics, prophets, and saints were directly influenced by their physical and social preconceptions of reality. Today Mohammed would likely see himself riding in a magnificent white vehicle throughout the energy dimensions of the universe. Instead of Saint John stating in Revelation, "I was in the spirit," he would likely say, "I was out-of-body."

This knowledge does not diminish the inspired writings of our early spiritual explorers; it only provides additional insight into the unseen meaning of these nonphysical explorations. Many of the early spiritual leaders who influenced and molded our major religions were out-of-body explorers. They documented their nonphysical journeys in accordance with their cultural perceptions of reality. The Bible is full of statements such as "I was in the spirit," "You must be born again to enter the kingdom of heaven," "The spirit moved me," and "Seek ye first the kingdom of God." These statements are clear references to their authors' nonphysical (spiritual) explorations of the universe. It's only natural that the early explorers of the nonphysical dimensions would call their discovery heaven; it's certainly a fitting name for a thought-responsive universe overflowing with endless energy levels of beauty and light.

Each of us is different, and what we experience when out-of-body will vary according to our social indoctrination and strongly held beliefs. The environments and objects encountered when out-of-body are often perceived through the filters of our mind.

It's essential to remember that any time you are exploring out-of-body, you can ask to see the true energy form of the object or environment you are experiencing. If you become confused or have questions concerning your observations, you can always request clarification.

Keep in mind that all form is energy; this applies to all environments, frequencies, and densities within the universe (including the physical). The objects, situations, and environments we perceive are shaped and formed by thought-energy for a specific purpose. Our understanding of this basic energy principle will help us interpret and react to the many nonphysical energy forms we encounter.

I have found that self-created nonphysical energy forms normally occur in the thought-responsive regions beyond the first nonphysical dimension. The first inner dimension is a parallel energy duplicate of the physical world and is a relatively stable energy environment that's resistant to thought-energy. Generally, perceived energy forms such as multilevel structures, vehicles, or bodies of water are a strong indication that you have ventured inward into the more thought-responsive areas of the multidimensional universe.

Guides

There are three primary ways to direct and control our out-of-body experiences. One way is to control our conscious thoughts (a difficult endeavor at best); another way is to ask for assistance from a more expansive part of ourselves—our higher self or soul. The third way is to request assistance from a guide or master with whom we feel comfortable. A guide can be anyone we respect: Jesus, Buddha, Saint Paul, a guardian angel, a saint.

When we request guidance, we are often directed to the experience that is the most favorable to our spiritual development. Nonphysical guides are seldom visible. Instead we may experience

224 a strong impression or feeling of their presence. In their wisdom they understand that their visual appearance would only distract us from our personal goal. When a guide is present, we often experience a warm feeling of love and security surrounding us. Within ourselves we know that we are being assisted and directed to the ideal experience.

The advantages of a guide are numerous. In the higher-frequency worlds our needs are transparent; our state of spiritual development, our inner blocks, limitations, fears, and abilities are clearly evident. A nonphysical guide can appraise our developmental needs and assist us to the situation best suited for our evolution.

The inner worlds of the universe are larger in size and diversity than our minds can begin to comprehend; unlimited energy levels and realities are available to explore. Without guidance it's easy to become confused or disoriented within any thought-responsive environment. Unlimited assistance is always available, but it is up to us to make the request. Guides normally will not interfere without a specific request.

Clarity

One of the best ways to enhance your awareness when out-of-body is to immediately focus and maintain your attention on a single idea or goal. If your attention begins to wander or your vision becomes fuzzy or dreamlike, firmly ask for complete clarity of your awareness. The most effective way of maintaining and enhancing your awareness and control is to request complete clarity of consciousness at the first sign of mental wandering.

Requesting clarity of thought is the key to prolonged out-of-body experiences. Using this technique it's possible to maintain an out-of-body experience for several hours. Every time your mind wanders, simply demand clarity by saying or thinking, "Clarity now!" It is often necessary to demand clarity immediately after separation, when moving to a new nonphysical location, or when traveling between energy environments or dimensions.

In the beginning, the easiest way to control and prolong your out-of-body experiences is to acquire the habit of demanding your clarity of awareness every few minutes. Eventually, as you gain experience, the clarity of your perceptions will become increasingly automatic.

It's important for us to recognize that we orchestrate our lives, both physical and nonphysical, by the power of our thoughts. When our lives feel out of control, it's because we have surrendered our internal control to others or have refused to accept our personal responsibility. For many of us, it's easier to point the finger of blame at others than to accept responsibility for our individual thoughts and actions. Some of the toughest lessons we are here to learn are directly related to thought control and personal responsibility. Our ability to focus and direct our thoughts is a central element of our personal evolution. The benefits we receive are beyond our expectations—our life is our reward.

CLARITY TECHNIQUE

A simple exercise is extremely effective for avoiding the disjointed or hazy awareness that some people report just after separation from the physical body. Immediately after separation, demand your complete clarity to be present: "Clarity now!" "I demand complete clarity!" or "Awareness now!" When making this request, avoid any phrase that includes a reference to your physical body or physical surroundings. For example, the statement "I demand full awareness in my body" will immediately snap you back to your physical body.

Always remember that when you are out-of-body you are experiencing a higher-frequency, less dense energy form and environment. Your new surroundings, including your nonphysical body, are much more responsive to thought-energy than the physical body. When making your request, keep it firm and specific and the results will be immediate and effective. The stronger and more focused the request, the more effective the results.

This technique can also be used to upgrade a lucid dream to a fully conscious out-of-body experience. The key is to repeat this procedure until the fogginess fades and your full awareness is present.

The clarity technique is a procedure I automatically do immediately following separation from my physical body. In addition, I repeat it anytime my vision or awareness is less than ideal. I have found that it not only sharpens nonphysical perceptions but also enhances control and memory recall.

Fear Reduction and Control

Fear can be an obstacle to successful out-of-body exploration. Our personal anxieties, both conscious and unconscious, create invisible walls around us, boxing us into a narrow comfort zone and hindering us from achieving our highest potential. The choices we make and the lives we live are often directed by the way we manage our individual fears.

When I was a young man, I had a high school friend who was considered one of the finest baseball players in Baltimore. After some media attention, his coach arranged for him to attend a major-league tryout session. But after weeks of encouragement from his coach and fellow players he told me a secret, "I'm afraid I'll fail. I'm just not good enough." He never did go to the tryout; his fear of failure was more than he could handle. Instead of going for his dream, he surrendered to his fear.

Many believe that the very act of separating from our physical body and exploring new realms of the universe is effective in reducing our personal fears and limits. After an out-of-body experience, it's common to hear people speak of their personal breakthroughs. Sometimes this is a realization or confrontation with an inner aspect of themselves; at other times it's the recognition that they are much more than just a physical creature. On a number of occasions I have had people tell me that they had somehow connected to a more expansive part of themselves. Whatever we call it—spirit, higher self, God, or universal mind—this connection is absolutely real to the participant. This experience is difficult to explain, for it extends beyond our current linear concepts of reality.

In all our lives there are pivotal moments that change our destiny. Our challenge is to face these moments and conquer our fears. Your discovery of out-of-body exploration may be one of these pivotal times. Your decision to explore beyond your physical boundaries may be a decision that changes your entire life. I can only say that it's definitely been a turning point in my life, and I thank God that I faced my fears and ventured forward. One thing that I have learned is that all fears are an illusion. Each of us is an immortal being possessing unlimited potential. Our true inner self cannot be harmed, nor can it die.

PANIC ATTACKS

During the early stages of an out-of-body exploration, some people report an intense rush of fear similar to a panic attack. Generally, this is caused by fear of the unknown and the initial physiological surprise of actually separating from your physical body. Panic attacks are often triggered by the unusual vibrations and sounds that sometimes accompany the shift of your awareness from the dense molecular body to your higher-energy counterpart. When first experienced, these vibrations and sounds can be startling, so it's important to remember that they are a natural part of out-of-body exploration. Many times, your recognition and understanding of these unusual sounds and vibrations are sufficient to eliminate or reduce any anxiety that may arise.

If panic attacks are a recurring problem, a simple soft affirmation may help. At the first sign of anxiety, repeat in your mind, "I am safe and secure" or "I am protected." Continue to repeat your affirmation until the fear subsides. Then follow the regular instructions by directing yourself away from your physical body—for example, "I move to the front door." It's commonly reported that after complete separation from the physical body is achieved, the initial anxiety disappears.

Keep in mind that out-of-body experiences are a natural transfer of consciousness—there is simply nothing to fear. This fact is verified daily by the thousands of people who have out-of-body experiences. Generally, panic attacks cease to be a problem after you have had a successful experience. At that point, you know for yourself that there is nothing to fear.

FEAR-REDUCTION TECHNIQUE

If fear continues to be a recurring issue, this technique will be helpful.

1. *Identify the fear.* Attempt to identify the nature of your fear. For example, are you afraid of the unknown? Of rapid change? Of the possibility of becoming lost? Your recognition of your fear is an excellent indicator of progress.

2. *Use the fear.* Fear is a form of energy. It increases your respiration, strength, and ability to concentrate. It's nature's energy boost, designed to enhance your capacity to deal with potential obstacles or challenges. When you feel fear, attempt to use it to your advantage. Use the energy generated by fear to increase your concentration and desire to achieve your personal goal of out-of-body exploration.

3. *Eject the fear.* Take a deep breath. As you exhale, visualize the fear being expelled from your body, mind, and emotions. You can mentally repeat to yourself, "My fear is moving away from me," "My fear is gone," "I rise above my fear," or "My fears are washed away." As vividly as possible, picture the fear moving away from you. Visualize it fading away forever.

4. *Replace your fear.* Replace the emotional feelings of fear with a positive, productive energy such as exhilaration, concentration, courage, or the thrill of adventure. Use an appropriate affirmation such as "I am safe and secure," "I enjoy my new adventure," or "Excitement flows through me."

HOT-AIR-BALLOON VISUALIZATION

The following visualization technique may assist you in overcoming fear and other obstacles to a successful out-of-body experience.

Take several deep breaths and completely relax. Begin to visualize a majestic, bright orange, hot-air balloon. As you approach the balloon, you can clearly see that it's ready for liftoff. The familiar smile of your guide welcomes you to another adventure beyond the limits of matter. As you step inside the basket, you look forward to another exciting journey.

With absolute joy, you cast off the ropes holding you to the earth. With an upward surge, your balloon begins to rise. An intense feeling of exhilaration builds as you effortlessly rise higher and higher and slowly drift over the treetops. Below, the homes and cars begin to look like toys—small and insignificant.

Looking down over the edge of the balloon's basket, you notice several large canvas bags. The bags look extremely full and heavy. On closer inspection, you recognize that the bags are filled with your fears and limits. Each bag is clearly labeled: fear of the unknown, fear of change, fear of failure, fear of new challenges, fear of death. Whatever fear or limit you currently experience in your life is clearly marked on the bags. Take a moment and recognize your individual fears and limits and see them hanging in the canvas bags.

As you drift above the treetops, you realize that you have stopped rising. The weight from the bags of fear and limits is holding you back, holding you down. Peering over the edge of your balloon, you can see that each bag is tied securely to your basket. With overflowing joy, you begin to untie bags of fear and watch each one plummet to earth. As each bag of fear is released, you can feel your balloon surge upward, going higher and higher. With childlike excitement, you can feel each fear drop away. You absolutely know that each fear is gone forever, that each limitation is a thing of the past.

Some of the bags of fear are so tightly tied that you need to cut them free. Your guide hands you a pocketknife, and with delight you begin cutting the tough strands of rope securing the remaining bags. As each rope is cut, you experience your lightness and freedom expanding. You feel the thrill of total liberation flowing through you as you go higher and higher. As you rise to new heights, your fears and limits are gone forever.

Control Overview

- You possess the exact amount of control that you believe you do, the exact amount that you accept and implement.

- The key to prolonging your out-of-body experience is to maintain the focus of your attention away from your physical body. The best way to achieve this is to become completely involved and interested in the nonphysical environment you are exploring. As you will soon discover, any thought of your physical body will instantly snap you back into it.

- You are the controlling cause of your experience, either consciously or subconsciously. You are the writer, director, and actor in every experience, situation, and encounter. This applies to all levels of the universe.

- Your method of movement is completely your decision. You can walk, float, fly, or drift. You can change your selected method of movement at any time to suit the situation encountered.

- If your perception is unclear or fuzzy, you can increase the clarity of your vision by firmly demanding an immediate improvement of your perception: "Clarity now!"

- Your nonphysical energy form is extremely flexible in size, shape, structure, and capabilities. You will probably experience the form that is most comfortable for you. This is generally a duplicate of your physical body. However, beyond the second energy membrane, you have the ability to consciously adapt and change your form to practically any shape necessary. This is achieved by concentrating upon a change in your self-conception.

- Feelings of fear are self-generated and are generally the direct result of a lack of information or knowledge when encountering a new situation or environment. Always remember that you are a powerful, nonphysical being; at your essence you are pure consciousness. You have nothing to fear, for you are immortal.

- As much as possible, attempt to maintain an open, nonjudgmental state of mind. Strongly held opinions, beliefs, and conclusions can influence what you experience and perceive, just as they do in the physical world.

- Remember to remain calm and centered during any changes or movement of your awareness.

- Recognize your ability to control your movement and your experience. Your thoughts are your personal vehicle and creative force. You simply go where your thoughts lead.

- Firmly request what you wish to explore, achieve, or perceive and be as specific as possible.

- Be prepared for rapid changes and/or inner motion when making requests.

- Fully expect to receive your requests—be open to receive.

- Ask for clarification if what you observe or experience is unclear. For example, "What does this nonphysical energy form represent?"

- Exercise your control. Just do it—there is no need for hesitation or second thoughts.

Your ability to navigate in a thought-responsive environment will largely depend on your thought control, knowledge, and personal ability to remain calm and focused when encountering rapid change. As in all things, the more prepared you are, the more productive the experience will be.

Always remember, you experience the degree of control you demand. Aim high.

CHAPTER 8

Advanced Explorations

Man's mind, stretched to a new idea, never goes back to its original dimension.
—Oliver Wendell Holmes

The potential of out-of-body exploration is absolutely unlimited. After we step from our physical limits, an exciting new frontier of human potential and exploration becomes clear. Old limits begin to melt away as our true potential is realized.

Each of us possesses unseen, untapped abilities that modern science is only beginning to comprehend. Controlled out-of-body experiences open the door to a new era of human development and exploration; however, it's up to us to explore the reality of this for ourselves—or to remain prisoners of our physical limits.

To give you a sense of the explorations that are possible, I have included a list of potential experiments later in this chapter. To achieve specific benefits or goals, you can also develop and pursue your own

234 experiments. When conducting any form of exploration or experiments, always remember to record the results as soon as possible. A voice-activated recorder is recommended.

To get started, you could try two experiments similar to those conducted at Stanford University's parapsychology facility.

The first experiment is quite easy to set up: before you begin your out-of-body technique, place a small item such as a paper clip, pencil, or coin at the edge of a table. During your out-of-body experience, consciously attempt to lower your personal density (frequency) and move the object. Record the results.

The second experiment is the viewing of a remote target when out-of-body. To set it up, have a friend select and draw a large (at least six inches in diameter) number, picture, or symbol and place it at a location you can't physically see. Ask him or her to display the target in a clearly visible location with which you are familiar, such as your friend's home. After you separate from your physical body, focus your complete attention on the target location and attempt to observe the target as accurately as possible.

Exploring the Universe

When exploring beyond your physical body, the first nonphysical dimension commonly observed is a parallel world consisting of energy many times less dense than matter. At first glance, it appears to be a duplicate of the physical world. After closer investigation, you will discover that this energy environment is similar to your physical surroundings but not identical. Objects such as chairs, doors, beds, and entire rooms will often look slightly different than they do in your physical surroundings.

The reason for these differences is simple. The objects and environments observed within the first inner energy level of the universe are not physical in substance. They are similar to energy molds of your physical surroundings. Each nonphysical item you see exists completely independent of the physical universe.

Numerous people have been led to believe that they are observing their physical surroundings from a new vantage point. They expect their nonphysical surroundings to be identical to their physical world, and when their expectations are unfulfilled, they easily become confused or disoriented. As a result, some conclude that their entire out-of-body experience was a dream, just because the environment observed didn't match their physical expectations. This misconception often occurs because we are conditioned to accept only dense forms as valid. As a result, our minds have a tendency to focus on the single reality we know and accept—matter.

Since we live in a physical environment and are immersed in a sea of physical stimuli, this indoctrination is to be expected. Our physical conditioning is a natural part of our socialization process. The key to overcoming this extensive physical indoctrination is to recognize it. The physical world we focus upon is but a tiny fraction of the universe. In reality, the physical forms we see around us are only the thin outer crust of the universe—the epidermis layer of the entire multidimensional universe.

Always remember that reality is relative; the environment we perceive as real is determined by our personal density and frequency. For example, when we are out-of-body, it's quite common for physical objects to appear vaporous and ghostlike. This occurs because matter, as observed from a higher-frequency vantage point, is no longer a solid reality to us. From your new perspective, the only firm reality to you is the energy frequency (density) corresponding to your own. Your knowledge of this energy principle is critically important when you are exploring a different vibrational universe. This knowledge will assist you in controlling your experiences.

As you progress in your explorations, you will begin to recognize a startling truth. You possess the power to move within the different energy areas of the universe by the act of focused thought.

236 You can consciously raise and lower your vibrational (density) rate; the observed result is a corresponding change in your surrounding environment. This discovery is significant because it practically eliminates the need for external (lateral) movement. You can essentially explore any frequency of the universe without moving. The physical concepts of distance, separation, and motion become irrelevant.

A second advantage of this advanced exploration method is greater self-control. It's easier to remain focused when you do not have to deal with simultaneous external and internal changes. It's also easier to retain your sense of stability and clarity.

Third, the method allows you to explore more effectively the innumerable frequency levels of the universe. Lateral motion within a given energy dimension is often limited to a narrow frequency band within that dimension.

And finally, it expands your ability to explore, perceive, and comprehend beyond current human understanding. Consciously altering your density (vibrational frequency) provides almost unlimited access within the nonphysical interior of the universe.

Our current concepts of motion are directly related to our physical indoctrination. Eventually, each of us will evolve to the point where we can simply "be" in any portion of the universe we choose. This is not a theory but an observable fact that can be verified by personal experience.

CONTROLLED INTERDIMENSIONAL MOVEMENT

1. Immediately after separation, move away from your physical body and become calm and centered. If necessary, request that your complete awareness or clarity be present. "Awareness Now."

2. While out-of-body, firmly demand to experience the next inner energy dimension. "I experience the next inner level (dimension) now!" Or pinpoint whatever interdimensional

area you would like to explore. The immediate result will be an intense inward motion that will last for several seconds. Remain as calm as possible; the sensation of inner motion can be intense and disorienting if you are unprepared. The experience is similar to being pulled inward, into the center of your consciousness.

3. After your inner motion has ceased, immediately center yourself by firmly requesting that your complete awareness be present. "Awareness now!" Be prepared; your new environment and viewpoint will be completely different.

Raising Our Internal Frequency

As you progress in your exploration within the higher-frequency energy levels of the universe, you may begin to notice changes in your state of awareness. Internal energy sensations, visions, experiences with light, and increased energy sensitivity are commonly reported.

The environments you encounter in the higher-frequency energy levels will become progressively more radiant with light. The very substance of your surroundings consists of a higher form of energy. For example, when you observe a simple flower or blade of grass you will see that it radiates an intense spectrum of light and color. A single blade of grass appears to be made of a thousand points of light. Each blazing point of light is pure, living consciousness.

As we explore deeper into the universe, there is a need for us to raise our internal vibratory rate—to increase our internal light. To effectively explore the higher levels of the universe, our vibratory rate must be adjusted to coincide with the energy frequency we are experiencing. If our internal frequency is not equal to the new environment we are visiting, we will experience a blinding light and a crushing sensation of intense energy pressing upon us. This

238   feeling is so uncomfortable that most people immediately retreat to their physical bodies.

When exploring the higher realms of the universe, we can enhance our internal vibrational rate by making a firm, sincere request. In effect, we can request a fine-tuning of our inner energy for the enhancement of our spiritual development. This fine-tuning of our unseen energy systems is an ongoing developmental process, normally occurring when we're asleep or dreaming. Most people are not consciously aware of these inner changes as they occur. For those who are aware, these changes are often perceived as waves of inner energy surging through the body. This process can last for seconds or minutes, depending upon the amount of adjustment required. I have found that the raising of our individual vibrational rate has a major effect upon our nonphysical capabilities. It's essential to enhance our personal energy frequency if we are to explore the higher realms of the universe. It is our responsibility to increase our personal light if we ever hope to escape from the illusion of matter. Always remember that heaven will not adapt to us; we must adapt to it.

Negative thoughts, anger, hatred, attachments, and ignorance block the natural radiation of our internal light. Destructive thoughts and emotions are a form of low-frequency energy that attaches to our inner energy-body like a cloak. When out-of-body you can immediately spot these negative vibrations in the energy field (aura) of anyone you are observing. Negative emotions such as hate, fear, anger, and greed become a part of the person who creates them. This negative energy acts like an energy-dampening field, blocking the inner light of soul from shining through at its normal intensity. During out-of-body exploration, the evolution of anyone you observe is clearly evident by the intensity of light radiating from that person. The brighter the internal light, the more evolved the individual.

Raising our personal vibratory rate begins with the removal of our internal energy blocks. This is why advanced spiritual

souls such as Jesus and Buddha spent so much time teaching the
Golden Rule. "Love they neighbor," "Do unto others . . ." They
fully realized that the more energy blocks we remove, the
brighter our light shines and the higher our natural frequency
rate becomes in the multidimensional universe.

The recognition of this principle is important to your immediate evolution. When your physical body dies, you will automatically go to the energy level (frequency) of the universe that
corresponds to your personal vibratory rate. As you will discover,
this is a natural energy process—the shift of consciousness from
one frequency to another. Those unique individuals who have
recognized and eliminated their energy blocks and raised their
personal frequency rate will experience the full magnificence and
light of the kingdom of heaven.

Amplifying the Vibrational State

It is possible to amplify the vibrational state from a slight internal vibration to a complete separation from the physical body.
This can be accomplished by mentally encouraging the slight vibrations to build, expand, and spread throughout the body. It's
quite common for some of us to awaken during various stages of
sleep and experience a slight internal vibration and/or numbness
at the back of the neck or in the legs or arms. This is often experienced during REM sleep, during lucid dreams, or during the
light stages of alpha, such as the hypnagogic state. Of course, the
key to this technique is to recognize the initial vibrations and
numbness when they occur. The best way to do this is to pay attention to the subtle energy fluctuations occurring during the
initial stages of sleep, dreams, and relaxation. Awareness of our
internal sensations, feelings, and perceptions is an important first
step in noticing our internal vibrations.

From now on, immediately upon awakening or when drifting
in and out of sleep, remain physically still and completely relaxed. Notice any internal energy changes, vibrations, numbness,

240 tingling, or other unusual sensations. When these sensations occur, mentally encourage the vibrations and accompanying sensations to expand throughout your body. Flow with the sensations and allow them to spread through your body and mind. After the vibrational sensations and numbness have spread throughout your body, direct yourself away from your body. Maintain your complete attention and thought away from your physical body and direct yourself to another area of your home.

As unusual as it may sound, this is a very natural thing to do. The key is simply to notice, and then encourage, the subtle nonphysical changes that occur within us.

Enhancing Memory Recall

Each time you end an out-of-body exploration or experiment, make a firm request for a complete memory transfer to your physical awareness. Your physical brain and memory function like a computer: the obtained nonphysical information must be accurately transferred and stored within your physical consciousness. The easiest way to accomplish this is simply to request it.

Many out-of-body explorers are unaware of this principle. The result can be a hazy, disjointed memory of their nonphysical experiences. As in the clarity technique, the emphasis you place upon your memory request will determine the effectiveness of the results. A firm, focused demand works best: "I remember all!"

Ideally, the request for enhanced memory should be made when you're ready to return to your physical form. This request will often propel you immediately back to your physical body.

Group and Partner Explorations

An out-of-body exploration group or partnership can provide considerable benefits for all involved. Since out-of-body experiences are a new form of exploration in our society, a nonphysical exploration group can offer valuable insights gained from firsthand experiences and also provide an open forum for new perspectives and techniques.

A group enables us to compare notes and learn from each other's experiences. As we fine-tune our natural abilities, the important areas of fear reduction, belief reappraisal, dream conversion, inner signals, and separation techniques can be explored and developed based on firsthand results. The group can also discuss and pinpoint any psychological limitations or blocks that appear.

As an added benefit, some powerful verification experiments can be conducted. For example, a group can create a target destination: a physical time and place where group members will meet while traveling outside their physical bodies.

In addition to group exploration, I highly recommend a buddy or partner system for out-of-body adventures. It's important to select someone who is serious about inner discovery. Consciously meeting a friend or lover while out-of-body is an incredible experience.

THE PARTNER TECHNIQUE

The partner technique is a variation of the Christos technique developed by G. M. Glaskin, an Australian journalist. The Christos technique was originally designed as a past-life regression method, but it was soon discovered that it initiated out-of-body experiences for substantial numbers of people.

The following technique is ideal for couples, partners, and groups. As the guide, you will be leading the meditation and occasionally moving around your partner, so it's important for you to be as quiet as possible.

Your partner lies on his (or her) back, eyes closed, head toward the north. To be as comfortable and relaxed as possible, he should remove his shoes and lie on a soft surface such as a bed, a floor mat, or pillows.

Now begin to gently massage your partner's anklebones in a gentle circular motion. The idea is to relax your partner as much as possible.

After about two minutes of the ankle massage, quietly move to your partner's head and place four fingers on his forehead, just above the bridge of the nose. Now slowly begin a gentle, circular rubbing to the lower portion of the forehead. With gradually increasing speed and pressure, continue to rub your partner's forehead until he reports a loud internal buzzing or humming sound. After the buzzing sound is heard, you can stop rubbing. Most people report hearing a sound within five minutes.

Now you will begin a verbal, guided meditation. Throughout the guided visualization, speak in a slow, relaxing tone, assisting your partner to become as relaxed as possible. Take your time and focus on relaxation as you begin the following guided visualization.

> Take several deep breaths and completely relax . . . completely relax . . . slow down and completely relax . . . begin to feel your inner energy flowing. . . . Feel your inner energy slowly moving from your head down your neck . . . feel it slowly move down through your shoulders. . . . You feel completely relaxed as your energy moves down through your chest. . . . The energy feels good as it continues moving down through your stomach . . . your hips . . . your thighs. . . . Now feel the energy moving down your calves . . . feel the energy moving past your ankles . . . you can see and feel the energy at the very bottoms of your feet. . . .

After the relaxation portion of this visualization, begin to lightly brush the bottoms of your partner's feet with your fingertips as you repeat the following.

> Visualize the energy at your feet extending and growing four inches through the bottoms of your soles. . . . Now you can see

and feel the extension of your feet by four inches. . . . Feel the
stretch of your feet extending four inches beyond the bottoms
of your feet. . . . Now, hold that extension for a few moments.
[After each extension is successfully visualized, your partner
can let you know by nodding.]

After your partner has visualized the four-inch stretch, have
him imagine the sight and sensations of his feet returning to
their normal position. Now, repeat this stretching at least three
times until your partner can easily visualize a four-inch extension
of his feet. Take your time and be patient. This initial stretching
is essential to the success of this technique, so feel free to repeat
it as many times as necessary.

After your partner has indicated his ability to extend his visualized feet, quietly move to the head and repeat the same stretching exercise with the upper body and head. (The guided visualization proceeds uninterrupted as you lightly touch the top of
your partner's hair and shoulders.)

Now, feel your energy flowing to the top of your head. . . . Feel
the top of your head begin to extend and grow. . . . See and feel
the top of your head and your upper body expand and grow
four inches. . . . See and feel your head and shoulders growing a
full four inches beyond their normal size. . . . Feel the stretch
of your entire upper body growing and expanding outward . . .
a full four inches beyond its physical limits. . . .

As before, repeat this process at least three times until your
partner can easily imagine the extension.

Return your partner's attention to his feet and verbally guide
him to extend his lower body by a full twelve inches. Repeat as
many times as necessary.

Move to your partner's head and guide him to a twelve-inch
extension of his entire upper body and then a return to normal
size.

244   Now, return to the feet and guide your partner to a full twenty-four-inch extension. This time, however, instruct him to hold the visualization and not return to a normal position. After the foot extension is complete, have your partner simultaneously stretch his upper body a full twenty-four inches. Repeat this procedure until your partner can clearly see and feel this total stretch of his body.

While the full twenty-four-inch stretch is being maintained, direct your partner to expand his complete body like a balloon being filled with air. For example:

> Now your entire body is expanding in size. . . . You can feel your inner self expand all over, like a balloon filling with air. . . . Your entire body is expanding all over . . . your entire body is expanding by twenty-four inches. . . . As your body expands, you can feel yourself getting lighter and lighter. . . . Like a balloon, you can feel yourself rising, rising. . . .

Now your partner is in an ideal state to achieve a fully conscious, out-of-body experience. At this point you can immediately begin a favorite out-of-body technique. For example:

> As you float, you can feel yourself becoming lighter and floating higher and higher above your body. . . . As you do, you repeat to yourself, "I am floating. I am floating. I am aware I am floating. I am floating free."

If done correctly, this technique provides a powerful preparation for any out-of-body visualization or affirmation.

Take your time and allow your partner to enjoy all the sensations associated with this technique. Feel free to enhance or lengthen the guided meditation to accommodate your partner's visualization skills. Ideally, allow at least half an hour when doing the guided visualization. After the verbal, guided portion of this technique, allow your partner at least twenty minutes of silence to accomplish his or her personal affirmations and visualization.

Although I've included only one technique designed specifically for partners, any of the visualization techniques can be easily adapted to a partner or group situation by designating someone to do the verbal guided visualization.

Accelerating Psychological Change and Self-Improvement

At some point in our lives we all seek a form of self-improvement or psychological change. In the past three decades, countless self-improvement techniques, books, tapes, and courses have become available: positive thinking, neurolinguistic programming, inner-child work, self-talk, rebirthing, Twelve Steps, biofeedback, and a host of others.

In general, our concepts of self-improvement are still linked to the conclusions arrived at decades ago by the founding fathers of modern psychology. Freud, the creator of psychoanalysis, and Jung, the founder of analytical psychology, believed that psychological change was a slow, deliberate process. Today this conclusion is accepted by psychologists and psychiatrists worldwide. Many consider psychological improvement to be the slow process of peeling away the outer layers of ego so that patients can see and understand the underlying cause of their current problems or blocks.

Every year millions of people spend considerable time and money attempting to achieve some form of psychological change. Many have been conditioned to believe that positive psychological change is a long, arduous road. Most psychiatrists and psychologists expect noticeable improvements to take from several months to several years. A few years ago, during a conversation with a psychologist, I was told bluntly, "Psychological change is a grueling task that takes a lifetime." My first thought was, *I'm glad I'm not paying you by the hour.* Studies have shown that the attitudes and expectations of the medical practitioner dramatically affect the results achieved; often the expectations, or lack of them, are transferred to the patient. If a psychologist expects positive psychological change to be a grueling lifelong task, it most certainly will.

Over the years I have found many of the basic conclusions of the billion-dollar self-improvement industry to be severely lacking. I believe that the time has come for us to ask some serious questions. How can we effectively improve ourselves when we don't know what we are, why we're here, and where we're going? How can we effectively improve something that we don't comprehend? Do self-improvement and positive psychological change require years of grueling introspection? I strongly believe that it is within our grasp to bypass the unending maze of self-analysis and cut to the heart of self-improvement. This observation is shared by a growing number of individuals and groups throughout the world.

For a moment just imagine what could be accomplished if there were a more direct and effective way to achieve positive psychological change and self-improvement. Consider, for example, the experience of Michael Crichton, the internationally known author of *Jurassic Park,* who describes one of his out-of-body experiences in his autobiography *Travels.* He initiated this out-of-body experience with the assistance of a personal guide and friend, Gary.

Anyway, the idea of the astral travel didn't seem too alarming, and I tried it with Gary. It is, after all, just another kind of guided meditation in an altered state. I visualized my chakras glowing brightly, spinning like white spirals. Then I visualized myself leaving through my third chakra, moving up to the astral plane—which to me appeared as a misty yellow place.

So far, so good. I began to see why people so often imagined heaven as misty or cloudy. This misty astral plane was agreeable. It was peaceful to be standing here, in all this yellow mist. I felt fine.

"Do you see anybody here?" Gary asked.

I looked around. I didn't see anybody.

"No."

"Stay there a minute and let's see if anybody comes."

Then I saw my grandmother, who died while I was in medical school. She waved to me, and I waved back. I wasn't surprised to see her up here. I didn't feel any particular need to talk to her.

So I just waited around. This astral plane was rather featureless. There weren't any palm trees or chairs or places to sit down. It was just a place. A misty yellow place.

"Do you see anybody else?" Gary said.

I didn't. Then:

"Yes. My father."

I felt worried. I hadn't had an easy time with my father. Now he was showing up while I was vulnerable, in an altered state of consciousness. I wondered what he would do, what would happen. He approached me. My father looked the same, only translucent and misty, like everything else in this place. I didn't want to have a long conversation with him. I was quite nervous.

Suddenly he embraced me.

In the instant of that embrace, I saw and felt everything in my relationship with my father, all the feelings he had had and why he had found me difficult, all the feelings I had had and why I had misunderstood him, all the love that there was between us, and all the confusion and misunderstanding that had overpowered it. I saw all the things he had done for me and all the ways he had helped me. I saw every aspect of our relationship at once, the way you can take in at a glance something small you hold in your hand. It was an instant of compassionate acceptance and love.

I burst into tears.

"What is happening now?"

"He's hugging me."

"What are you feeling?"

"It's . . . all over," I said.

What I meant was that this incredibly powerful experience had already happened, complete and total, in a fraction of a second. By the time Gary had asked me, by the time I burst into tears, it was finished. My father had gone. We never said a word. There was no need to say anything. The thing was completed.

"I'm done," I said, and opened my eyes. I had bounced right out of the trance state.

I couldn't really explain it to Gary—I couldn't really explain it to anybody—but part of my astonishment at the experience was at the speed with which it had occurred. Like most people who have had therapy, I had an expectation about the pace of psychological insights. You struggle. Things happen slowly. Years may go by without much change. You wonder if it is making any difference. You wonder if you should quit or hang in. You work and you struggle and you make your hard-won gains. But what of this experience? In less time than I took to open my mouth to speak, something extraordinary and profound had happened to me. And I knew it would last. My relationship with my father had been resolved in a flash. There hadn't even been time to cry, and now that it was over, crying seemed after-the-fact. I had no desire to cry. The experience was already finished.

This made me wonder if my ideas about the normal speed of psychological change might be incorrect. Perhaps we could accomplish massive changes in seconds, if we only knew how. Perhaps change took so long only because we did it the wrong way. Or perhaps because we expected it to take so long.

The following is a personal confrontation I experienced with my own fears.

Journal Entry, September 14, 1992

I verbally repeat an affirmation, "Now I'm out-of-body," thirty to forty times as my body drifts to sleep.

I awaken floating just above my body. I am aware of a connection at the base of my spine and somehow visualize this attachment to be a large insect holding me to my body. I instantly fall back into my body and break this unusual connection. Immediately I again float upward out of my body. I feel people touching me, gently rocking me side-to-side. I hear my mother's voice as she calls my name. I know I'm out-of-body but my perceptions are semidreamlike. I say aloud, "Clarity now!" I feel a surge of energy and an intense sensation of lightness and enhanced perception.

Suddenly I'm in a new environment. I'm standing in a maze of rooms completely different from my physical home. Again I ask for clarity and receive an instant improvement of my vision. Directly in front of me are two stairways: one goes up into a golden-colored room; the other leads into a dark basement.

As I stare down into the darkness, I see a large, slowly moving form. It appears to be headed toward me. As it comes closer, I see the outline of a huge hairy creature, a giant sloth, standing nine feet high; it has a bear's head and the face of a dog. My entire being is paralyzed with fear. I desperately want to run, but I hold my position. Slowly, the creature climbs the stairs and wraps its huge hairy arms around my neck and body. All I can think is, *This thing can snap my neck in a heartbeat.*

Suddenly the creature gives me a warm hug and licks my face like a dog. All my fear dissipates as I realize that this ugly creature is powerless to harm me. An intense feeling of empowerment and joy explodes through me; I feel completely free from my fear and limits. The creature looks directly into my eyes, smiles, and disappears. A surge of energy flows through me as I recognize a new form of freedom—an absolute freedom from fear.

I return to my physical body with a new vision of myself. Somehow I know that I have confronted an inner representation of my deepest, darkest fears and have conquered them by holding firm. I feel completely empowered, absolutely knowing that I can achieve whatever I desire. Now I realize that I can overcome my greatest enemy—my own fears.

Controlled out-of-body experiences give us the unique opportunity to confront and resolve the underlying energy-cause of any psychological issues we may have. The mirror experience related in chapter 5 is another example of this process in action. It should be emphasized that this is an advanced method of self-improvement that can create a powerful experience of confrontation. It is not recommended for individuals who are psychologically unstable.

Advanced Healing

Science has proved that many of the medical problems so prevalent in our society are the direct result of our emotions and thoughts. We influence our physical bodies by the way we use, move, and hold energy within us. For example, stomach ulcers, skin ailments, physical addictions, and depression are often caused by our thought and emotional patterns.

Controlled out-of-body exploration gives us the opportunity to consciously experience the unseen energy frequencies and patterns that affect our physical body. When out-of-body we are directly experiencing our personal energy substructure, our subtle nonphysical energy system. This gives us a tremendous opportunity to make energy adjustments at the very core of our being. Energy restructuring accomplished within the nonphysical energy-body must eventually manifest changes within the outer physical body.

The following is a highly advanced technique that goes directly to the underlying energy-cause of physical illness. Using this healing technique, it is possible to influence and balance the unseen energies flowing within yourself or another person.

Begin by doing your favorite out-of-body technique. Immediately after separating from your physical body, request complete clarity of awareness: "Clarity now!" Repeat the clarity request until your consciousness is crystal clear.

When your full awareness is centered in your nonphysical body, begin to mentally and verbally request the healing light and energy of God (the universe) to enter you. Ask for and clearly feel the positive healing energies of the universe flowing within you. Sincerely request the healing light of the universe to permeate every level of your energy-body. Allow yourself to be completely immersed within the intense healing light.

If you desire, verbally request the healing energy to be directed to a specific person, or within a specific part of your own physical body. "I request the pure energy of the universe to assist and heal *name of person*." Or, "The healing power of the universe flows throughout my body and mind." When you direct your thoughts toward your physical body, you will likely return to it.

After returning to the physical, remain still and feel the energy and light flowing through every cell and system in your body. Take your time and welcome the energy flow into your entire body. Feel the vibrational adjustments necessary for you to obtain your optimum health.

Be open to receive. Be open to a complete adjustment of your body's vibrational rate. It's important that you are open to receive your request—so many times people ask for things without being open to receive them. "I am open to receive the healing energy within me." This is a powerful request at any level of the universe.

Be thankful for your experience. You have received a special gift of energy awareness, adjustment, and healing. Use your gift to assist others to recognize and awaken the inner healing energy that flows through all of us.

During the initial phases of this technique, remain as detached as possible toward your physical body. Any focused thought directed toward your physical form will instantly snap you back to your body.

Don't underestimate the power of this technique. This form of nonphysical energy adjustment is the true cause of all physical miracles throughout recorded history. The person doing this technique is acting as an open channel for the power of God; within this state of consciousness, all things are possible.

Accelerating Our Spiritual Growth

For hundreds of millions of people around the world, the ultimate goals of spiritual development are self-realization and God realization. These spiritual goals are known by various names in different cultures: Christ consciousness, enlightenment, spiritual union, oneness with God, and illumination. Since the dawn of time, spiritual seekers, monks, prophets, and saints have spent their lives attempting to experience these goals. Unfortunately, our modern religions have wandered from their rich heritage of spiritual experience. Tragically, many modern religions and churches have become a poor reflection of the original spiritual experiences and teachings upon which they were built. The concept of personal spiritual experience has become an unexplored and mysterious phenomenon unknown to many religious leaders and their churches. As a result, millions of people settle for manmade beliefs and interpretations of their scriptures.

Today, we no longer need to depend upon the interpretations and beliefs of others. Using out-of-body exploration, we can obtain and verify for ourselves the spiritual answers we seek.

As you will soon discover, one of the fastest and most direct ways to experience your spiritual essence and obtain firsthand knowledge of heaven is to learn out-of-body exploration. Controlled out-of-body experiences give us the unique ability to achieve any spiritual goal upon which we focus. The spiritual power of this is absolutely verifiable, but it is up to you to take action; it is up to you to take the steps and move beyond the limits of your physical body.

In the physical world it's easy to become lost in the dense illusions and ignorance around us. It's easy to become immersed in the sea of man-made beliefs, doctrines, and traditions; it's easy to be trapped in the physical labyrinth. Those who truly seek spiritual growth and wisdom soon discover that it is not found in the external world. Spiritual growth is an internal journey of awareness, a journey deep within ourselves to the essence of our being. Spiritual growth is the personal experience and knowledge of our true self, our very soul.

The following technique is highly recommended for anyone seeking accelerated spiritual development, knowledge, and answers.

ADVANCED SPIRITUAL TECHNIQUE

Begin by doing your favorite out-of-body technique. Immediately after separation from your physical body, firmly request clarity, "Clarity now!" When you are fully aware and centered within your nonphysical body, ask to experience your soul (higher

254 self). Make this request a firm verbal demand for immediate action. "I experience my soul (higher self) now!"

Instantly, you will be propelled within yourself at tremendous speed. The sensation is one of extreme inner movement, like being drawn into a powerful vacuum deep within yourself. Endless layers of light and color flash by your awareness as you're pulled deeper and deeper within. (Some people report a sensation of shooting upward into space.) After several intense seconds, this motion will come to an abrupt halt.

Be prepared. When first experienced, this rapid inner motion of our awareness can be startling; hold on, have faith, and remain as calm as possible. I believe the experience of inner or upward motion is the transfer of our awareness from our relatively dense nonphysical body to the higher-frequency existence of pure consciousness (soul).

The result of this technique is beyond all expectations. You will experience and know your true self, independent of all form and substance. Limits melt away as an incredible spiritual dimension of pure light and knowledge opens within you.

Experiencing your higher self (soul) is the very heart of spiritual development; now you have a tremendous opportunity to discover the answers to the oldest mysteries of your existence. You can receive an answer or solution to any physical challenge or limitation you may currently experience. Within this state of awareness, miracles can be achieved. Your ability to comprehend and influence the denser levels of the universe is magnified beyond all human comprehension.

Don't underestimate the power of this technique; the conscious experience of being your true self is an awakening that will change your life. While in this state of consciousness, your ability to obtain answers is unlimited; you experience your spiritual essence beyond all physical concepts of time, space, and form.

You finally know the greatest mystery of your existence—what you truly are.

Out-of-Body Experiments and Explorations

- Observe, investigate, and explore the unseen energy substructure of the universe.

- Investigate your new environment: its form, substance, solidity, and stability.

- Conduct experiments using thought-energy; closely observe changes in your environment.

- Travel to a friend's or relative's home and observe the environment and activities. Record the time and place for verification.

- Conduct experiments with your nonmolecular density. Attempt to increase or decrease your body's density. Apply pressure on your arm. Can you feel it?

- Touch an object in your new environment. Can you feel it? Does it have density, or does your hand pass through it?

- Ask to visit and communicate with a "passed on" loved one.

- Closely observe the energy structure of your "new body."

- Conduct experiments with nonmolecular energy. Observe cause and effect, inertia, gravity, and the unique energy forces that exist in the new environment.

- While out-of-body, observe your prevailing thoughts. Do they affect the environment around you in any way? Now, focus upon a single thought. How does your concentration affect the environment?

- Ask for a specific quality such as increased comprehension, vision, or understanding. Observe any changes in your perception ability.

- Scan the horizon. How far can you see? Are there changes to the environment as you look around?

- Request a specific form, such as a chair, to appear in front of you. Does it? If so, does this object possess three-dimensional density? Now, ask this object to disappear. Does it?

- Investigate the possibilities of space exploration without the limits of a conventional spacecraft.

- Travel to your favorite physical location and observe and record the environment and events.

- Explore the possibility of your past lives.

- Meet and communicate with a nonphysical guide or resident.

- Explore the existence of sex in a different vibrational state.

- Ask to experience your higher self, your soul (highly recommended).

- Observe your life—past, present, and probable future—from a more expansive viewpoint.

- Ask to understand and resolve a physical problem that is causing you difficulty.

- Observe and explore the primal source of matter as we know it.

- Ask for insight into or clarification of any difficult question.

- Ask to observe the source and purpose of your current reality.

- Ask to see and communicate with a biblical angel.

- Explore and experience "heaven"—the nonphysical vibrational levels of the universe.

- Experiment with the transmission of healing energy to a physically ill friend or associate. Observe and record the results.

- Closely observe the connection between your energy-body and your physical body. Is there any visible connection?

- Firmly ask to see the true essence of the energy forms around you. Observe any changes in your environment.

- Ask to observe a thought—its form, function, and characteristics.

- Ask any question and be prepared to "experience" the answer.

- Observe your physical body from a more expansive perspective.

- Experience, explore, and begin to chart the multidimensional universe.

- Manipulate energy (form) by the conscious focus of your thought.

- Explore with a partner or mate (a highly recommended verification experience).

- Ask to observe the birth of a child from a nonphysical perspective.

- Explore the possibilities of time travel and the possibilities of sequential time and sequential existence.

Questions About Our Existence

Throughout recorded history, every great exploration and discovery started with a simple question. What is on the other side of the ocean? What is on the other side of our solar system? Now, with increasing intensity, we are asking deeper questions. What is on the other side of matter? What kind of energy and life exists just beyond our current technological vision?

Out-of-body exploration raises many questions—so many that the list could fill a book. Here, I present a small sampling of questions that I believe serious out-of-body explorers can answer if they are willing to devote the necessary time and energy. These questions make excellent research and exploration areas for out-of-body partners or research groups. The questions are endless, but so are our potential abilities to discover answers when we transcend our temporary physical vehicles.

What do the nonphysical environments look like?

What is their structure?

Why are only some of these environments thought-responsive?

_____

Does a universal form of nonphysical government exist?

Are there laws or rules?

Are there penalties for breaking rules?

Does a universal nonphysical police force exist?

What are angels?

Is there a nonphysical or spiritual hierarchy?

Does God directly interact or communicate with nonphysical inhabitants?

How do nonphysical inhabitants live?

What is their normal day like?

Is it anything like physical existence?

Do cities, towns, communities, or nations exist?

Do cultures, ethnic groups, or races continue to exist?

How do the energy centers (chakras) of our body affect or influence our daily life?

How do our energy centers and nonphysical bodies function as a complete energy system?

What is the correlation between the energy centers and our ability to have out-of-body experiences?

Can our energy-body assume any shape or form?

Are physical disease and illness the molecular result of unseen nonphysical energy disturbances?

At what point during pregnancy does consciousness (soul) enter the fetus?

Does this vary from person to person or is it universal?

Can physical diseases or illnesses be healed or improved by making energy adjustments to the nonphysical substructure of an individual?

Can a future event or disaster be averted or altered by influencing and adjusting the unseen energy substructure of the universe?

Can future physical events be accurately analyzed, interpreted, and predicted by observing the energy interactions existing within the interior of the universe?

Can we travel in time when out-of-body?

Is it possible that events in time are simultaneous?

Is reincarnation a reality?

Is it an evolutionary system?

How does it function?

Do angels actually exist?

If so, what do they look like?

What is their function?

Are they a nonhuman species?

Do the biblical heavens exist?

What does heaven really look like?

How many heavens are there?

How do they differ from one another?

Is the biblical heaven the inner energy dimensions of the universe?

Does God interact with human evolution or is it an automatic system of development?

———————

What is our true form or essence, if any?

Why are we using these temporary biological bodies?

What do we hope to learn or gain?

What does the interior of the universe look like?

What is it made of?

Is it a series of energy dimensions?

Is there a distinguishable border between the different energy dimensions?

If so, what is this border?

How does it function?

What is its purpose?

What are miracles?

Are they the alteration and restructuring of the nonphysical energy substructure of the universe?

What do people look like when they sleep or dream?

Do they float slightly above their bodies?

Are dreams internal creations or our unconscious interpretations of nonphysical events?

Do dreamers normally separate from their physical body?

How does our species' evolution correlate with out-of-body experiences?

Are out-of-body experiences an evolutionary step for our species?

Is evolution actually the movement of consciousness from simply physical organisms to increasingly complex nonphysical states of being?

What actually occurs at physical death?

Where do we go?

Is death a natural part of our evolution?

Why are we here?

Do we have a specific (unconscious) goal or plan on which we are working?

Did we select our parents?

If so, why and how?

Does nonphysical food exist and is it necessary for survival?

Do physical-like families and relationships continue after death?

Does physical-like sex exist?

Are nonphysical babies conceived?

The questions are endless. The answers are simply waiting for us to expand our vision beyond the dense molecular crust of the universe. This is not a theory but an evolutionary fact of our existence. For many of us, the time has come to take a step beyond the physical limits we see around us. This step is the logical transition and evolution each of us will experience in the near future.

Questions and Comments

Can out-of-body experiences be proved?

Out-of-body experiences can be proved only by the participant. The ivory-tower conclusions held by many researchers are completely archaic and meaningless in the light of a single personal experience. Many people desperately attempt to fit this unique state of consciousness into their accepted model of reality. For example, several scholars have concluded that out-of-body experiences are actually lucid dreams; their conclusions conveniently fit their traditional concepts of the mind.

What does it feel like to separate from your physical body?

Many people report a high-energy vibrational feeling and temporary physical numbness during separation; this is often accompanied by an intense buzzing, humming, or roaring sound.

These sounds and sensations normally dissipate after separation is complete.

What does the out-of-body environment look like?
The environment perceived depends upon the vibrational frequency (density) of the participant. Many people report a physical-like environment. This environment does not necessarily correspond to their immediate physical environment.

How long does it take to have an out-of-body experience?
Each person is different; however, a large percentage of people who practice daily techniques report an experience in less than thirty days.

Why should I invest my time and effort in out-of-body exploration?
The only way to know something absolutely is to experience it for yourself; anything less is theory, speculation, and belief. Out-of-body exploration offers us the unique opportunity to experience and explore beyond the limits of our physical senses. It gives us the ability to obtain firsthand knowledge of our existence.

What will my "new" body look like?
Most people report a higher-energy duplicate of their physical body. The form we experience is a direct result of our expectations and beliefs. In general, most people will see themselves as they appear in the physical world.

Will I be able to see, hear, and feel as I do now?
In your early out-of-body explorations, you will most likely experience your surroundings with a physical-like perception. Our perception capabilities are linked to our expectations; the more open we are to expanded perceptions beyond our physical

264   senses, the more available these enhanced capabilities become. For example, some people report 360-degree vision, enhanced hearing, and the ability to read thoughts.

During my out-of-body experiences I sometimes feel out of sync and have difficulty seeing or moving. How can I overcome this limitation?
This is commonly reported. To increase your clarity and mobility, simply demand (verbally or mentally) that your complete awareness be present: "Complete awareness now!" or "Clarity now!" Whatever personal ability or perception you need to improve your out-of-body experience can be obtained by making a firm request. Repeat your request as often as needed, and remember to make each request a firm demand for immediate results.

Will an out-of-body experience change my religious beliefs?
According to an in-depth study of 350 participants published in 1992 by Dr. Melvin Morse, "Out-of-body experiences do not seem to alter one's professed values." Many people even report that their religious beliefs have been confirmed and strengthened by their out-of-body experiences.

What is the radiant light so often reported during a near-death experience?
This is the higher-frequency light of the inner dimensions being seen by someone not accustomed to its brilliance. The light is commonly seen emanating from the entrance to a tunnel.

What is the human aura?
The aura is the energy field that emanates from all life-forms.

What is the tunnel effect commonly reported during near-death experiences?
This is the opening of the first inner energy membrane. It occurs automatically when a person dies and moves to the interior

of the multidimensional universe. The tunnel immediately closes after the individual passes through into the next dimension.

Does the biblical silver cord exist?

The biblical concept of the silver cord is accurate. According to my observations, it is not actually a cord but a thin, fibrous substance similar in appearance to a spider's web. The silver cord appears to function as the connection between the physical body and the first inner energy-body of all life-forms. Though its complete function is unknown, it's logical that it may act as an inner energy conduit. One thing is certain, when the cord is severed, the biological life ends.

Do animals have souls?

Absolutely. Without a soul (conscious energy) no living creature can exist. To be more accurate, the soul possesses and uses a biological vehicle, not vice versa.

What is the purpose of physical existence?

Physical existence allows us to learn from experience. In a sense, the physical dimension is a slowed-down molecular environment ideally suited for the training of developing consciousness. The personal challenges we encounter in our biological life are the lessons we need for our personal development. We learn by being, by doing—by firsthand experience.

How can I determine the dimension or energy level I am exploring?

In general, the more similar the immediate environment is to your physical surrounding, the closer you are to the physical dimension. As you raise your vibratory rate, you will automatically move inward within the nonphysical dimensions. The perceived environments become progressively less dense and increasingly thought-responsive as you move inward away from matter.

Can out-of-body experiences be harmful?

No. They are a natural experience reported in every culture and society of the world. In over twenty years of personal research, I have never heard of anyone being harmed or injured in any way.

Can drugs be used to induce an out-of-body experience?

The key to a valid, productive out-of-body experience is absolute mental focus and control. Without complete control, the interdimensional realities experienced during out-of-body explorations cannot be accurately distinguished from self-created internal hallucinations or imagery. Control is the key to a productive, meaningful experience, and control is the first thing lost when using any kind of mind-altering substance. I strongly believe that nonphysical explorers should not use drugs. Why contaminate your biological vehicle when effective results can be achieved naturally?

Is it possible that I won't be able to find my way back to my physical body?

No. In thousands of reported experiences there is no documented evidence of such an occurrence. We instantly return at the slightest thought of our physical body.

Can my body or mind be possessed when I leave it?

No. There is always an interactive energy connection between your physical body and your inner energy-bodies.

What is the church's official viewpoint on out-of-body experiences?

The Christian church does not have an official or unified viewpoint concerning out-of-body exploration. I have encountered a wide variety of opinions on this subject. Many theologians consider out-of-body experiences a unique spiritual blessing—a personal confirmation of their religious faith and beliefs. Others are perplexed and uncertain where such experiences may fit in their belief system. A few are inclined to fear any phenomenon they don't understand, and automatically classify out-of-body experiences as something to be avoided. Today, increasing numbers of theologians consider out-of-body explorations to be a profound spiritual experience and solid personal verification of immortality.

Every time I feel I'm about to separate from my body, a wave of intense fear overwhelms me. How can I overcome this?

This wave of fear is a common, instinctual response to a new experience. One of the best ways to overcome it is to immediately begin repeating a safety affirmation such as "I'm safe and secure," "I'm protected," or "I'm safe and calm." Any brief, positive statement that helps you relax and feel secure will be effective. As you repeat your affirmation, begin to direct your attention away from your body. This can easily be achieved by thinking about another area in your home or by saying to yourself, "I float away from my body." After a couple of successful experiences, your fear will diminish and eventually disappear.

Is out-of-body exploration safe for everyone?

Yes, with one exception. Anyone who has acute psychological problems should avoid this form of exploration. In general, people having difficulty dealing with their physical reality can only complicate the situation by introducing other realities into their lives.

What is the most important step in gaining full, conscious control of the out-of-body experience?

The key is to repeat the clarity technique whenever your awareness is hazy or out of sync. "Clarity now!" or "Awareness now!"

268   *What is the difference between dreams and out-of-body experiences?*

The difference is quite dramatic to the participant. During an out-of-body experience, the participant is often as conscious as you are now. Dreams, on the other hand, are experienced as a rapidly changing motion picture projected within your awareness. At least three factors not found in a dream are normally present in an out-of-body experience: your ego self-awareness is present; you consciously control your movement; and you can consciously verify your experience.

Conclusion

The enormous potential of controlled out-of-body exploration may well be the most important discovery of the twentieth century. Only by exploring beyond our physical limits can we ever hope to comprehend the essence of ourselves and our universe. Eventually, our species will evolve beyond dependence on physical vehicles and technology. Until then, the progressive explorers will be those courageous individuals who go beyond the limits of science, religion, and their physical perceptions.

An unquenchable desire for knowledge is propelling a select number of explorers beyond the security of their physical homelands. These resourceful adventurers are exploring and charting the universe beyond the dense, outer crust of matter. This exploration and charting of our unseen energy-universe are of worldwide importance. Only nonphysical exploration can pierce the dense, outer layer of matter and expose the invisible, underlying structure of our universe.

270　It's time we recognize that the decaying molecular forms we see around us are not the only reality in the universe. It's time we know the truth that lies behind the molecular facade of life.

Just beyond our vision exist vast realms of energy and life waiting to be discovered. As the twenty-first century approaches, the time has come for us to explore and discover the truth of our existence—to break free from the conclusions and assumptions of others, to see and know for ourselves.

Each of us faces an important choice. We can remain complacent, hoping and praying that our beliefs are accurate, or we can make a decision to explore and discover for ourselves. Ask yourself, what can you possibly lose by expanding your vision and comprehension beyond the limits of matter?

Your decision to explore will mold your future, your evolution, and your life beyond all expectations. All of us possess the God-given ability to explore and discover the answers for ourselves. The answers are never hidden, but are patiently awaiting our recognition and discovery. The inner search for the answers to our existence is the very essence of human growth and evolution. No one can hand you this or quote it from a book.

An exciting new frontier of exploration is before you—endless levels of energy just waiting to be discovered. Today you have the rare opportunity to be one of the pioneers, to explore beyond the dense outer crust of the universe and see the truth for yourself. The ultimate adventure is waiting, and you have nothing to lose but your limits.

Affirmations: Repeated positive statements spoken, thought, or written in the present tense. For example, "Now I'm out-of-body!"

Apparitions: Nonphysical inhabitants who have lowered the personal frequency of their energy-bodies and are temporarily visible within the physical world.

Aura: The energy field emanating from all life-forms.

Black holes: Interactive energy conduits between the physical and nonphysical dimensions.

Cataleptic: The experience of being unable to move the physical body. This sometimes occurs during separation from and return to the physical body. It is a temporary condition resulting from our energy-body being out of phase with our physical body. Physical sensations generally return within a minute or less.

Cluster experiences: Multiple out-of-body experiences occurring in a series. This is a normal experience and is similar to slipping in and out of body. Cluster experiences are commonly reported during physical illness and when physical death is close.

Consciousness continuum: Consciousness extending its awareness from the nonphysical source through numerous energy frequencies until it eventually expresses itself within the outer physical dimension.

272 *Consensus environments:* Areas of the universe created and sustained by the group consciousness of a large number of nonphysical inhabitants. These environments are resistant to individual thought-energy.

Energy-body: A general term referring to the nonphysical or spiritual form we experience when out-of-body. Energy-bodies are necessary for consciousness (soul) to function within the various nonphysical frequencies of the universe.

Energy dimensions: Distinct and stable energy systems or frequencies of the universe; separate universes of energy existing at defined frequency rates. Energy dimensions are separated from one another by their individual and unique vibrational frequencies. For example, the physical universe is a single energy dimension.

Energy environment: A general term used to describe a specific nonphysical area within a dimension. Countless energy environments can exist within a single dimension.

Energy membrane: The convergence point of two different energy systems (frequencies of energy); the energy border or barrier separating two energy dimensions or systems.

First energy-body: The nonphysical form often experienced while out-of-body. This energy form, although invisible to current technology, exists closest in density and frequency to the physical body. Commonly referred to in traditional metaphysical literature as the astral or etheric body.

Human radiation: A distinct feeling of energy emanating from a nonphysical human being when out-of-body.

Hypnagogic state: The subtle state of consciousness experienced between waking awareness and sleep. We pass through this creative state, in which mental imagery is especially vivid, every time we go to sleep.

Lucid dream: A dream in which a degree or percentage of awareness is present.

Multidimensional universe: The entire universe, seen and unseen; a continuum of energy consisting of an unknown number of energy frequencies or levels. As we explore inwardly away from matter, the inner, nonphysical energy dimensions become progressively less dense and increasingly thought-responsive. The visible physical universe is the dense outer molecular crust of the entire universe.

Natural energy environments: Unformed energy areas currently unaffected by thought. They are easily manipulated by conscious and subconscious thought-energy.

Near-death experience: An experience reported by millions of people who are declared clinically dead and then resuscitated. They often experience a separation from their physical body, movement through a tunnel leading to a bright light, and a new environment.

Nonconsensus environments: Nonphysical areas of the universe that appear formed and developed but are currently not sustained and supported by conscious energy. They readily respond to individual focused thought.

Nonhuman radiation: Unique and distinctive energy emanations originating from nonphysical beings who have never had a physical human experience.

Nonphysical inhabitants: Any living beings existing within the nonphysical dimensions without current physical bodies.

274 *Out-of-body experience (O.O.B.E. or O.B.E.):* The separation of consciousness from its temporary biological vehicle. Also commonly called astral, etheric, or mental projection.

Physical life-forms: Temporary cellular vehicles (biological life) used by consciousness (soul) for expression within the dense outer dimension of the universe. Physical vehicles are required to experience, explore, and interact within the physical dimension, just as nonphysical vehicles are required to experience and explore within the nonphysical dimensions.

Physical universe (dimension): The visible universe; the dense outer crust of the complete multidimensional universe. The physical dimension makes up but a small fraction of the entire universe (less than 1 percent).

Second energy-body: A second energy form, less dense than the first energy-body, existing at a higher (finer) frequency than the first nonphysical body. Its internal frequency corresponds to the second inner energy dimension.

Silver cord: The traditional biblical term for the nonphysical connection between the first inner energy-body and the biological body. In many respects, it is similar to an energy umbilical cord capable of stretching for immense distances. In appearance, though, it is not cordlike but is observed as thin, fibrous filaments connecting the biological body to its densest nonphysical counterpart.

Soul: Pure consciousness existing independent of all energy-bodies or forms; the pure essence of all life-forms. Soul exists beyond all form and substance as we know it but uses forms of energy for its expression in the denser regions (dimensions) of the universe. Our current physical body is one of these temporary energy-bodies used by the soul to experience, explore, and perceive within this dense outer dimension of the universe.

Thought forms: Nonphysical energy formed by thought. These forms, which may appear as anything we can imagine, are often responsive to focused thought-energy. The density and longevity of thought forms vary dramatically; without continuing thought reinforcement, they slowly decay and revert to natural clouds of nonphysical energy.

Thought transference: The universal communication method used within the nonphysical dimensions. This communication is commonly experienced as an internal recognition of a progression of vivid images entering the mind. These images can convey emotions and thought simultaneously.

Tunnel experience: The temporary opening of an energy membrane. This energy opening is often reported during a near-death experience.

Vibrational state: Internal vibrations and sounds often reported during the preliminary stages of an out-of-body experience. Buzzing and humming sounds accompanied by electrical-like vibrations, numbness, and catalepsy are commonly reported.

Visualization: The process of creating mental imagery for a specific purpose.

OUT-OF-BODY
SURVEY

An overwhelming need exists for greater insight into out-of-body experiences. The purpose of this survey is to obtain as much data as possible about non-physical experiences and the environments observed. Your participation in this survey will help to expand our knowledge about the out-of-body phenomenon. Send your responses to William Buhlman, 39500 Fourteen Mile Road, Suite 129, Walled Lake, MI 48390.

Name _____

Address (optional) _____

Sex   M   F   Date of birth: _____

RACE OR ETHNIC GROUP
_____ White
_____ Black
_____ Hispanic
_____ Native American
_____ Asian
_____ Other (please specify)

CURRENT RELIGIOUS PREFERENCE/ AFFILIATION
_____ Catholic
_____ Protestant
_____ Jewish
_____ Muslim
_____ Buddhist
_____ Other (please specify)
_____ None

Current occupation _____

CURRENT MARITAL STATUS
_____ Single
_____ Married
_____ Remarried
_____ Separated
_____ Divorced
_____ Widowed

EDUCATIONAL LEVEL
_____ Grade school
_____ Some high school
_____ High school graduate
_____ Some college or presently attending college
_____ College graduate
_____ Some postgraduate work
_____ Earned advanced degree (please specify)

278   1. Please describe your out-of-body experience in detail, including your feelings, thoughts, and actions.

2. At what time of day did the experience occur?

3. What physical position was your body in during your out-of-body experience? Lying down? Reclined in an easy chair? Were you lying on your back or side? Please describe.

4. How would you describe your emotional and mental state before and during the experience?

5. Was your physical body asleep when the experience occurred?

6. How did you leave your physical body? Rolling out, floating, spinning, sitting up? Please describe.

7. Did you experience any feelings of fear or anxiety?

8. Did you feel any internal sensations or hear any sounds before or during the experience? Please describe.

9. Has the experience changed your perception of life and death?

10. Do you feel that the experience has provided evidence or proof that you continue beyond your physical body?

11. Did your state of consciousness differ from your normal physical awareness? If so, how?

12. Did you see and touch your "new" body? Did your body possess density and form?

13. Could you touch or move through obstacles such as walls and doors? If so, what did it feel like? What did these structures look like when you were out-of-body?

14. How did your experience differ from a dream?

15. Did you enjoy the experience? Would you like to do it again?

16. Do you feel the experience has changed you? If so, how?

17. Have you received any physical or psychological benefits from your experience? If so, please describe.

18. Has the experience changed your understanding of your existence? How?

19. Did you see or experience a tunnel, door, or opening of any kind?

20. Did you have a dream before your out-of-body exploration?

21. Did you have any difficulty adapting to your new environment?

22. How long did your experience last? Did you notice any difference between the experienced time and the physical time?

23. How many days or attempts did it take for you to have an out-of-body experience?

24. Have you conducted any of the experiments or explorations introduced in chapter 8? Please describe.

25. Did you encounter any other life-forms during your experience?

26. Did you observe your sleeping physical body?

27. Describe in detail what the nonphysical environment looked like. What forms, colors, densities, and lighting did you experience? How did the environment compare with your physical surroundings?

28. How clear were your vision and awareness during your experience? Did you do the clarity technique? If so, what was the result?

29. How long was your physical body asleep before your out-of-body experience?

30. Which out-of-body technique is the most effective for you?

31. Did you experience an impenetrable barrier or wall?

32. Describe your nonphysical body—its form, substance, and capabilities.

33. Did your thought processes, personality, or ego differ from your physical state of consciousness? Please describe in detail.

34. Did you notice an increased sensitivity to electrical systems, equipment, watches, computers, TVs, lights, and so on, after your out-of-body experience?

adventure: sense of, 136. *See also* exploration

affirmations, 182, 189–90; for panic attacks, 227–28; techniques, 172, 187–94; visualization with, 190–91

animals: met in out-of-body experiences, 35–36; souls of, 265

answers: increased desire for, 132; obtaining personal, 134; about our existence, 134, 270; about out-of-body experiences, 262–68

apparitions, multidimensionality and, 97, 98

Aspect, Alain, 110

assistance: for clarity, 15–16, 66, 185, 213, 224–26, 231, 264, 267; for memory, 240; from nonphysical beings, 40–42, 167, 168, 223–24; with separation from physical body, 167; from subconscious mind, 183, 185

astral projection, term for out-of-body experience, 7

astronomers: big bang theory, 101; black holes, 103–5; and invisible matter, 77–79, 88, 100

Astronomers, The (Goldsmith), 78

aura, human, 264

basics: energy mechanics, 221; out-of-body exploration, 209–10

beliefs: basis for, 57; in consensus reality, 67; knowledge vs., 130, 135; about out-of-body experiences, 150; out-of-body experiences influenced by, 222–23, 231; out-of-body experiences influencing, 264; reappraisal of, 144. *See also* religions

Bell, John Stewart, 110, 117–18

benefits, of out-of-body experiences, 139–40; of nonconsensus areas, 94–95; of nonphysical forms, 46; for physically challenged people, 137–39; transformative, 129–41. *See also* personal development

Bible: out-of-body experiences in, 222; silver cord, 265

big bang theory, 101, 103

birth, in evolution, 115, 116, 124

black holes, 79–82, 83, 101, 103–5, 106

Blake, William, 84–85, 86

Blavatsky, Madame, 84

Bohm, David, 69, 79, 89, 110, 119

Bohr, Niels, 79, 109

Born, Max, 109

Bosch, Hieronymus, 84, 86

282

brain: and consciousness, 108, 151; function of, 21, 108
breathing, in out-of-body experience, 33
bridges, in multidimensional universe, 80–81, 103–4
buddy system, for out-of-body experiences, 241

Cabbard, Glen, 131
calm: inner, 135; maintaining, 154, 155, 158, 231
Capra, Fritjof, 106–7, 119
Carnegie, Dale, 143
catalepsy, 212
Chopra, Deepak, 118
Christian churches, and view of out-of-body experiences, 266–67
Christos technique, 241
clarity: request for, 15–16, 66, 185, 213, 224–26, 231, 264, 267; technique, 225–26. See also focus
Clarke, Arthur C., 37
Clauser, John, 110
cluster out-of-body experiences, 64
commitment, to out-of-body experience, 146–47
communication: reading thoughts, 264; thought transference, 216; with visual representations of ideas, 39. See also assistance
consciousness, 107–8; continuum of, 112–15; after death, 87; in dreams, 183–84; dual, 66–67, 219; evolution of, 51, 62, 68, 107, 108, 115–21, 124–25, 136; group, 67, 93; hypnagogic state, 160–64; light as, 237; in nonphysical states,

30, 63, 66–67, 268; in physical states, 30, 66–67; reality created by, 67–69, 93, 96; science using, 111–12; tunneling effect, 105–6. See also thoughts
consensus reality, 67, 92–94, 96, 122
control, 154–55, 211–32; clarity request for, 15–16, 66, 185, 213, 224–26, 231, 264, 267; consciousness of, 268; fears and, 41, 148, 213, 226–30; of frequency rates, 31, 238; in hypnagogic state, 160–61; keys to, 212–19; and mind-altering substances, 266; overview, 230–32; of thoughts, 96–97, 219–23, 225; of vibration stage, 158, 212
creative ability: in hypnagogic state, 160–61; recognition of, 134; to shape surroundings, 68, 96, 174–76. See also imagination; thoughts
Crichton, Michael, 246–49

Dancing Wu Li Masters (Zukav), 106–7
dark matter, 78–79, 88, 100, 106
Darwinian theory, 115
Davisson, Clinton, 109
death: choices after, 121–22; in continuum, 113; in evolution, 115, 116; fear of, 132; frequency rates, 100; immortality verified, 131; life after, 24, 92, 117; realizations concerning dying, 132; right temporal lobe stimulated during, 136. See also near-death experiences
de Broglie, Louis, 79, 109

density: changes over time, 62; and
structure of universe, 89. *See also*
frequency rates; matter

dimensions: first inner, 67, 93–94,
216, 223, 234; interdimensional
movement, 236–37. *See also* multidimensionality; parallel dimensions; physical life

Dirac, Paul, 109

Doré, Gustave, 86

dreams: in consciousness continuum,
114; conversion to out-of-body experience, 181–87; daily log, 182;
difference from out-of-body experiences, 268; lucid, 114, 183–84,
207, 226, 262; recall increased, 4;
signals, 185–87, 207

drugs, and out-of-body experiences,
266

Dyer, Wayne, 118

Eadie, Betty, 120

early morning technique, 191–94

Eddington, Arthur, 79, 81

Edison, Thomas, 160–61

Einstein, Albert, 118–19; Einstein-
Rosen Bridge, 80, 82, 86, 106,
109; and energy tunnels, 86;
famous equation, 77; and four-
dimensional continuum, 79–80,
112; and grand unification, 125–26;
on imagination, 174; and mysticism, 3, 79; photon theory, 108;
relativity theory, 79, 98, 109

Einstein-Rosen Bridge, 80, 82, 86,
106, 109

electromagnetic wave spectrum, 52,
75–76, 125

Emerson, Ralph Waldo, 129

"empty" space, 96–97

energy: basic mechanics, 221; clouds,
57–58; in consensus environments,
92–94; continuum, 70–72, 88–90,
106, 113; environmental durabil-
ity, 95; expansion, 101–3; fear represented in, 217, 249–50; hands
of, 38–39; matter and, 52–53,
70–71, 77; membranes, 61–62, 87,
98–100, 264–65; multifrequency,
72; in natural environments,
95–96; in nonconsensus environments, 94–95; spectrum, 75–76;
subtle, 175; system, 63, 77–78;
thought, 90–96, 219–23; tunnels,
84–87, 100, 264–65. *See also*
forms; life; vibrations

energy-bodies, 263; appearance and
substance of, 15, 24–25, 33–35;
consciousness, 30, 63, 66–67, 268;
after death, 24; in exploration
stage, 154; first, 29–30, 33–34,
67; frequency rate, 30–31, 62–63,
237–39; multiple forms, 29–35,
61–62, 67, 231; progressively "less
humanoid," 62; in reentry stage,
154; second, 31–32, 67; in separation stage, 165–67; similarities
with physical body, 32, 33; as temporary vehicle, 33; thoughts forming, 24–25, 33, 166–67; thoughts
propelling, 14, 16, 93–94, 154,
231, 235–36. *See also* nonphysical
forms

energy dimensions. *See* dimensions

energy environments. *See* nonphysical
environments

284

Everett, Hugh III, 80–81, 82, 110, 118
evolution: of consciousness, 51, 62, 68, 107, 108, 115–21, 124–25, 136; future, 121–25; of human species, 62, 68, 132–33; personal, 51, 62, 68–69, 225, 239; of science, 108–12, 126
experiments, 233–68; pencil, 14, 16, 17, 234; questions about our existence, 257–62; recording, 234; suggested experiments, 234, 255–57. *See also* techniques
exploration stage, 154; basics, 209–10. *See also* experiments
extrasensory perception: multidimensionality and, 97; process of, 175

Far Journeys (Monroe), 166
fears, 231; conquering, 41, 94–95, 148–49, 213, 226–30, 249–50, 267; energy representations of, 217, 249–50; panic attacks, 213, 227–28, 267; recognizing, 144; reduction technique, 228–29; of separation from physical body, 227–28, 267
Feynman, Richard, 110
Finkelstein, David, 81, 110
focus: with affirmations, 188; maintaining, 155, 158, 176–77, 182, 218, 230; objects of, 177–80; request for clear, 15–16, 66, 185, 213, 224–26, 231, 264, 267; in ritual technique, 204
forms: all energy, 223; multidimensionality of, 70; representational value of, 48, 63; as soul, 63;

thoughts molding, 24–25, 33, 57, 67, 223. *See also* matter; nonphysical forms; physical forms
Freedman, Stuart, 110
frequencylike nature, of physical particles, 108, 125
frequency rates: apparitions/poltergeists, 98; control of, 31, 238; death, 100; and energy dimensions, 89; energy membranes and, 61–62; fine-tuning, 238; hands of energy adjusting, 38–39; Hemi-sync tapes, 202–3; in interdimensional movement, 236; multifrequency energy, 52, 72; personal, 30–31, 39, 62–63, 236, 237–39; raising, 237–39; reality measured by, 71. *See also* radiation frequencies; vibrations
Freud, Sigmund, 245
Fronsdal, Christian, 81

Gawain, Shakti, 118
Germer, Lester, 109
Glaskin, G. M., 241
goals: out-of-body, 146–47; written, 147–48, 183
Goldsmith, Donald, 78
grand unification theory, 125–26
Greyson, Bruce, 117, 130
group consciousness, 67, 93
group explorations, 240–45
guides, nonphysical, 40–42, 168, 223–24

hands of energy, adjustments by, 38–39
harm: in out-of-body experience, 266; and violence reduction, 134, 135

healing: advanced, 250–52; spontaneous, 133
hearing: in out-of-body experience,
33, 263–64. *See also* sounds
heaven, religious concepts of, 83–84,
93, 122–23, 222
Heisenberg, Werner, 77, 79, 109
Heitler, Walter, 69
Hemi-sync tapes, 202–3
Herbert, Nick, 119
Holmes, Oliver Wendell, 233
hostility, reduced, 135
Hubble, Edwin, 100–101
Huxley, T. H., 143
hypnagogic state, 160–64
hypnosis, 194–202; self-hypnosis,
18, 196–202
hypnotherapists, selecting, 196

illness: spontaneous out-of-body
experiences during, 63–64. *See also*
healing
imagination: enhanced, 136; in hypnagogic state, 161; in visualization,
174–76
immortality, verification of, 131
intelligence, increased, 136
interconnectedness: of all nonphysical
dimensions, 88–90; of physical and
nonphysical life, 51–52, 72, 90;
theorem, 117–18
interdimensional movement, exercise, 236–37

Jacob's Ladder (Blake), 84–85
James, William, 171
Jeans, James, 79
John, Saint, 221–22
Jones, Fowler, 131

Journeys Out-of-the-Body (Monroe), 95
Jung, C. G., 245

Kerr, Roy P., 81–82, 104, 110, 118
killing, repugnance for, 134
knowledge: vs. beliefs, 130, 135;
increased, 135
Kramers, H. A., 109
Kruskal, Martin, 81, 82, 104, 110,
118
learning: physical life for, 50–51,
265. *See also* personal development
life: as challenges/obstacles, 149;
after death, 24, 92, 117; increased
respect for, 134; increased zest for,
135; interconnectedness of physical
and nonphysical, 51–52, 72, 90;
purpose of, 50–51, 57, 265. *See also*
consciousness; nonphysical environments; past lives; physical life
Life After Life (Moody), 117
light: dual (particle-wave) nature of,
71–72, 106; energy clouds, 58; and
frequency level, 237–39; multidimensional, 52; during near-death
experiences, 86, 264
limits: recognizing, 144; of science,
103, 151; transcending, 123–24,
148–49
London, Fritz, 69
Lucas, George, 119
"many worlds interpretation," 80–81

matter: and energy, 52–53, 70–71, 77;
evolution through, 124; invisible/
dark, 77–79, 88, 100, 106; multidimensionality of, 79–84; and reality, 235; as transformation tool,
116. *See also* physical forms

286   meditation: in consciousness continuum, 114; in partner technique,
242

meetings, face-to-face, with nonphysical beings, 134

meetings, out-of-body, 37–72; with
animals, 35–36; group, 241; with
guides, 40–42, 168, 223–24; with
people, 5–6, 20–21, 22–24, 39–45,
48–49

membranes, energy, 61–62, 87,
98–100, 264–65

memory recall, enhanced, 136, 240

Minkowski, Hermann, 109

miracles, 252, 254

mirror technique, 180–81

Misner, Charles, 81

Mohammed, 222

Monroe, Robert, 62, 95, 119, 166,
202

Monroe Institute of Applied Sciences,
202–3

Moody, Raymond, 86, 117, 130, 150

Morse, Melvin, 86, 130, 264

movement, 230; interdimensional,
236–37; "moving inward," 30–31,
93; thought-propelled, 14, 16,
93–94, 154, 231, 235–36

movies, and evolution of consciousness, 118, 120–21

Muldoon, Sylvan, 26

multidimensionality, 52; of energy-
bodies, 29–35, 61–62, 67; of energy frequencies, 52, 72; of forms,
70; of light, 52; of universe, 79–84,
87–127. *See also* parallel dimensions

mysterious: experience of, 3–4; scientists ascribing to, 3, 79

mysticism, quantum physics and, 79,
106–8

Mysticism and the New Physics (Talbot),
107

natural ability, developing, 143–69

natural energy environments, 92,
95–96

near-death experiences: in consciousness continuum, 114; energy membrane, 98, 100; and expanding
universe, 103; light during, 86,
264; moving inward, 93; right
temporal lobe stimulated during,
136; studies/writings, 86, 117,
120; and temporary physical vehicle, 152–53; tunnel effect, 86, 87,
100, 105–6, 264–65

Neumann, John von, 69, 109

nonconsensus energy environments,
92, 94–95

nonphysical environments, 92–97,
263; with cloudlike forms, 215;
duplicate of physical environment,
216; interconnectedness of all dimensions of, 88–90; interconnectedness with physical life, 51–52,
72, 90; rapidly changing, 218;
"rules of the road," 212–19; separate from physical-like surroundings, 28; thought-responsive, 57,
67–69, 90–96, 174–75, 219–23,
235–36. *See also* dimensions; energy; nonphysical forms

nonphysical forms: cloudlike, 215;
density changes over time, 62; as
energy system, 63; fluctuating, 63;
in parallel dimension, 18, 52, 67,

69–70, 79–82; for personal benefit, 46; qualities observed, 14–32, 51–52; thoughts molding, 24–25, 33, 57, 67, 223. *See also* energy-bodies; matter; meetings, out-of-body

Nordstrom, G., 82, 104

Pagels, Heinze, 105, 119

panic attacks, 213, 227–28, 267

parallel dimensions, 18, 52, 69–70, 79–82, 216, 223, 234; and black holes, 79–82, 104; consensus reality, 67; physicists and, 79–82, 87, 118; tunnels and, 87, 106

Parallel Universes (Wolf), 111–12

particles: elemental, 77, 108, 125; frequencylike nature, 108, 125; particle-wave nature of light, 71–72, 106

partner explorations, 240–45

past lives: possible experiences of, 49–51, 58–59, 64–66; recognized/experienced, 133; regression therapy, 117, 195, 241

Pauli, Wolfgang, 79, 109

Peale, Norman Vincent, 118

pencil experiments, during out-of-body experience, 14, 16, 17, 234

Penfield, Wilder, 136

people: met in out-of-body experiences, 5–6, 20–21, 22–24, 39–45, 48–49. *See also* guides

personal development: accelerated, 131, 133–34, 245–50; evolution, 51, 62, 68–69, 225, 239; nonconsensus reality benefiting, 94–95; nonphysical forms created for, 46,

94–95; out-of-body experiences natural for, 155–56; as purpose of life, 50–51, 57, 265; spiritual, 133, 253–55; transformative, 129–41. *See also* fears

physical body: brain, 21, 108, 151; conditioned acceptance of, 152–53; consciousness, 30, 66–67; healing, 133, 250–52; observed from out-of-body, 11–12; during out-of-body experience, 266; in reentry stage, 154; similarities with nonphysical body, 32, 33. *See also* returning to physical body; separation from physical body

physical forms: in multidimensional universe, 92; and parallel dimension of nonphysical forms, 18, 52, 67, 69–70, 216; as reality, 70–71, 235; as temporary vehicles, 33, 107, 152–53. *See also* matter; physical body

physical life: black holes as conduits from, 104; conditioning and indoctrination in, 150–53; evolution in, 115–16, 124; increased respect for, 134; interconnectedness with nonphysical life, 51–52, 72, 90; purpose of, 50–51, 265; science limited by, 103, 151. *See also* physical forms; senses

physically challenged people, benefits for, 137–39

physics: big bang theory, 101; black holes, 79–82, 83, 101, 103–5; and dual nature of light, 71–72, 106; and evolution of consciousness, 118–19; evolution of, 108–10; and

288 physics (*continued*)
grand unification theory, 125–26;
increased interest in, 67; interconnectedness theorem, 117–18; and
interconnectedness of universe, 89;
and invisible matter, 77–79, 88,
100; and parallel universes, 79–82,
87, 118; tunneling effect, 105–6.
See also quantum theory
pineal gland, 26, 136
Planck, Max, 79, 108
Podolsky, Boris, 109
proof, of out-of-body experiences, 262
psychic abilities: as creative process,
175; increased, 132; multidimensionality and, 97
psychic phenomena, multidimensionality and, 97–98
psychological change: accelerated,
133–34, 245–50. *See also* personal
development
psychological problems (acute), and
out-of-body experiences, 250, 267

quantum theory, 77, 151; consciousness creates reality, 69; interconnectedness of universe, 89; "many
worlds interpretation" and, 80–81;
and mysticism, 79, 106–8; and
parallel universes, 118
quarks, 77, 108
questions: about our existence, 134,
257–62; about out-of-body experiences, 262–68; self-evaluation,
144–46. *See also* answers

radiation frequencies: in electromagnetic wave spectrum, 52, 75–76,
125; our immersion in, 52; visual
limitations with, 75–76. *See also*
nonphysical forms
rapid eye movement (REM) sleep, 191
reality: consensus, 67, 92–94, 96,
122; greater awareness of, 131;
imagination creating, 174–76; of
interconnected universe, 89; nonconsensus, 92, 94–95; of physical
surroundings, 70–71, 235; psychological problems with, 267; re-
appraising our concepts of, 143–53;
relativity of, 107, 235; thoughts
creating, 41, 67–69, 94, 95. *See also*
life
recall: dream, 4; memory, 136, 240;
after out-of-body experience, 214,
240
reentry stage, in out-of-body experiences, 154
Reissner, H., 82, 104
Reissner-Nordstrom black hole, 82
relativity: of reality, 107, 235; theory
of, 79, 98, 109
religions: heaven concepts, 83–84,
93, 122–23, 222; nonphysical concepts, 150–51; out-of-body experiences in, 171, 222; out-of-body
experiences influencing beliefs
in, 264; and spiritual experience,
252–53; unnecessary fighting between, 57; views of out-of-body
experiences, 266–67
repetition (ceremonial technique),
204–5
results, initial, 205–7
returning to physical body: capacity
for, 266; memory request during,

240; reentry stage, 154; tugging signal for, 218; unintentional, 154–55, 156, 213

Revelation, Book of, 221–22

right temporal lobe, stimulation of, 136

Ring, Kenneth, 86, 117, 130

ritual technique, 204–5

Robbins, Tom, 136

Rodenberry, Gene, 119

Rosen, Nathan, 79–80, 86, 109

Rubin, Bruce Joel, 118

Rubin, Vera, 78

safety, of out-of-body experiences, 266, 267

Schopenhauer, Arthur, 211

Schrödinger, Erwin, 79, 109

Schwarzschild throat, 104

science: big bang theory, 101, 103; black holes, 79–82, 83, 101, 103–5; and evolution of consciousness, 117–19; evolution of, 108–12, 126; and invisible matter, 77–79, 88; limited by physical world, 103, 151; new frontier of, 126–27. *See also* physics

Seckel, David, 75

self, true, 63, 253–55

self-concept: and changing form, 231; and concepts of reality, 143–44, 152; conditioned, 152; expanded, 133

self-control. *See* control

self-evaluation, and ability for out-of-body experience, 144–46

self-hypnosis, 196–197; candle blown out in, 18; script, 197–202

self-improvement, 245–50. *See also* personal development

self-respect, increased, 134

senses: in out-of-body experience, 32–33, 216, 263–64; in target technique, 179–80. *See also* hearing; sight

separation from physical body, 164–68; direct, 167; fear of, 227–28, 267; floating out, 165; panic attacks, 227–28; pulling energy-body out, 166–67; requesting, 166; requesting assistance with, 167; rolling out, 166; sensations of, 25–27, 153, 154, 262–63; sitting up and out, 165–66; stage of, 153; success at, 155; vibrations and, 26, 153, 156–58, 164–66, 215

Siegel, Bernie, 118

sight: blurred, 32, 213; limitations of, 75–79; out-of-body, 32–33, 213, 263–64; in target technique, 179

silver cord, biblical, 265

Slater, John, 109

sleep: rapid eye movement (REM), 191. *See also* dreams

smell, in target technique, 179–80

souls: animals', 265; experiencing, 254; without form, 63; religious teachings, 151

sounds: to induce out-of-body experiences, 202–4; in out-of-body experiences, 8–9, 26–27, 153–59, 212, 214, 215, 227; panic attacks with, 227; sound-frequency techniques, 202–3; Tibetan monks' technique, 203–4

space-time: continuum, 89; curvature, 98–99, 106; four-dimensional, 79–80
Spielberg, Steven, 118
spirituality, increased, 133, 252–55
spontaneous healing, 133
spontaneous out-of-body experiences,
63–64
Stanford University, experiments, 234
Stapp, Henry Pierce, 69, 110
success: four steps to out-of-body,
154–56; system of, 205
Szertes, G., 81

Talbot, Michael, 107, 119
Tao of Physics (Capra), 106–7
target technique, 172, 177–80
taste, in out-of-body experience, 33
techniques, 7–8, 171–210; affirmation, 172, 187–94; choosing,
172–73; Christos, 241; clarity,
225–26; dream conversion, 181–87;
early morning, 191–94; fear reduction, 228–29; hypnosis, 194–202;
ideal mind-set, 207–8; partner,
241–45; repetition (ceremonial
technique), 204–5; review, 208–9;
separation, 164–68; sound, 202–4;
spiritual advance, 253–55; visualization, 173–81, 229–30
temperature, in out-of-body experience, 33
thoughts: affirmations focusing, 188;
controlling, 96–97, 219–23, 225;
"empty" space and, 96–97; energy-
body conforming to, 24–25, 33,
166–67; in first nonphysical dimension, 93; group consensus reality, 67, 93; negative, 96, 238; nonphysical environments responsive
to, 57, 67–69, 90–96, 174–75,
219–23, 235–36; nonphysical
senses created by, 33; propelling
capacity, 14, 16, 93–94, 154, 231,
235–36; reading, 264; reality-
creating, 41, 67–69, 94, 95; in
scientific observations, 77; self-
limiting, 96; transference, 216;
written goals and, 147–48
Tibetan Book of the Dead, 171
Tibetan monks, sounds used by,
202, 203
touch: in out-of-body experience, 33,
216; in target technique, 179
transformation, 129–41; qualities of,
130–37
Travels (Crichton), 246–49
tunnels, 84–87, 213; black holes,
104; energy membranes and, 87,
100, 264–65; in near-death experiences, 86, 87, 100, 105–6,
264–65; physics' tunneling effect,
105–6
Twemlow, Stuart, 117, 130, 131,
133, 134, 156
Twitchell, Paul, 26, 41, 119

universe: bridges, 80–81, 103–4;
expanding, 100–103; exploring,
234–37, 269–70; interconnectedness, 88–90; multidimensional,
79–84, 87–127. See also dimensions
Verne, Jules, 119–20
vibrations, with out-of-body experiences, 8–10, 16–17, 154–55;
adjustments by hands of energy,

38–39; amplifying, 239–40; control of, 158, 212; in nonphysical body, 15; panic attacks with, 227; recognizing and responding to, 156–60; and separation stage, 26, 153, 156–58, 164–66, 215; stage of, 153, 156–60, 212. *See also* frequency rates

violence, reduced, 134, 135

virtual reality, and evolution of consciousness, 121

vision. *See* sight

visualizations: with affirmations, 190–91; as early morning alternative, 192; and fear reduction, 228; hot-air-balloon, 229–30; in hypnagogic state, 161; made easy, 176–77; for out-of-body experience, 7–8, 158, 162–64, 172, 173–81; in partner technique, 242–45; techniques, 173–81, 229–30

weather changes, in out-of-body experiences, 43–44

Weiss, Brian, 117, 133

Wheeler, John, 81

Wigner, Eugene, 69

Wolf, Fred Alan, 79, 111–12, 114, 118

Yukawa, Hideki, 110

Zukav, Gary, 106–7, 118